Praise for The Ethics of Influence

"In this era of intransigence and intolerance, *The Ethics of Influence* is a vitally needed book. It embraces what all of us—left, right, and center—mutually want: a balance between the goals of welfare, autonomy, dignity, and self-government. What's more, it is a hoot to read. Roll Over Mill and Marx; tell Hayek and Gramsci the news."
-George A. Akerlof
Nobel Laureate in Economics, 2001

"As more governments and businesses turn to 'nudging,' pioneer Sunstein turns his brilliant mind to building an ethical framework for these powerful approaches. New findings on public attitudes to nudges – showing surprisingly high levels of support even among traditionally skeptical Americans – are combined with Sunstein's trademark clarity of thought to offer a timely framework that will be influential across the world."
-David Halpern
CEO, Behavioural Insights Team, and author, Inside the Nudge Unit

"In a book full of convincing detail but free of dogmatism, Sunstein walks us through the case for and against nudges. Nudges are, in some circumstances, the best tool government has at its disposal – cheaper than financial incentives, more freedom-preserving than mandates, and more effective than information. Our government is sometimes ethically required to nudge us. Nonetheless, nudges raise legitimate ethical concerns, foremost among them that they can be manipulative. Sunstein ultimately makes a powerful argument for the widespread use of nudges by government, but without shortchanging the ethical arguments on both sides."
-Anne Barnhill
Assistant Professor of Medical Ethics and Health Policy
University of Pennsylvania

"One need not agree with all of Cass Sunstein's arguments about nudging to admire him for doing more than anyone to champion the importance of behavioral science for public policymaking. Owing to him, it is an increasingly recognized ethical imperative to measure government actions not only against societal values but also against evidence."

-Ralph Hertwig
Director, Center for Adaptive Rationality,
Max Planck Institute for Human Development, Germany

"Cass Sunstein knows more than anyone about nudging, and in this very insightful book he brings his acute reasoning to understanding the ethics behind choice architecture. Here he considers sources from Mill to Hayek to Ostrom, and argues that choice architecture is unavoidable and in many cases that it's the right thing to do. Just as importantly, he talks about when nudging is wrong and when it is manipulative. All in all, it is an essential book for anyone interested in the ethics of behavioral intervention, either by governments or firms."

-Eric J. Johnson
Norman Eig Professor of Business, Columbia University

"Behavioural regulation has spread to governments worldwide. This brilliant book tackles the many myths that have evolved around the use of behavioural economics in politics. Cass Sunstein explains in clear words how (and why) the core values of an Ethical State – welfare, autonomy, dignity, and self-government – are indeed best served by governments that carefully base their policies on an empirical foundation and use behavioural insights as additional effective policy tools."

-Professor Lucia A. Reisch
Behavioural Economist, Copenhagen Business School

"We typically consider ourselves rational actors, whose dignity derives from our autonomy. In fact, our behavior is easily shaped by other actors and by external factors, often outside our awareness and control. When government intervenes to influence our behaviors, often to improve our lives, we recoil. But if government remains uninvolved while other interests are free to shape our world, how autonomous are we then? Sunstein confronts our naïveté with a penetrating discussion about how to balance government influence against personal dignity, manipulation against autonomy, and behavioral facts against political ideals. This book is an engrossing read."

-Eldar Shafir
William Stuart Tod Professor of Psychology & Public Affairs,
Princeton University, Co-author of Scarcity

THE ETHICS OF INFLUENCE

In recent years, "nudge units," or "behavioral insights teams," have been created in the United States, the United Kingdom, Germany, and other nations. All over the world, public officials are using the behavioral sciences to protect the environment, promote employment and economic growth, reduce poverty, and increase national security. In this book, Cass R. Sunstein, the eminent legal scholar and best-selling coauthor of *Nudge*, breaks new ground with a deep yet highly readable investigation into the ethical issues surrounding nudges, choice architecture, and mandates, addressing such issues as welfare, autonomy, self-government, dignity, manipulation, and the constraints and responsibilities of an ethical state. Complementing the ethical discussion, *The Ethics of Influence: Government in the Age of Behavioral Science* contains a wealth of new data on people's attitudes toward a broad range of nudges, choice architecture, and mandates.

CASS R. SUNSTEIN is Robert Walmsley University Professor at Harvard University. From 2009 to 2012, he was Administrator of the White House Office of Information and Regulatory Affairs. He is the founder and director of the Program on Behavioral Economics and Public Policy at Harvard Law School. Mr. Sunstein is the author of many articles and books, including the best-selling *Nudge: Improving Decisions about Health, Wealth, and Happiness* (with Richard H. Thaler, 2008), *Simpler: The Future of Government* (2013), *Why Nudge?* (2014), *Conspiracy Theories and Other Dangerous Ideas* (2014), *Wiser: Beyond Groupthink to Make Groups Smarter* (2014), *Valuing Life: Humanizing the Regulatory State* (2014), *Choosing Not to Choose: Understanding the Value of Choice* (2015), and *Constitutional Personae: Heroes, Soldiers, Minimalists, and Mutes* (2015).

CAMBRIDGE STUDIES IN ECONOMICS,
CHOICE, AND SOCIETY

Founding Editors
Timur Kuran, *Duke University*
Peter J. Boettke, *George Mason University*

This interdisciplinary series promotes original theoretical and empirical research as well as integrative syntheses involving links between individual choice, institutions, and social outcomes. Contributions are welcome from across the social sciences, particularly in the areas where economic analysis is joined with other disciplines, such as comparative political economy, new institutional economics, and behavioral economics.

Books in the Series:
TERRY L. ANDERSON AND GARY D. LIBECAP,
Environmental Markets: A Property Rights Approach 2014

MORRIS B. HOFFMAN,
The Punisher's Brain: The Evolution of Judge and Jury 2014

PETER T. LEESON,
Anarchy Unbound: Why Self-Governance Works Better Than You Think 2014

BENJAMIN POWELL,
Out of Poverty: Sweatshops in the Global Economy 2014

THE ETHICS OF INFLUENCE

Government in the Age of Behavioral Science

CASS R. SUNSTEIN

Harvard University

CAMBRIDGE
UNIVERSITY PRESS

CAMBRIDGE
UNIVERSITY PRESS

One Liberty Plaza, New York, NY 10006, USA

Cambridge University Press is part of the University of Cambridge.

It furthers the University's mission by disseminating knowledge in the pursuit of
education, learning, and research at the highest international levels of excellence.

www.cambridge.org
Information on this title: www.cambridge.org/9781107140707

First published 2016

Printed in the United States of America by Sheridan Books, Inc.

A catalogue record for this publication is available from the British Library.

Library of Congress Cataloging in Publication Data
Sunstein, Cass R., author.
The ethics of influence : government in the age of behavioral science / Cass R. Sunstein.
New York, NY : Cambridge University Press, 2016. | Series: Cambridge studies in economics,
choice, and society | Includes bibliographical references and index.
LCCN 2015051000 | ISBN 9781107140707 (Hardback)
LCSH: Public policy (Law)–Psychological aspects. | Public policy
(Law)–United States–Psychological aspects. | BISAC: POLITICAL SCIENCE / Public Policy /
Economic Policy.
LCC K378 .S86 2016 | DDC 172/.1–dc23 LC record available at
http://lccn.loc.gov/2015051000

ISBN 978-1-107-14070-7 Hardback

For my students

Contents

Acknowledgments

This book has been on my mind for many years, but it ultimately emerged from an essay on the ethics of choice architecture and nudging, delivered at a conference on that topic at Humboldt University in Berlin in January 2015. I am most grateful to participants in the conference for many valuable thoughts and suggestions. For obvious historical reasons, many Germans are keenly aware of the risks that can come from government influence (and manipulation); the discussion in Berlin was particularly valuable for that reason. For similar reasons, I am grateful to participants in a spirited colloquium at the Max Planck Institute in June 2015, and particularly to my hosts, Ralph Hertwig and Gerd Gigerenzer.

In addition, my thinking has been greatly informed by a special issue on this topic for the REVIEW OF PHILOSOPHY AND PSYCHOLOGY, available at http://link.springer.com/journal/volumesAndIssues/13164. I am most grateful to the various contributors to that issue for their contributions, and to the editors, Adrien Barton and Till Grüne-Yanoff, for arranging it and for many helpful suggestions.

Many people provided comments on one or more of the chapters. Timur Kuran offered wise suggestions on the manuscript as a whole. Till Grüne-Yanoff provided a careful reading of a near-final draft, which resulted in numerous improvements. Thanks to Anne Barnhill, Elizabeth Emens, Craig Fox, Matthew Lipka, Heidi Liu, George Loewenstein, Martha Nussbaum, Eric Posner, Arden Rowell, Lucia Reisch, Maya Shankar, Richard Thaler, the late Edna Ullmann-Margalit, and Adrian Vermeule for helpful discussions and valuable suggestions of many different sorts. Special thanks to Thaler for joint work on the topics of nudging and choice architecture, which has of course informed everything presented here. Special thanks also to Reisch for a wonderful coauthorship that provided the basis for Chapter 7 and for generous permission to use that material here.

Many thanks as well to David Halpern, who has headed the spectacularly successful Behavioural Insights Team in the United Kingdom, for a variety of valuable discussions over the years. I am also grateful to my agent, Sarah Chalfant, and Karen Maloney, my editor, for their support, wisdom, and advice. For excellent research assistance, I am grateful to Heidi Liu and Patrick Grubel.

The book is dedicated to my students, which means that it is dedicated to thousands of people. I have been blessed (and that is the right word) to be able to work with, and to learn from, truly extraordinary students at the University of Chicago and Harvard (and for shorter periods, at Columbia and Yale). From the distant past, thanks to a sample of amazing thinkers and human beings: Richard Cordray, Catherine Epstein, Lisa Heinzerling, Jessica Hertz, Michael Herz, and Larry Kramer. From the very recent past and the present, another sample: Daniel Kanter, Heidi Liu, and Mary Schnoor. From the current undergraduate class, thanks to three scholar-athletes, who have had the kindness to indulge me on the squash court as well as on academic matters: Isabelle Dowling, Michelle Gemmell, and Jake Matthews.

I am more honored than I can say to have had a chance to work with you all – and by you, I mean the thousands, not just the samples – and I thank you from the bottom of my heart. It's also been a ton of fun.

I have drawn here on other work, done more or less contemporaneously with this book. I am grateful to the respective journals for permission to draw on *The Ethics of Nudging*, 32 YALE J. REG. 493 (2015); *Automatically Green,* 38 HARV. ENV. L. REV. 127 (2014) (coauthored with Lucia Reisch); *Fifty Shades of Manipulation,* 1 J. MARKETING BEHAVIOR 213 (2016); and *Do People Like Nudging,* ADMINISTRATIVE LAW REVIEW (Forthcoming 2016). I am also grateful to the HARVARD LAW REVIEW for permission to draw on *Nudges vs. Shoves,* 127 HARV. L. REV. FORUM 210 (2014), on which I also drew for a chapter of CHOOSING NOT TO CHOOSE (2015).

CHAPTER I

The Age of Behavioral Science

We live in an age of psychology and behavioral economics – the behavioral sciences.

For-profit companies are using behavioral research every day. They want to learn how people think and to use that learning to make money. Charitable organizations consult behavioral scientists to find out how they might attract donors and increase donations. For their part, public officials are increasingly turning to the behavioral sciences to promote their goals. They are influencing people in multiple ways in order to reduce poverty, to increase employment, to clean the air, to improve health, to encourage people to vote, and to increase safety on the highways. What are the ethical constraints on their actions?

From the ethical point of view, there are large differences between coercion and influence. A single person can certainly coerce another: A thief, armed with a gun, tells you, "Your money or your life." Coercion might also be said to occur when employers inform their employees that unless they submit to certain requests, they will lose their jobs. Many of the most objectionable forms of coercion come from governments, which may threaten people with jail, or with large fines, if they do not do exactly what public officials want. In his great book *On Liberty*,[1] John Stuart Mill argued that coercion was unacceptable unless it was designed to prevent "harm to others." Mill's target was the use of force.

Mere influences seem far less objectionable. If a beggar sitting on a street corner asks you for money, you are free to refuse. The same is true if an employer asks you to do certain tasks, while also making it clear that you are at liberty to decline. If a friend manipulates you into doing what she wants you to do, rather than what you want to do, you might not be

---

[1] *See* JOHN STUART MILL, *On Liberty, in* THE BASIC WRITINGS OF JOHN STUART MILL: ON LIBERTY, THE SUBJECTION OF WOMEN, AND UTILITARIANISM (2002/originally published 1863).

thrilled, but at least you haven't been forced (and you might admire her for
her ingenuity). A government might engage in public education campaigns, or even propaganda, but if people are allowed to ignore what
public officials say, the problem, and the risks to liberty and well-being,
might not seem all that severe.

That is certainly a reasonable view, and as we will see in some detail,
most people seem to hold it – not only in the United States, but in
Sweden, Germany, Italy, France, the United Kingdom, Hungary, and
Denmark as well. But it would be a mistake to underestimate the effects
of influence and the extent to which it can be used for good or for evil. We
keep learning about its nature, and its subtle and sometimes decisive
power. Dale Carnegie's 1936 classic, *How to Win Friends and Influence
People*,[2] has sold many millions of copies, in part because of its terrific and
often hilarious insights into how to move people in the directions you
want. Some of Carnegie's advice is pretty innocuous (but smart): "Don't
criticize, condemn, or complain." (It really is a good idea to avoid com-
plaints.) "Give honest and sincere appreciation." "Become genuinely interested in other people." "Talk in terms of the other person's interest." Some
of his advice is clever: "The only way to get the best of an argument is to
avoid it." (Carnegie thinks that you can't win an argument, and it would
be foolish to argue with him about that.) A few of his ideas might be
thought to get close to an ethical line: "Start with questions to which the
other person will answer yes." "Let the other person feel the idea is his or
hers." (Very effective, even though it can be counted as a form of
manipulation.)

Carnegie's book is wise, even brilliant, and somehow also humane,
because it treats human foibles with kindness, gentleness, and humor
rather than contempt. Everyone should read it (and read it again, every
few years). But it is a product of Carnegie's own experiences and
intuitions, rather than of empirical study. The preeminent modern
discussion, initially published in 1984, is Robert Cialdini's *Influence*,[3]
which offers six principles, all of them with strong empirical foundations.
One of these is *reciprocity*: People like to return favors, and if you give
someone something (a discount, a little cash, and a token), you'll probably
get something back. Another principle is *social proof*: If a lot of people
seem to think something, or to do something, others will be inclined to

[2] DALE CARNEGIE, HOW TO WIN FRIENDS AND INFLUENCE PEOPLE (1936).
[3] ROBERT CIALDINI, INFLUENCE (1984).

think it or do it too. (A good way to change behavior is to tell people that other people are now doing what you want them to do.) Another is *scarcity*: People find things more attractive when they seem hard to get or sharply limited in availability.

If you know about these principles, you will be in a far better position to sell things (including yourself) to others. Public officials and governments can do the same thing, Maybe that's fine, but we can easily imagine uses of Cialdini's work that would seem ethically questionable or worse. And in the last forty years, psychologists and behavioral economists have taught us immeasurably more about how human beings can affect one another.

A lie is a form of influence, and it is usually unacceptable, not least if it comes from governments. Outside of highly unusual circumstances, public officials should not lie. A statement might be literally true, and hence not a lie, but nonetheless deceptive or manipulative; if a friend deceives or manipulates you, he isn't being particularly friendly. To be sure, politicians would be well advised to read Carnegie and Cialdini and make use of what they learn. (Many politicians have a good intuitive sense of their ideas.) But most people would agree that politicians should not manipulate people – certainly as a general rule. What counts as manipulation? What are the ethical constraints on influence, when it comes from government?

To answer that question, we need some kind of framework. Ethical states focus above all on four values: welfare, autonomy, dignity, and self-government. If they are concerned with human welfare – and they had better be – such states will try to increase the likelihood that people will have good lives. Partly for that reason, they will allow people to go their own way, and in that sense respect personal autonomy (at least most of the time). If they are concerned with dignity – and they had better be – they will treat people with respect (all of the time). They will ensure that people can govern themselves, which means that people must have the authority to control their leaders.

The four values call for firm constraints on what governments can do, whether they are engaging in coercion or merely imposing influence. Authoritarian states do not allow autonomy; they do not respect dignity; they forbid self-government; they tend not to promote people's welfare. But the four values also require governments to act, not merely to refrain from acting. However we define it, human welfare does not come from the sky. Self-government is a precious achievement, requiring a certain kind of architecture. People who are subject to violence, uneducated, or desperately poor cannot be autonomous, or cannot enjoy such autonomy as they may have. A dignified life requires background conditions and social support.

It is true that the four values require investigation. Perhaps one of them is central and the others are derivative. Many people would give pride of place to dignity; many others insist that human welfare is central. We might also find conflicts among the values – as, for example, when the pursuit of welfare undermines autonomy, or when self-government places individual dignity at risk. But it is often possible to make progress by bracketing the deepest theoretical questions, and by seeing if some approaches compromise none of the values and can attract support from people who are committed to all of them, or who are uncertain of their relationship. I hope to show that many of the most promising approaches have exactly those virtues.

It is also true that many people distrust government. They believe that it is biased or ignorant, or buffeted about by powerful interest groups. They do not want it thinking all that much about how to improve people's lives, whether through coercion or even through influence. Individuals and free markets should be doing that, not public officials. But that is a pretty extreme position, and even if some version of it is right, government has to lay the groundwork – for example, by protecting property rights and by enforcing contracts. Efforts to lay the groundwork will coerce and influence, and even the most minimal state must be justified and compared to the alternatives. Perhaps it will promote people's welfare and increase their freedom, but perhaps not.

To know, we have to investigate some ethical questions. We also have to know a lot about the relevant facts – and if we do not, we will have to be honest that we are speculating. What does an ethical state do? What does it avoid? What makes a state unethical? What kinds of distinctions, if any, should we make between acts and omissions?

If we keep the four governing values in mind, we will be in a better position to answer such questions. We will be inclined to favor acts of government that promote those values, and to reject acts of government that violate one or more of them. As we shall see, we will be especially well disposed toward approaches that preserve freedom of choice, but that also steer people in directions that promote human welfare, dignity, and self-government. Much of my discussion here will be devoted to such approaches and to seeing how and when they can avoid crossing ethical lines.

A Growing Movement

Government has many tools in its toolbox. It can prohibit and it can require. It can use the criminal law. It can threaten and it can promise. It can tax and it can subsidize. It can do much more.

Coercion runs into distinctive objections. It abridges freedom of action, for better or for worse; it can reduce economic growth; and it can have unintended bad consequences. A ban on cigarette smoking, for example, would create black markets, and in the United States, the era of Prohibition was mostly a disaster. To be sure, coercion has an important place, even in the freest societies. No reasonable person thinks that murder, rape, and assault should be allowed, and if the goal is to protect health, safety, and the environment, a nation will have to rely on mandates and bans. But if freedom and welfare matter, coercion is often best avoided, and so the last decade has seen a remarkably rapid growth of interest in choice-preserving, low-cost tools, sometimes called *nudges*.[4] For example, many governments are keenly interested in disclosing information; in providing reminders and warnings; and in using default rules, which establish what happens if people do nothing. Some of those approaches can save a lot of lives.[5]

For public institutions, many of the most popular tools, and perhaps increasingly many, involve nudges, understood as interventions that maintain people's freedom of choice, and uses of *choice architecture*, understood as the background conditions for people's choices. (I will explore definitional issues in more detail later.) In the United States,[6] the United Kingdom,[7] Germany,[8] and many other nations, governments have enlisted people with expertise in behavioral science, with the goal of identifying approaches that will help to achieve widely shared social ends – increasing economic growth, cutting the cost of government, promoting compliance with the law, improving public health, reducing poverty and corruption, protecting the environment, and increasing national security. As we shall see, national surveys suggest that most citizens, in countries with highly

[4] Catalogs can be found in OECD, REGULATORY POLICY AND BEHAVIORAL ECONOMICS (2014). European Commision, Behavorial Insights Appiled Policy: Overview across 32 European Countries.
[5] An especially good demonstration is BEHAVIORAL ECONOMICS AND PUBLIC HEALTH (Christina A. Roberto and Ichiro Kawachi eds., 2015).
[6] See, e.g., Cass A. Sunstein, Simple (2013); Courtney Subramanian, *"Nudge" Back in Fashion in White House*, TIME, August 9, 2013.
[7] See, e.g., DAVID HALPERN, INSIDE THE NUDGE UNIT (2015); Tamsin Rutter, *The Rise of Nudge – The Unit Helping Politicians to Fathom Human Behaviour*, THE GUARDIAN, July 23, 2015.
[8] See, e.g., Philip Plickert and Hanno Beck, *Kanzlerin sucht Verhaltensforscher*, FRANKFURTER ALLGEMEINE ZEITUNG, August 26, 2014.

diverse histories and cultures, approve of nudges. While many people oppose coercion as such, they show far less skepticism about nudging.

Most advanced nations already have some kind of Council of Economic Advisers, focusing on economic growth and decreasing unemployment. Should they also have a Council of Psychological Advisers, focusing on behavioral science and choice architecture, and exploring when people could benefit from a nudge? Maybe some already do. The United Kingdom has its own high-profile "nudge unit." In 2015, President Barack Obama memorialized the efforts of the United States with an executive order, formally committing the nation to uses of behavioral sciences. The importance of this executive order cannot be overstated in view of its likely role in making behavioral science a permanent part of American government (see Appendix C).

Consider three exemplary initiatives from the United States – which have analogues in many nations – and ask whether any of them raises serious ethical problems.

1. In 2010, the Federal Reserve Board adopted a regulation to protect consumers, and especially poor consumers, from high bank overdraft fees.[9] The regulation forbids banks from automatically enrolling people in "overdraft protection" programs; instead, customers have to sign up. In explaining its action, the Board drew on behavioral research showing that "consumers are likely to adhere to the established default rule, that is, the outcome that would apply if the consumer takes no action."[10] The Board also referred to the phenomenon of "unrealistic optimism" – suggesting that consumers might well underestimate the likelihood that they will not overdraw their accounts.

2. In 2014, the Food and Drug Administration (FDA) proposed to revise its "nutrition facts" panel, which can be found on almost all food packages.[11] The panel is a nudge, and the FDA wanted it to be as clear and helpful as possible. Drawing directly on behavioral science, the FDA stated that the new label could "assist consumers by making the long-term health consequences of consumer food choices more salient and by providing contextual cues of food consumption."[12] Explaining

---

[9] Federal Reserve Board Requirements for Overdraft Services, 12 C.F.R. § 205.17 (2010).
[10] Federal Reserve System Electronic Fund Transfers, 74 Fed. Reg. 59038 (2009).
[11] U.S. Food & Drug Administration, *Preliminary Regulatory Impact Analysis: Nutrition Facts/Serving Sizes* 2 (2014), *available at* www.fda.gov/downloads/Food/GuidanceRegulation/GuidanceDocuments RegulatoryInformation/LabelingNutrition/UCM385669.pdf.
[12] *Id.* at 5.

that consumers might need this information, the FDA added that the "behavioral economics literature suggests that distortions internal to consumers (or internalities) due to time-inconsistent preferences, myopia or present-biased preferences, visceral factors (e.g., hunger), or lack of self-control, can also create the potential for policy intervention to improve consumer welfare."[13] I will have more to say about some of these terms later, but the basic idea is that consumers might focus on immediate pleasures and neglect long-term health consequences. A good nutrition facts panel could help.

3. In 2014, the FDA proposed to assert authority over a range of tobacco products.[14] In explaining its action, it referred to behavioral research, emphasizing that "consumers may suffer from time-inconsistent behavior, problems with self-control, addiction, and poor information, which prevent them from fully internalizing the benefits of reducing tobacco use."[15] The FDA added that there are "opportunities for regulation of tobacco products to enhance social welfare for the population at large. Time inconsistency exists when consumers use lower rates of discount for consequences far in the future than for consequences close to the present. Time-inconsistent consumers make current decisions that they would not make from the perspective of their future selves."[16]

From these examples, it should be plain that in the United States, psychology and behavioral science are playing a major role in important policy domains. The Consumer Financial Protection Bureau, created in 2010, is particularly interested in using behavioral research to protect consumers in financial markets. Consider its excellent mantra: "Know before you owe."[17] Among its main goals are clarity and simplification, so that consumers can understand what they are signing, and so that they can engage in genuine comparison shopping. In financial markets, companies might well have an incentive to baffle people or to offer terms that are tempting and attractive, but not really beneficial.[18] The Bureau is working to counteract that problem, with close reference to how people actually think. It turns out

---

[13] *Id.* at 6.
[14] Department of Health and Human Services, U.S. Food & Drug Administration, *Deeming Tobacco Products to Be Subject to the Food, Drug, and Cosmetic Act* 6 (2014), *available at* www.fda.gov/downloads/AboutFDA/ReportsManualsForms/Reports/EconomicAnalyses/UCM394933.pdf.
[15] *Id.* at 15. [16] *Id.* at 10.
[17] *See* Consumer Financial Protection Bureau, *Credit Cards: Know before You Owe, available at* www.consumerfinance.gov/credit-cards/knowbeforeyouowe/.
[18] *See* George Akerlof and Robert Shiller, Phishing for Phools (2015).

that making sensible comparisons can be hard – how does one mortgage really stack up against another? – and simplification can help a lot.

In 2014, the United States created its behavioral insights team, called the White House Social and Behavioral Sciences Team (SBST). The team is overseen by the White House Office of Science and Technology Policy and is engaged in a range of projects designed to test the effects of various policies, with close reference to behavioral research. With some simple interventions, it has produced major success stories, helping more members of the military service to save for retirement, more students to go to college, more veterans to take advantage of education and job-training benefits, more farmers to obtain loans, and more families to obtain health insurance.[19] For example, just one behaviorally informed email, specifying the three steps needed to enroll in a workplace savings plan, and explaining the potential value of making even small contributions, nearly doubled the enrollment rate for members of the military service.

In 2010, the United Kingdom became the first to create a Behavioural Insights Team (BIT), with the specific goal of incorporating an understanding of human psychology into policy initiatives.[20] David Halpern, the leader of BIT, is an expert on behavioral science and has spearheaded a wide range of reforms to save money and to extend lives. When it was a formal part of the Cabinet Office, BIT's official website stated that its "work draws on insights from the growing body of academic research in the fields of behavioural economics and psychology which show how often subtle changes to the way in which decisions are framed can have big impacts on how people respond to them."

Influenced by the underlying psychological research, the Team enlists the acronym "EAST" to capture its approach: Easy, Attractive, Social, and Timely.[21] BIT has used behavioral science to promote initiatives in numerous areas, including smoking cessation,[22] energy efficiency,[23] organ

[19] See Social and Behavioral Sciences Team, *Annual Report* (2015), *available at* www.whitehouse.gov/ sites/default/files/microsites/ostp/sbst_2015_annual_report_final_9_14_15.pdf.

[20] See Tamsin Rutter, *The Rise of Nudge – The Unit Helping Politicians to Fathom Human Behaviour* (July 23, 2015).

[21] See generally Owain Service et al., *EAST: Four Simple Ways to Apply Behavioral Insights* (2015), *available at* www.behaviouralinsights.co.uk/wp-content/uploads/2015/07/BIT-Publication-EAST_ FA_WEB.pdf.

[22] See Behavioural Insights Team, *Applying Behavioral Insight to Health* (2010), *available at* www.gov .uk/government/uploads/system/uploads/attachment_data/file/60524/403936_BehaviouralInsight_ acc.pdf, at 8.

[23] See Behavioural Insights Team, *Annual Update 2011–2012, available at* www.gov.uk/government/ uploads/system/uploads/attachment_data/file/83719/Behavioural-Insights-Team-Annual-Update- 2011-12_0.pdf.

donation,[24] consumer protection,[25] and tax compliance.[26] BIT has had some big successes. For example:

- A message designed to prompt people to join the Organ Donor Registry added no fewer than 100,000 people to the Registry in a single year;[27]
- Automatically enrolling individuals in pension schemes increased saving rates for those employed by large firms in the UK from 61 to 83 percent;[28]
- A behaviorally informed approach increased tax payment rates from delinquent taxpayers by over 5 percentage points.[29]

In 2014, the Team moved from the Cabinet Office to become a partly privatized joint venture, a self-described "social purpose company" owned by the government, the team's employees, and Nesta (an innovation charity).[30]

Other nations have expressed keen interest in the work of the Behavioural Insights Team, and its operations have significantly expanded. Several cities in the United States, including New York and Chicago, are working with BIT or enlisting behavioral ideas. The idea of "nudge units," of one or another kind, is receiving worldwide attention. In Germany, Australia, Denmark, Sweden, Canada, Singapore, Israel, the Netherlands, South Korea, and Mexico, among other countries, behavioral insights have been used in discussions of environmental protection, financial reform, energy policy, and consumer protection. In 2014, a study by the Economic and Social Research Council found that no fewer than 136 nations have incorporated behavioral findings into some aspects of public policy, and that 51 "have developed centrally directed policy initiatives that have been influenced by the new behavioural sciences."[31]

Behavioral science has drawn considerable (and mounting) attention in Europe, in particular. The Organisation for Economic Development and Cooperation (OECD) has published a Consumer Policy Toolkit that

---

[24] *See* Behavioural Insights Team, *Applying Behavioral Insight to Health* (2010), at 10.
[25] *See* Behavioural Insights Team, *Annual Update 2011–2012*.   [26] *Id.*
[27] *See* Owain Service et al., *EAST: Four Simple Ways to Apply Behavioral Insights* (2015), at 32.
[28] *Id.* at 4.   [29] *Id.* at 5.
[30] *See, e.g.,* Patrick Wintour, *Government's Behavioural Insight Team to Become a Mutual and Sell Services*, THE GUARDIAN, February 4, 2014.
[31] Mark Whitehead et al., *Nudging All over the World 4* (2014), *available at* https://changingbehaviours .files.wordpress.com/2014/09/nudgedesignfinal.pdf.

recommends a number of initiatives rooted in behavioral findings.[32] A report from the European Commission, called *Green Behavior*, enlists behavioral science to outline policy initiatives to protect the environment.[33] In the European Union, the Directorate-General for Health and Consumers has also shown the influence of psychology and behavioral economics.[34] Private organizations, notably including the European Nudge Network, are using behavioral insights creatively to promote a variety of environmental, health-related, and other goals. Emphasizing behavioral findings, Singapore has initiated a large number of reforms in this domain.[35] A Norwegian group, GreeNudge, focuses on environmental protection.[36]

There has been particular interest in using psychological and behavioral research in the areas of poverty and development, with considerable attention from the World Bank, whose 2015 report was devoted entirely to this topic.[37] In the words of Jim Yung Kim, president of the World Bank, "insights into how people make decisions can lead to new interventions that help households to save more, firms to increase productivity, communities to reduce the prevalence of diseases, parents to improve cognitive development in children, and consumers to save energy. The promise of this approach to decision making and behavior is enormous, and its scope of application is extremely wide."[38]

As the World Bank report demonstrates, behaviorally informed approaches might help combat corruption and inefficiency, and also make existing programs more effective, in part by combating low take-up rates and improving well-intentioned but counterproductive initiatives that are not alert to how people think. It is worth underlining the problem of low take-up rates.[39] Many private and public institutions have important

---

[32] ORGANISATION FOR ECONOMIC CO-OPERATION AND DEVELOPMENT, CONSUMER POLICY TOOLKIT (2010).

[33] *See generally* European Commission, Science for Environment Policy, *Future Brief: Green Behaviour 2012, available at* http://ec.europa.eu/environment/integration/research/newsalert/pdf/FB4_en.pdf.

[34] *See* Directorate General for Health and Consumers, *Consumer Behaviour: The Road to Effective Policy-Making 2010, available at* http://dl4a.org/uploads/pdf/1dg-sanco-brochure-consumer-behaviour-final.pdf.

[35] *See* DONALD LOW, BEHAVIORAL ECONOMICS AND POLICY DESIGN: EXAMPLES FROM SINGAPORE (2011).

[36] GreeNudge, *How We Work, available at* www.greenudge.no/how-we-work/.

[37] *See generally* World Bank, *World Development Report, Mind, Society, and Behavior* (2015), *available at* www.worldbank.org/content/dam/Worldbank/Publications/WDR/WDR%202015/WDR-2015-Full-Report.pdf.

[38] *Id.* at xi.

[39] *See* Saurabh Bhargava and Dayanand Manoli, *Psychological Frictions and the Incomplete Take-Up of Social Benefits: Evidence from an IRS Field Experiment,* 105 AM. ECON. REV. 3489–3529 (2015).

programs that could relieve suffering (by providing economic help), increase opportunities (by offering training), and reduce violence (by promoting self-help). Unfortunately, many people do not participate in these programs. Smarter design, with a few good nudges, could help a lot.

Ethics and Personal Agency

Notwithstanding all of these developments, uses of nudging and choice architecture have sometimes run into serious objections, particularly from those who are concerned that citizens might be manipulated or treated without respect, as if they were incompetent or mere children. Suppose that you have lived under an authoritarian government, one that is in the midst of a transition to democracy. The use of nudges might be unwelcome; it might seem to be a holdover from an earlier era. Maybe some nudges look like propaganda. Or suppose that you live in Germany and that memories of East Germany, and the Stasi, remain fresh. At least in the abstract, the very idea of choice architecture might seem alarming. Or suppose that you live in the United States or the United Kingdom, with their deep traditions of support for free markets and suspicion of government. Even if those traditions are not unbroken, you might want to make sure that choice architects are properly constrained and monitored.

I have said that the ethical issues largely turn on whether nudges promote or instead undermine welfare, autonomy, dignity, and self-government. Many forms of choice architecture, and those that deserve support, promote some or all of those ideals and compromise exactly none of them. In many cases, nudges are ethically required, not forbidden. In ordinary life, we have a duty to warn people who are at serious risk. A government that fails to produce such warnings is often failing to live up to its ethical obligations. Disclosure of information about the nutritional content of food can promote both welfare and autonomy. Automatic voter registration – common in many nations – can promote self-government.

As we shall also see, the ethical analysis of nudges is similar to the corresponding analysis for other tools, such as fines, bans, and mandates. It follows that much of the discussion here bears on the wide range of tools that government might use to make people's lives better. If welfare is our guide, for example, we will be drawn to careful consideration of the costs and benefits of what government proposes to do. Analysis of costs and benefits is far from perfect, but it is the best way of finding out whether reforms will increase human welfare or instead reduce it. The idea of dignity raises serious questions about mandates and bans. Some mandates do not treat human beings with respect.

But as we shall also see, the topics of nudging and choice architecture raise distinctive issues, suggesting that noncoercive influences can threaten both autonomy and dignity. In particular, concerns for dignity and for personal agency often motivate the most intuitive objections to nudges. If the government is engaged in nudging, might our own agency be at risk? Might we be objects or targets of public officials, rather than authors of the narratives of our own lives? Might government manipulate us? Behavioral science certainly offers lessons about how people can be influenced, and the line between influence and manipulation is not always clear.

People who ask such questions sometimes think that it is not enough for government to give people the formal *opportunity* to choose; it should ensure that they actually *exercise that opportunity*. All nudges preserve the opportunity to choose, but some of them call for its exercise, by prompting or requiring "active choosing." For example, an employer might ask ("prompt") people, at the beginning of their employment, to say whether they want to enroll in a health care plan, or it might require them, as a condition for employment, to state their wishes. There is a pervasive question whether institutions should ask or require people to choose, perhaps by supplementing, or "boosting," their ability to choose well.[40] Some of the best nudges are indeed "boosts." They are specifically designed to help people to be better choosers, and also to encourage or require them to indicate what they want.

I shall argue that at least if they are taken in general or in the abstract, the ethical objections to nudging lack force, and for two different reasons. *First*, both choice architecture and nudges are inevitable, and it is therefore pointless to wish them away. *Second*, many nudges, and many forms of choice architecture, are defensible and even mandatory on ethical grounds, whether we care about welfare, autonomy, dignity, self-government, or some other value. But it remains true that some nudges, and some forms of choice architecture, are unacceptable. The most obvious and important reason is that they have illicit ends. They might be intended, for example, to entrench the current government, or to help powerful private groups, or to advantage certain racial or religious majorities. But even when the ends are legitimate, public officials owe citizens a duty of transparency, and they should avoid manipulation.

---

[40]   Till Grüne-Yanoff and Ralph Hertwig, *Nudge Versus Boost: How Coherent Are Policy and Theory?*, 25 MIND & MACHINES 1 (2015).

Of course trust is central. If people do not trust public officials, they will be skeptical of nudges, even if they are even more skeptical of mandates and bans. Despite the inevitability of nudging and choice architecture, many people will say to such officials: Who are you to nudge me? *What gives you the right?* As we will see, the evidence suggests that when people are distrustful of government, they will be less likely to approve of nudging. That makes perfect sense, especially because much nudging is indeed avoidable. People who are inclined to dislike government power, and being subject to it, will not be happy about nudges.

The best way for officials to obtain trust is simple: be trustworthy. As we will see, transparency and accountability can help in this endeavor. And as we shall also see, the apparently rhetorical question (what gives you the right?) masks the real issues. Of course it needs an answer, but it has far more rhetorical force than deserves.

Government's Burden of Justification

All government action, including nudges, should face a burden of justification (and sometimes a heavy burden). Whether or not a nation's constitution specifically imposes that burden, public officials should be required to give acceptable, and sufficiently weighty, reasons for their actions. If the government requires disclosure of information, or establishes default rules to promote savings or to protect privacy, or urges schools to promote healthy eating (perhaps through cafeteria design), it must explain and defend itself.

One of my principal themes is this: The fact that people retain freedom of choice, and are ultimately permitted to go their own way, does not give public officials any kind of license to do whatever they want.[41] A choice-preserving approach has many advantages, but it might have illicit ends, or it might count as a form of unacceptable manipulation. But in many cases, a legitimate explanation is available.

To simplify a less-than-simple story: Suppose that we believe that the goal of social ordering (including those forms for which government is responsible) is to promote human welfare. We want people to have good lives (as they themselves understand that idea). If so, we will favor welfare-promoting nudges. Consider, for example, a disclosure requirement for credit card companies or mortgage providers, designed to promote

---

[41] Note as well that a disclosure requirement is a mandate, and no mere nudge, for the people on whom the requirement is imposed. It might be a nudge for consumers but a requirement for producers. I will say more about this point later.

informed choices, and likely to achieve that goal. Perhaps that requirement will help people from getting into serious economic trouble. Policies of that kind might be required on ethical grounds.

Or suppose that we believe in individual autonomy and dignity. If so, we will favor nudges and choice architecture that promote those values. Consider, for example, an effort to prompt people to make their own choices about what kind of retirement plan they want, by asking them precisely that question when they begin employment. That approach would seem to promote both autonomy and dignity. (It is possible, of course, that distrust of government, and faith in markets, will incline us to minimize government nudging on grounds of welfare, autonomy, or dignity.[42] I will get to that point in due course.)

If we value democratic self-government, we will be inclined to support nudges and choice architecture that can claim a democratic pedigree and that promote democratic goals. Any democracy has a form of choice architecture that helps define and constitute its own aspirations to self-government; authoritarian nations, of course, have their own forms of choice architecture, which make self-government impossible. A constitution can be seen as a kind of choice architecture for choice architects, one that disciplines and orients them. A self-governing society might well nudge its citizens to participate in the political process and to vote. Certainly political parties engage in such nudging, and increasingly with the help of behavioral science. It is hardly illegitimate for public officials to encourage people to vote.

In 2015, Oregon adopted a system of automatic voter registration, a form of choice architecture that is unambiguously designed to promote participation in the political process through exercise of the franchise.[43] Oregon also offered an opportunity to opt out, thus allowing citizens to say that they do not want to be voters. Oregon's idea is both simple and important: People should not have to fill out paperwork, or surmount hurdles, to become voters. So long as the problem of fraud can be handled (and it can be), even small and seemingly trivial hurdles are a bad idea, because they can have large and destructive effects. California has followed Oregon's example, and other states should too. It already has close analogies all over Europe, where automatic registration is often favored.[44]

---

[42] Edward L. Glaeser, *Paternalism and Psychology*, 73 U. CHI. L. REV. 133 (2006).

[43] *See, e.g.,* Associated Press, *Oregon Becomes First State with Automatic Voter Registration*, March 16, 2015.

[44] European Union Agency for Fundamental Rights, *Is There a Requirement under Law to Register to Vote?, available at* http://fra.europa.eu/en/publications-and-resources/data-and-maps/comparative-data/political-participation/register-vote.

That nudge raises an important general question, which is whether there might be other contexts in which it might make sense to make people right-holders by default. To have freedom of speech and religion, you don't have to opt in. No paperwork has to be filed. You have those freedoms by default. Are there other areas where the same should be said – but isn't?

Of course no one should approve of nudges or choice architecture in the abstract or as such. Some nudges, and some forms of choice architecture, do indeed run into convincing ethical objections. Both fascist and communist nations have used propaganda for insidious or malign purposes. Authoritarian nations nudge their citizens in ways that deserve widespread social disapproval. Suppose that a nation establishes a default rule stating that unless voters explicitly indicate otherwise, they will be presumed to support the incumbent leader in the election. Or suppose that a nation establishes a default rule to the effect that unless citizens indicate otherwise, their estates will revert to the nation's most powerful political party upon their death. There is ample reason to question a default rule of this kind even if citizens are authorized to opt out.

I have suggested that there is also a pervasive question about manipulation. The very concept is important, because most people do not want to be manipulated (at least most of the time; a little manipulation can be fun), but also vexed, because ordinary language does not offer a simple definition. As we shall see, transparency and accountability are indispensable safeguards, and both nudges and choice architecture should be transparent. Even if so, there is a risk of manipulation, and that risk should be avoided. Many of the most interesting and complex ethical questions involve manipulation, and I will devote a lot of attention to that concept here.

A Preview

More specifically, I will be defending eight principal conclusions.

1. It is pointless to raise ethical objections to nudging or choice architecture as such. The private sector inevitably nudges, as does the government. No government can avoid some kind of choice architecture. We can object to particular nudges, and particular goals of particular choice architects, but not to nudging in general. For human beings (or for that matter dogs and cats and mice), choice architecture is present, whether we see it or not. It is tempting to defend nudging on the part of government by saying that the private sector already nudges

(sometimes selfishly and sometimes invidiously) – but this defense is not necessary, because government is nudging even if it does not want to do so.

2. In this context, ethical abstractions (about, e.g., autonomy, dignity, legitimacy, and manipulation) can create serious confusion. We need to bring those abstractions into contact with concrete practices. Nudging and choice architecture take many diverse forms, and the force of an ethical objection depends on the specific form. It is important to avoid the trap of abstraction. In his Marginalia on Sir Joshua Reynolds, William Blake wrote, "To Generalize is to be an Idiot. To Particularize is the Alone Distinction of Merit – General Knowledges are those Knowledges that Idiots possess." Characteristically, the great poet put it much too strongly. But he had a point.

3. If welfare is our guide, much nudging is actually required on ethical grounds, even if it comes from the government. A failure to nudge might be ethically problematic and indeed abhorrent, at least if we do not insist on controversial (and possibly incoherent) distinctions between acts and omissions.[45] It is usually unacceptable not to warn people before subjecting them to serious risks; a failure to warn is a failure to nudge. So too, serious ethical problems can be raised by a failure to use an appropriate default rule, certainly if we aim to promote people's welfare.

4. If autonomy is our guide, much nudging is also required on ethical grounds. Some nudges actually promote autonomy by ensuring that choices are informed. Some nudges promote choice making, for those who want to choose, and others facilitate choice avoidance, for those who choose not to choose. In both cases, nudges promote autonomy. Some nudges free people to focus on their real concerns; there is a close relationship between autonomy and time management. People cannot be autonomous if they are unable to control their own time, or even the allocation of their limited attention. A failure to nudge might seriously compromise autonomy. Good default rules do not reduce our autonomy, they increase it.

5. Choice architecture should not, and need not, compromise individual dignity, though imaginable forms could do both. To the extent that good choice architecture allows people to be agents, and to express

[45] On acts, omissions, and government, see Cass R. Sunstein and Adrian Vermeule, *Is Capital Punishment Morally Required? Acts, Omissions, and Life-Life Tradeoffs*, 58 STAN. L. REV. 703 (2005).

their will, it promotes dignity. Reminders are helpful, and unless they take unusual forms, they do not undermine dignity. Default rules are pervasive, and taken simply as such, they are perfectly compatible with dignity. Nonetheless, it is true that the value of dignity (explicitly recognized in the German constitution[46] and playing a significant role in American constitutional law as well) does impose a barrier to some forms of choice architecture and some nudges.

6. Self-government calls for certain nudges, and it legitimates others, and it forbids still others. If we are concerned with self-government, we are likely to approve of nudges that encourage people to participate and to vote. If certain default rules emerge from the democratic process, they have a degree of legitimation for that reason. If public officials use nudges to entrench themselves, there is an evident problem. The line between acceptable campaign strategies and unacceptable self-entrenchment might not always be clear, but it would not be ethical for the incumbent party to ensure that its candidates are always listed first on ballots, or that their names are in an appealing color or a larger font.

7. Many nudges are objectionable because the choice architect has illicit ends, such as political or religious favoritism, or the inculcation of bigotry or intolerance. If the ends are legitimate, and if nudges are fully transparent and subject to public scrutiny, a convincing ethical objection is far less likely. Important constraints on unethical nudges come from forbidding illegitimate ends and from full transparency – though both ideas raise their own share of questions.

8. Even if the underlying ends are legitimate, and even if transparency is guaranteed, there is room for ethical objections in the case of manipulative interventions, certainly if people have not consented to them. The concept of manipulation deserves careful attention, especially because manipulation takes many forms and can compromise both autonomy and dignity. Some forms of manipulation are built into the fabric of everyday life, including relationships between employers and employees, friends, and even spouses. Advertisements and storefronts manipulate. Nonetheless, manipulation can run into serious ethical concerns, perhaps especially when it comes from governments.

Now let us turn to some details.

---

[46] Article 1, paragraph 1 of the German constitution states: "Human dignity shall be inviolable. To respect and protect it shall be the duty of all state authority."

CHAPTER 2

Choice and Its Architecture

Every government relies on coercion. Public officials forbid murder, rape, and assault. They impose rules to safeguard property rights and to make the highways safer (people have to drive on the right, or maybe the left), and people who violate those rules may well face a risk of jail. In numerous areas, officials mandate and they ban, even if they are generally and sincerely committed to freedom.

What's Coercion? Which Tools?

To be sure, the idea of coercion is far more complex than it first appears. When governments coerce people, they often do so by saying: *If you act in ways that we do not like, you will face a risk of punishment.* The risk might be large; maybe it is 100 percent, or close to it. The risk might be small; maybe it is 1 percent, or even lower. The punishment might be severe (the death penalty), or it might be lenient (a small fine). In any event, those who are subject to coercion usually face a choice: Obey the law, or face a penalty. Of course some people are subject to actual physical restraint. But most of the time, we say that people are "coerced" when they face a credible threat of punishment if they act in a way that officials dislike.

Government might avoid a threat of punishment and might speak instead of incentives. Some of those incentives are positive: If you engage in certain behavior, you will get a benefit, perhaps in the form of money. For example, those who buy fuel-efficient cars might be given some sort of tax subsidy. Some of those incentives are negative: If you want to pollute, you have to purchase a license, or if you engage in certain misconduct, you will have to pay a fee. The line between negative incentives and punishment is not altogether clear. If the goal is to discourage behavior, a very large fee might be more effective, and a lot more unpleasant, than a very small punishment. In fact a large fee might be a punishment. But if the government resorts to what it calls a punishment, it is usually trying to convey a strong message, which is that the underlying action is morally wrong. A fee need not have that connotation. Laws have meaning, and the meaning of punishment is quite distinct.

When do mandates, bans, and incentives make sense? When is it ethical for government to deploy them? Economists have a reasonable working theory, which points to "market failures." For electricity providers, the market failure might involve a problem of natural monopoly: Perhaps only one provider can efficiently operate in an area, and government legitimately intervenes to restrict the exercise of monopoly power. For food safety, the market failure is usually thought to involve information: Consumers often lack information about the safety of the foods they are eating, and government can intervene, either to provide that information or to regulate in a way that ensures that people will not be eating food that will make them sick. Workers might also lack information, leading them to face serious risks to their safety and health.

For environmental protection, the market failure comes in the form of externalities (or "spillovers"): Polluters impose harms on others, who are not in a position to do much about those harms. Sometimes the problem of externalities is described as one of transactions costs: It is not easy for people to get together and bargain about the problem. Clean air and clean water are "public goods" – those that cannot be provided to one person without effectively being provided to many or all. In the presence of public goods, some kind of regulation may be required, because people cannot easily provide them on their own. To do so, they have to overcome a collective action problem, and everyone will have an incentive to defect from any agreement. To be sure, social norms might solve the problem, by making it seem immoral or shameful for people to defect[1] – which argues in favor of nudges in support of those norms. And indeed, some norms do solve collective action problems; that is one of the most important functions of social norms. But in many circumstances, nudges and norms are not enough, and a more aggressive response will be required, perhaps in the form of punishment, perhaps in the form of regulation, perhaps in the form of a tax.

Behavioral scientists have also emphasized "behavioral market failures," which occur when people make decisions that reduce their own welfare.[2] Suppose, for example, that people are unduly focused on the short term, thinking that today matters, but tomorrow not so much, and next week

---

[1] *See* EDNA ULLMANN-MARGALIT, THE EMERGENCE OF NORMS (1975).
[2] *See* OREN BAR-GILL, SEDUCTION BY CONTRACT (2013).

not at all. If so, they might make serious errors. Or suppose that people suffer from optimistic bias or overconfidence, thinking that they don't have to worry about serious health risks. If so, they might not take reasonable precautions. Or suppose that people's attention is limited, so that they do not focus on important aspects of goods or activities, and that in free markets, some companies exploit that failure, leading people to make foolish choices.[3] Or suppose that people suffer from serious problems of self-control, endangering their financial situations and their health.[4]

In the face of behavioral market failures, as with standard market failures, government has an assortment of tools. Economists would want to "match" each failure to a particular tool. If the problem is one of externalities, some kind of corrective tax seems to be a good idea. If the problem is a lack of information, then the first line of defense is to provide that information. If people focus on the short term, then an educational campaign might broaden their viewscreen.

Of course many people reject purely economic approaches to these issues. Perhaps we should begin with a principle of individual autonomy, and perhaps that principle should provide the basis for our inquiries into what government ought to be doing. Even if so, we might end up with broadly similar conclusions about actual practices. In fact I will be suggesting precisely that. Or perhaps we care about fair distribution. Perhaps some people are poor and other people are rich, and perhaps that inequality reflects unfairness. Perhaps some people are subject to systematic inequality, perhaps because they lack decent opportunities, perhaps because they are disabled, perhaps because of the color of their skin. An ethical state might want to take steps to help.

Our World and Welcome to It

Nudges steer people in particular directions but also allow them to go their own way. A reminder is a nudge; so is a warning. A GPS device nudges; a default rule nudges. Disclosure of relevant information (about the risks of smoking or the costs of borrowing) counts as a nudge. A recommendation is a nudge. Save More Tomorrow plans, allowing employees to sign up to set aside some portion of their future

---

[3] *See, e.g.,* Nicola Lacetera et al., *Heuristic Thinking and Limited Attention in the Car Market,* 102 Am. Econ. Rev. 2206 (2012).

[4] An important general treatment is George Akerlof and Robert Shiller, Phishing for Phools (2015).

earnings in pension programs, are nudges. The same is true of Give More Tomorrow plans, which allow employees to decide to give some portion of their future earnings to charity.

Private institutions can and do nudge; the same is true of government. Some nudges by private institutions are ethically questionable, because they verge on deception or manipulation. The same is certainly true of some nudges from the public sector. Every legal system creates some form of choice architecture, and every legal system will nudge. No one doubts that some kinds of coercion are acceptable, and they embody certain forms of choice architecture. But many forms of choice architecture do not coerce.

Without incentives

To qualify as a nudge, an intervention must not impose significant material incentives.[5] A subsidy is not a nudge; a tax is not a nudge; a fine or a jail sentence is not a nudge. To count as such, a nudge must preserve freedom of choice. If an intervention imposes significant material costs on choosers, it might of course be justified, but it is not a nudge.

Some nudges work because they inform people. Others work because they make certain choices easier; people often choose the path of least resistance. Some such nudges, such as default rules, work because of the power of inertia and procrastination. Some nudges work because of social influences. If you are told what other people do, you might do it too, because you think it's probably a good idea to do what they do. And even if you aren't sure, you might not want to violate social norms, and so you'll go along. A default rule might be effective for just that reason; it has the power of suggestion. It might well contain information about what people do and also about what people *think* people should do. Inertia and suggestion can be a powerful combination.

If you are automatically enrolled in some kind of retirement plan, you might not bother to opt out, or you might think, "I'll opt out tomorrow" – and tomorrow never comes. Some nudges work because they make some fact or option or risk salient when it previously was not ("reminder: this bill is due"). Uses of color and large fonts can be nudges; people are more likely to see candy bars in green wrappers as healthy.[6] Advertisers certainly

---

[5] On some of the complexities here, *see* CASS R. SUNSTEIN, WHY NUDGE? 57–59 (2014).

[6] *See generally* Jonathon P. Schuldt, *Does Green Mean Healthy? Nutrition Label Color Affects Perceptions of Healthfulness*, 28 HEALTH COMMUNICATION 814 (2013).

nudge. When the government runs educational campaigns to reduce drunk driving or smoking, it is engaged in nudging.

Whenever people make decisions, they do so in light of a particular choice architecture, understood as the background against which they choose. A choice architecture will nudge. Any cafeteria has a design, and the design will affect what people select, with potentially large effects on health. Cafeterias nudge, even if those who design them do not intend any nudging.[7] Workplaces have architectures, which can encourage or discourage interactions, with major consequences for how people relate to one another, and for how often they collaborate. If people's offices are proximate, all sorts of creativity might emerge. (The University of Chicago Law School, where I taught for more than two decades, greatly benefits from open, proximate offices.)

Department stores have architectures, and they can be designed so as to promote or discourage certain choices, such as leaving without making a purchase. With its baffling and somewhat frustrating design, making it hard for people to leave, IKEA is a master of choice architecture. (Assembling IKEA furniture, which is a bit of a nightmare, has even become a form of couples therapy, though I would predict that such therapy sessions do not end well.[8]) Even if the layout of a department store is a result of chance, or does not reflect the slightest effort to steer people, it will likely have consequences for what people end up selecting.[9] Of course department stores know that.

Airports have architectures, and many of them are specifically designed so as to encourage shopping, sometimes by making it impossible to go through customs or passport control without passing a large number of stores. If people see certain items first, they are more likely to buy them.[10] If articles or books are first on a list, people will be more likely to read them – even if they are economists.[11] If you want people's attention, it's always good to be first.

---

[7] See BRIAN WANSINK, SLIM BY DESIGN 116 (2014).

[8] Peter Holley, *A Therapist Has Devised the Scariest Couples Exercise Ever: Assembling Ikea Furniture*, WASHINGTON POST, April 30, 2015, *available at* www.washingtonpost.com/news/morning-mix/wp/2015/04/30/a-therapist-has-devised-the-scariest-couples-exercise-ever-assembling-ikea-furniture/.

[9] See WANSINK, SLIM BY DESIGN (2014).

[10] Eran Dayan and Maya Bar-Hillel, *Nudge to Nobesity II: Menu Positions Influence Food Orders*, 6 JUDGMENT AND DECISION MAKING 333 (2011).

[11] See Daniel R. Feenberg et al., *It's Good to be First: Order Bias in Reading and Citing NBER Working Papers* (Nat'l Bureau of Econ. Research, Working Paper No. 20401, 2014), *available at* www.nber.org/papers/w21141.

Law

The law of contract is permeated with default rules, which establish what happens if people say nothing. Of course silence cannot make a contract, but when people have entered into a contractual relationship, default rules determine how gaps should be filled. These rules have major effects on our rights and our lives. Your legal relationships with your employer, your mortgage provider, your rental car company, your hotel, your credit card company, and even your spouse and your children consist in large part of default rules. Welfare and job training programs typically come with defaults.

Suppose that the contracting parties are silent on whether employment is "at will" or "for cause," establishing whether an employer may end the relationship for any reason at all, or indeed for no reason. If so, the law must supply a default; neither possibility is foreordained by nature, and neither comes from the sky. Whether you have job security might well be a product of a default rule, provided by the legal system. Or consider "implied warranties" of various sorts, which people can waive if they want, but which provide the background for people's bargaining.[12] The law to one side, a cell phone, a tablet, and a computer will inevitably come with defaults, which can be changed if people decide to do so.

Default rules may or may not be highly visible, but they nudge. They often operate like a GPS device, and they can even help to shape our preferences and our values. Suppose that you are told that you have a right not to be discriminated against on the basis of age – but that you can waive the right to sue for age discrimination, for a fee (perhaps at the time of retirement). Now suppose that you are told that you have no right to be discriminated against on the basis of age – but that you can buy the right to sue for discrimination, for a fee. In the first case, you might well demand a high amount to give up your right, and you might well think that no amount is high enough. (That would be pretty extreme, but you might think it.) In the second case, you would probably be willing to pay a far lower amount to buy the right. The idea of an "endowment effect" – meaning the effect of the initial grant of the right in increasing people's valuation of goods – captures the basic point.[13] People value goods more highly if they own them in the first instance. Both private and public

---

[12] *See* Richard Craswell, *Contract Law, Default Rules, and the Philosophy of Promising*, 88 Mich. L. Rev. 489, 516 (1989).
[13] *See* Richard Thaler, Misbehaving 12–19 (2015).

institutions initially grant entitlements, and to that extent they influence preferences and values. Markets cannot exist without initial grants, and so it is pointless to wish them away.

Default rules tend to create a feeling of entitlement, and once people have a feeling of entitlement, they may well demand a good deal to give up what they have. In this respect, a default rule can preserve freedom of choice, but it might not be neutral. It might well affect how, and how much, people value things.

To some people, this is a disturbing or even threatening fact. They are not at all enthusiastic about the idea that their values, and significant aspects of their lives, are influenced by default rules, which they did not themselves select, and which might well come from the practices, judgments, or wishes of other people. (As we shall see, many people object to nudges because they prize individual agency.) Nonetheless, that influence is in place, and it is not helpful to ignore it.

It is also important to see that attention is a scarce resource. In this respect, it is a lot like money, and we have to find good ways to allocate it. Attention is pervasively subject to influences, whether they are imposed consciously or not. Suppose that an institution adopts complex and difficult applications for loans, for educational opportunities, for refinancing mortgages, for permits, for training, for financial benefits of any kind. If so, people may not apply; a great deal of money might be lost as a result.[14] This point has implications for regulatory design and for actual and appropriate nudging. It suggests that the private sector may help or hurt people by focusing their attention in certain ways. The same is true for the public sector, whether or not it seeks to do so. A regulation might be written or applied in a way that makes certain features of a situation especially salient, and salience is a nudge.

For the future, we could imagine new forms of choice architecture that are designed to improve antipoverty programs;[15] environmental programs (see Chapter 7); energy programs; retirement and social security programs;[16] anti-obesity programs;[17] educational programs;[18] health care

---

[14] *See* Benjamin J. Keys et al., *Failure to Refinance* 1, 5 (Nat'l Bureau of Econ. Research, Working Paper No. 20401, 2014), *available at* www.nber.org/papers/w20401.

[15] *See* SENDHIL MULLAINATHAN AND ELDAR SHAFIR, SCARCITY 168 (2013).

[16] *See* Ryan Bubb and Richard Pildes, *Why Behavioral Economics Trims Its Sails*, HARV. L. REV. 1593, 1614 (2014).

[17] *See* WANSINK, SLIM BY DESIGN 106 (2014).

[18] *See* Adam Lavecchia et al., *Behavioral Economics of Education: Progress and Possibilities* 30 Nat'l Bureau of Econ. Research, Working Paper No. 20609, 2014), *available at* www.nber.org/papers/w20609.

programs; and programs to increase organ donation.[19] We could also imagine forms of choice architecture that are designed to combat race and sex discrimination,[20] to help disabled people, and to promote economic growth. A great deal of future work needs to be devoted to choice architecture in these and related domains.[21]

There is no question that certain nudges, and certain kinds of choice architecture, can raise serious ethical problems. Consider, for example, a government that uses nudges to promote discrimination on the basis of race, sex, or religion. Any fascist government might well (and almost certainly does) nudge. Hitler nudged; so did Stalin. Terrorists nudge. Even truthful information (e.g., about crime rates) might fan the flames of violence and prejudice. (If people learn that crime is widespread, they might be more likely to engage in crime, because it is the social norm.) Groups or nations that are committed to violence often enlist nudges in their cause. Even if nudges do not have illicit ends, it is possible to wonder whether those who enlist them are treating people with respect.

I have suggested that the most prominent concerns about nudging and choice architecture point to four foundational commitments: welfare, autonomy, dignity, and self-government. Some nudges could run afoul of one or more of these commitments. It is easy to identify welfare-reducing nudges that lead people to waste time or money; an unhelpful default rule could fall in that category, as could an educational campaign designed to persuade people to purchase excessive insurance or to make foolish investments. Nudges could be, and often are, harmful to the environment. Pollution is, in part, a product of unhelpful choice architecture. When crime and corruption are pervasive, it is because of forms of choice architecture that allow them to prosper, or perhaps even encourage them.

---

[19] For an interesting empirical result, *see* Judd Kessler and Alvin Roth, *Don't Take 'No' for an Answer: An Experiment with Actual Organ Donor Registrations* 27 (Nat'l Bureau of Econ. Research, Working Paper No. 20378, 2014), *available at* www.nber.org/papers/w20378 (finding that required active choosing has a smaller effect, in terms of getting people to sign up for organ donation, than prompted choice).

[20] *See* Iris Bohnet, What Works: Gender Equality by Design (2016); Iris Bohnet et al., *When Performance Trumps Gender Bias: Joint Versus Separate Evaluation* 16 (2013), *available at* www .montana.edu/nsfadvance/documents/PDFs/resources/WhenPerformanceTrumpsGenderBias.pdf.

[21] *See* World Bank, World Development Report, Mind and Society: How a Better Understanding of Human Behavior Can Improve Development Policy 86 (2015) (exploring how behaviorally informed policies might promote development, in part by combating poverty).

The Trap of Abstraction

To come to terms with the ethical questions, it is exceedingly important to bring first principles in contact with concrete practices. For purposes of orientation, it will be useful to give a more detailed accounting of potential nudges that might alter choice architecture. One reason is to avoid the trap of abstraction, which can create serious confusion when we are thinking about public policy. For example, the work of the Behavioural Insights Team in the United Kingdom and the Social and Behavioral Sciences Team in the United States has produced significant changes in behavior, including dramatic increases in the take-up of important programs, but generally without raising serious ethical issues. A look at concrete practices puts the ethical issues in far better perspective.[22]

Motivating Nudges

Default rules are probably the most obvious and important nudges. Others include

- disclosure of factual information (e.g., about the caloric content of foods);
- simplification (e.g., of applications for job training or financial aid);
- warnings, graphic or otherwise (e.g., on cigarette packages);
- reminders (e.g., of bills that are about to become due or of the availability of benefits);
- increases in ease and convenience (e.g., through website, airport, or cafeteria design);
- personalization (e.g., through a communication that focuses on the personal situation of recipients, that specifies a personal appointment time, or that informs people of potential actions);
- framing and timing (e.g., through a clear statement that people are entitled to certain benefits, or by sending reminders and messages at a time when people are likely to be paying attention);
- increases in salience (e.g., by making potential benefits very clear to those who might enjoy them);

---

[22] See DAVID HALPERN, INSIDE THE NUDGE UNIT (2015); Social and Behavioral Sciences Team, Annual Report (2015), available at www.whitehouse.gov/sites/default/files/microsites/ostp/sbst_2015_annual_report_final_9_14_15.pdf.

- uses of social norms (e.g., disclosure of how one's energy use compares to that of one's neighbors);[23]
- nonmonetary rewards, such as public recognition;
- active choosing (as in the question: *What retirement plan do you want?* or *Do you want to become an organ donor?*); and
- precommitment strategies[24] (through which people agree, in advance, to a particular course of conduct, such as a smoking cessation or weight loss program).

All of these approaches preserve freedom of choice; they allow people to go their own way. They could also be mixed and matched. For example, doctors could default smokers into a smoking cessation program, subject to opt-out. They could accompany the program with reminders and information disclosure. Doctors might also nudge smokers – perhaps through active choosing – into a smoking cessation program that contains economic incentives (e.g., with a monetary reward for quitting for six months). People might be asked: *Do you want to enroll in a program by which you will get some money if you quit smoking?* Or they might be asked: *Do you want to enroll in a program by which you will lose some money if you do not quit smoking?* Evidence shows that such programs have significant beneficial effects.[25] Public officials might disclose information about the risks of smoking while also enlisting social norms to try to reduce tobacco use; here too, the two approaches might work well together.

It is important to acknowledge that some nudges preserve freedom of choice for one population (such as consumers), while mandating action from some other population (such as producers). Suppose that the government requires large employers to adopt automatic enrollment plans either for retirement or for health insurance. If so, employees are nudged, but employers are coerced. Or suppose that the government requires chain restaurants or movie theaters to display calories to consumers (as in fact the Affordable Care Act mandates). If so, customers are nudged, but restaurants are coerced. Some nudges from government take the form of requiring some group X to nudge some group Y. Other nudges do not impose any

[23] *See generally* Hunt Allcott, *Social Norms and Energy Conservation*, 95 J. PUBLIC ECON. 1082 (2011).

[24] *See generally* Ian Ayres, CARROTS AND STICKS: UNLOCK THE POWERS OF INCENTIVES TO GET THINGS DONE (2011) (reviewing the power of self-commitment devices to change people's behaviors).

[25] Scott D. Halpern et al., *Randomized Trial of Four Financial-Incentive Programs for Smoking Cessation*, 372 NEW ENG. J. MED. 2108–2117 (2015).

requirements at all; they are really like a GPS device, giving everyone the option to say, "I will go my own way, thank you very much!"

Nudges can have substantial effects on both individual lives and social welfare. Their effects might be comparable to that of mandates, bans, and incentives. Consider a few examples:

- In Denmark, automatic enrollment in retirement plans has had a much larger effect than substantial tax incentives.[26] It is worth pausing over this remarkable finding. A mere shift in the default rule, from opt-in to opt-out, has a much bigger impact than giving people real money to encourage them to opt in.

- In the United States, simplification of the financial aid form, to assist people who seek to attend college, has been found to have as large an effect, in promoting college attendance, as a several thousand dollar increase in financial aid.[27] In principle, simplification should not be expected to have such significant impacts, but it can often do the work of large monetary incentives.

- At a university in Sweden, a switch in the default setting on printers, from single-sided to double-sided, produced a 15 percent decrease in the use of paper. The effect occurred immediately and remained intact after six months.[28] This effect was far larger than that of education and moral suasion (which was approximately zero) and also projected to be larger than that of significant economic incentives for conserving paper.

- In the United States, efforts to inform consumers of how their energy use compares to that of their neighbors has had the same effect in reducing energy use as a large spike (8–20 percent) in the short-term cost of electricity.[29]

What accounts for such effects? In behavioral science, many people distinguish between two families of cognitive operations in the human mind: System 1, which is fast, automatic, and intuitive, and System 2, which is slow, calculative, and deliberative.[30] When you recognize a smiling face,

[26] Raj Chetty et al., *Active vs. Passive Decisions and Crowdout in Retirement Savings Accounts: Evidence from Denmark* 38 (Nat'l Bureau of Econ. Research, Working Paper No. 18565, 2012), *available at* www.nber.org/papers/w18565.

[27] *See* Eric Bettinger et al., *The Role of Simplification and Information in College Decisions: Results from the H&R Block FAFSA Experience* (Nat'l Bureau of Econ. Research Working Paper No. 15361, 2009), *available at* www.nber.org/papers/w15361.

[28] Johan Egebark and Mathias Ekstrom, *Can Indifference Make the World Greener* (2013), 76 J. ENVTL ECON. & MGMT. 1–13 (2016).

[29] *See generally* Hunt Alcott, *Social Norms and Energy Conservation*, 85 J. PUBLIC ECON. 1082 (2011).

[30] *See generally* DANIEL KAHNEMAN, THINKING, FAST AND SLOW (2011).

add two plus two, or know how to get to your bathroom in the middle of the night, System 1 is at work. When you first learn to drive, or when you multiply 563 times 322, you must rely on System 2.

It is important to see that System 1 can and does get things right. Through fast and frugal heuristics, people often perform exceedingly well. Professional tennis players have educated Systems 1, and they know exactly what shot to hit in an instant. And System 2 is hardly unerring. On multiplication problems, people often make mistakes.

Nonetheless, System 1 is distinctly associated with identifiable behavioral biases. People often show "present bias," focusing on the short term and downplaying the future.[31] For better or for worse, most people tend to be unrealistically optimistic.[32] In assessing risks, people use heuristics, or mental shortcuts, that often work well but that sometimes lead them in unfortunate directions.[33] With respect to probability, people's intuitions go badly wrong, in the sense that they produce serious mistakes, including life-threatening ones.[34]

To be sure, there is, in some circles, intense controversy about the appropriate evaluation of the automatic system and about the extent to which it should be associated with error. Our intuitions work well enough in the situations in which we ordinarily find ourselves.[35] But there is no question that those intuitions can misfire, and that a good nudge, and good choice architecture, could provide a great deal of help. In fact those who celebrate fast and frugal heuristics, and the "ecological rationality" that they exhibit, often draw attention to the importance of good choice architecture – and the harm and confusion that can result if the choice architecture is bad.[36]

Some nudges, offered by government agencies, attempt to strengthen System 2 by improving the role of deliberation and people's considered judgments. One example is disclosure of relevant (statistical) information,

---

[31] For references and discussion, see SUNSTEIN, WHY NUDGE? (2015).

[32] *See generally* TALI SHAROT, THE OPTIMISTIC BIAS (2011).

[33] *See* KAHNEMAN, THINKING, FAST AND SLOW (2011).

[34] For a powerful demonstration, *see* Daniel L. Chen et al., *Decision-Making under the Gambler's Fallacy: Evidence from Asylum Judges, Loan Officers, and Baseball Umpires* (2014), *available at* http://papers.ssrn.com/sol3/papers.cfm?abstract_id=2538147.

[35] This position is vigorously defended in GERD GIGERENZER ET AL., SIMPLE HEURISTICS THAT MAKE US SMART (2000); for general discussion, see MARK KELMAN, THE HEURISTICS DEBATE (2011). In my view, the outcome of this occasionally heated debate does not have strong implications for policy, practice, or ethics. Everyone should agree that heuristics generally work well; that is why they exist. Everyone should also agree that in important cases, boundedly rational people make mistakes. When they make mistakes, some kind of nudge might help. To be sure, the best nudge may or may not involve education, as discussed later.

[36] *See generally* GERD GIGERENZER, SIMPLY RATIONAL (2015); GERD GIGERENZER, RISK SAVVY (2014).

framed in a way that people can understand it. These kinds of nudges, sometimes described as "boosts," attempt to improve people's capacity to make choices for themselves. We might put "debiasing" strategies in the same category. Such strategies might be specifically designed to counteract present bias or optimistic bias[37]; consider reminders that bills are due, or statistical warnings about distracted driving or smoking. Other nudges are designed to appeal to, or to activate, System 1; graphic warnings are an example. We should distinguish between System 2 disclosures, designed simply to give people information and to ask them to process it, and System 1 disclosures, designed to work on the automatic system. Some nudges do not appeal to System 1, strictly speaking, but turn out to work because of its operation – as, for example, where default rules have large effects because of the power of inertia.[38]

A nudge might be justified on the ground that it helps either to exploit or counteract a behavioral bias, such as inertia and procrastination. As we shall see, some people vigorously object to such efforts on ethical grounds, especially if they seem to target System 1. They think that such nudges are a form of manipulation. But a behavioral bias is *not* a necessary justification for a nudge, and nudges need not target or exploit System 1 in any way. Disclosure of information can be helpful even in the absence of any bias. A default rule simplifies life and might therefore be desirable whether or not a behavioral bias is involved. A GPS is useful even for people who do not suffer from any such bias.

As the GPS example suggests, many nudges, and many forms of choice architecture, have the goal of *increasing navigability* – of making it easier for people to get to their preferred destination. Such nudges stem from an understanding that life can be simple or hard to navigate, and helpful choice architecture is desirable as a way of promoting simple navigation. To date, there has been far too little attention to the close relationship between navigability and (good) nudges. Insofar as the goal is to promote navigability, the ethical objections are greatly weakened and might well dissipate. Another way to put it is that nudges can make social life more "legible."

Though choice architecture and nudging are inevitable, some particular nudges are certainly avoidable. A government might decide not to embark on a campaign to discourage smoking or unhealthy eating. It could ignore

---

[37] *See generally* Christine Jolls and Cass R. Sunstein, *Debiasing through Law*, 35 J. LEGAL STUD. 199 (2006).

[38] *See* Eric Johnson and Daniel Goldstein, *Decisions by Default*, in THE BEHAVIORAL FOUNDATIONS OF POLICY 417–427 (Eldar Shafir ed., 2013).

the problem of obesity. It could try to refrain from nudging people toward certain investment behavior. To that extent, it is reasonable to wonder whether government should minimize nudging. If we distrust the motives of public officials, or believe that their judgments are likely to go wrong, we will favor such minimization.

Three Distinctions

For purposes of evaluating the ethical questions, three distinctions are particularly important.

1. *Harm to self, harm to others.* Harm-to-self nudges should be distinguished from harm-to-others nudges. Some of the most familiar nudges, such as automatic enrollment in savings plans, are designed to protect people from making mistaken decisions about their own lives (where mistakes are measured by their own lights; see Chapter 3). Some of those familiar nudges can be characterized as paternalistic, at least if choice architects have chosen them in order to protect people against their own errors. But some of those nudges strain the boundaries of the concept of paternalism. Disclosure of risk-related information, or efforts to increase understanding or navigability, might not qualify as paternalistic. If choice architects frame risk-related information so that people can actually understand it, are they acting paternalistically? Perhaps not. Whether paternalistic or not, the goal of many nudges, and many influences, is to protect people from harming themselves, or to make it easier for them to benefit themselves.

Other nudges are designed to respond to some kind of market failure or otherwise to reduce harms to third parties; consider efforts to discourage criminal activity, to encourage people to pay their taxes, or prevent harm to the environment. In the latter category, we can distinguish among (1) nudges designed to reduce externalities, (2) nudges designed to counteract prisoner's dilemmas, and (3) nudges designed to solve coordination problems.[39] If third parties are harmed, and if the choice architect's goal is to reduce those harms, we are not speaking of any kind of paternalism at all. We are speaking, much less controversially, of reducing adverse third-party effects. For nudges that fall in this category, a governing question should be: Do they increase social welfare, rightly understood[40]? Cost-benefit

---

[39] On coordination, with implications for productive nudges, *see* Edna Ullmann-Margalit, *Coordination Norms and Social Choice*, 11 ERKENNTNIS 143 (1977).

[40] Of course there is a great deal of dispute about how social welfare is rightly understood. For a valuable discussion, see MATTHEW ADLER, WELL-BEING AND FAIR DISTRIBUTION (2011).

analysis is the best available way of operationalizing that question, though it has significant gaps and limitations,[41] and though distributional considerations might turn out to be relevant.

As we have seen, there is broad agreement that it is perfectly legitimate for government to respond to market failures.[42] If the government is trying to reduce a collective action problem that produces high levels of pollution, it does not raise the kinds of ethical concerns that come into play if the government is acting paternalistically. It follows that market failure nudges should not be especially controversial in principle, though we might worry over questions of effectiveness. In the face of a standard market failure, a mere nudge may not be enough; coercion might well be justified (perhaps in the form of a corrective tax, perhaps in the form of a regulatory mandate). But sometimes social norms go a long way toward solving collective action problems, and a nudge might prove to be complementary to coercion; in some cases, it might even work as a substitute.

2. *Nudges and education.* Educative nudges should be distinguished from nudges that lack educative features. Educative nudges, or "boosts," attempt to inform people, or to build their competence, so that they can make better choices for themselves. Such nudges might be designed to overcome or correct behavioral biases by promoting learning – or more modestly, by creating a choice architecture in which those biases will not manifest themselves. Other nudges are meant to help people without increasing their knowledge or understanding; default rules have this characteristic.

If the focus is on increasing people's own powers of agency, educative nudges should not be controversial on ethical grounds. Indeed, they should be welcomed, because they create a kind of "capital stock" that can benefit people for the rest of their lives. If government can design a form of choice architecture that enables people to learn more about financial choices or health care, there should be no reason for objection, at least in principle. But here again, the benefits might not justify the costs,[43] and they can also run into problems of effectiveness.[44]

It is important to emphasize that many people prize education and educative nudges, and they are far more suspicious of nudges that do not

[41] *See generally* Cass R. Sunstein, Valuing Life (2014). Within economics, a pervasive question is whether interpersonal comparisons of utility are possible. *See generally* Interpersonal Comparisons of Utility (Jon Elster ed., 1991).

[42] *See* Stephen Breyer, Regulation and Its Reform 13–35 (1984).

[43] *See* George Loewenstein et al., *Disclosure: Psychology Changes Everything*, 6 Ann. Rev. of Econ. 391, 392 (2014).

[44] *See* Lauren Willis, *The Financial Education Fallacy*, 101 Am. Econ. Rev. 429, 430 (2011).

educate and that in a sense reward and possibly promote passivity (which might infantilize people). Thus Jeremy Waldron writes: "I wish, though, that I could be made a better chooser rather than having someone on high take advantage (even for my own benefit) of my current thoughtlessness and my shabby intuitions."[45] This suspicion is sometimes justified: Often the best approach does involve education and active choosing. But it would be extravagant, and far too dogmatic and rigid, to insist that the word "often" means "always" or even "usually." Life is short and people are busy, and often (!) a good default rules is a blessing, even a form of mercy.

People benefit from default rules with respect to cell phones, tablets, health insurance policies, and rental car agreements. If people had to obtain sufficient education on all of the underlying issues, they would quickly run out of time. In many cases, a default rule is desirable, because it would promote good outcomes (again, from the standpoint of choosers themselves) without requiring people to take the functional equivalent of a course in (say) statistics or finance.[46] There is a recurring question whether in particular circumstances, the costs of education justify the benefits. For those who make many decisions, it would be impossibly demanding to insist on the kind of education that would allow active choices about all relevant features of products, relationships, and activities. Default rules may well be best. Everything depends on the facts, but there is a reasonable argument that with respect to certain retirement issues, default rules are preferable to financial education.[47]

It is true that education or educative nudges can have large advantages over default rules, because the former provide people with that "capital stock" from which they can draw in making their own decisions.[48] If educative nudges, or boosts, do provide such a stock, then they might be better in terms of both robustness and persistence.[49] With respect to robustness, an otherwise effective default rule might be undermined by compensating behavior – as, for example, where a healthy eating default (say, for lunch) ends up produce unhealthy eating at a later time (say, for snacks or dinner). Education might be better on this count. Importantly, behavior that is induced by defaults does tend to persist, so long as the

---

[45] *See* Jeremy Waldron, *It's All for Your Own Good*, NY Rev. of Books (2014), *available at* www .nybooks.com/articles/archives/2014/oct/09/cass-sunstein-its-all-your-own-good/.

[46] *See generally* Lauren Willis, *The Financial Education Fallacy*, 101 Am. Econ. Rev. 429 (2011).

[47] *See id.*   [48] I am grateful to Till Grüne-Yanoff for help with the ideas in this paragraph.

[49] *See generally* Till Grüne-Yanoff, *Why Behavioral Policy Needs Mechanistic Evidence*, Economics and Philosophy (2015).

defaults do. But if the defaults are changed, behavior might well fall back. Education can produce more lasting change.

For all these reasons, educative nudges might be preferred. But in some cases, default rules are better because they do not impose significant demands on choosers, because they are more effective, and because the area is one for which education is not particularly important.[50]

3. *Nudges and behavioral biases.* Nudges that enlist or exploit behavioral biases should be distinguished from nudges that do no such thing. In particular, we have seen that some nudges enlist or exploit System 1 whereas other nudges appeal to System 2. Efforts to target, or to benefit from, behavioral biases tend to be more controversial on ethical grounds than efforts to appeal to deliberative capacities. The reason is that the former may appear to be more manipulative and less respectful of people's capacity for agency. Consider, for example, a graphic warning that triggers strong emotional reactions, or a default rule that is chosen precisely on the ground that as a result of inertia and procrastination, people will not alter it. We might prefer choice architecture that promotes learning and active choosing, because it does not target people's behavioral biases against them. On this view, there is room for particular objection to any approach that enlists or exploits behavioral biases. I will return to this point, but it follows that the most controversial nudges are paternalistic, noneducative, and designed to enlist or exploit behavioral biases.

One final clarification: Some nudges are designed not to promote the interests of choosers, but to give fairness the benefit of the doubt, by promoting particular understandings of (say) equality. Consider the problems of discrimination on the basis of race, sex, sexual orientation, and disability. These forms of discrimination have been promoted by social norms and also by nudges from both private and public institutions. They can be counteracted in the same way. Educational campaigns are sometimes designed to have this effect, and much more can be done through various forms of choice architecture. Discrimination is often fueled by such architecture, and it can be reduced in the same way. Disability discrimination is the most obvious example, but the point applies to discrimination of all kinds; for example, women are often victims of choice architecture that disadvantages them.

Of course the law might well ban certain forms of discrimination, as through civil rights legislation. And if a society wants to decrease income inequality, the income tax is usually the most effective approach, and it is

---

[50] For discussion, see Cass R. Sunstein, Choosing Not to Choose (2015).

no mere nudge. The idea of fairness takes multiple forms, and laws that call for maximum hours and minimum wages are often defended in its name. But many forms of choice architecture, and many nudges, are also designed to promote fairness – as, for example, by invoking social norms or default rules that favor charity and generosity. (Consider automatic enrolment in charitable giving plans or the idea of Give More Tomorrow.) If so, there need be no issue of paternalism. The ethical judgment would turn on the question whether the government legitimately acts in the interest of fairness, as it understands it.

Choice Architecture and Visible Hands

Here is a tale from the novelist David Foster Wallace: "There are these two young fish swimming along and they happen to meet an older fish swimming the other way, who nods at them and says 'Morning, boys. How's the water?' And the two young fish swim on for a bit, and then eventually one of them looks over at the other and goes 'What the hell is water?'"[51]

This is a tale about choice architecture. Such architecture is inevitable, whether or not we see it. It is the equivalent of water. Weather is itself a form of choice architecture, because it influences how people decide; on snowy days, people are especially likely to purchase cars with four-wheel drive, which they will return to the market unusually quickly.[52] Human beings cannot live without some kind of weather. Nature nudges. The common law of contract, tort, and property is a regulatory system, and it will nudge, even if it allows people to have a great deal of flexibility.

In this light, choice architecture is inevitable. Human beings cannot wish it away. Any store, real or online, must have a design; some products are seen first, and others are not. Any menu places options at various locations. Television stations are assigned different numbers, and strikingly, the number matters, even when the costs of switching are vanishingly low; people tend to choose stations with lower numbers.[53] A website has a design, which will affect what and whether people will choose.[54]

---

[51] David Foster Wallace, *In His Own Words* (2008), *available at* http://moreintelligentlife.com/story/david-foster-wallace-in-his-own-words.

[52] Meghan R. Busse et al., Projection Bias in the Car and Housing Markets (Nat'l Bureau of Econ. Research, Working Paper No. 18212, 2014), *available at* www.nber.org/papers/w18212.

[53] *See* Gregory Martin and Ali Yurukoglu, *Bias in Cable News: Real Effects and Polarization* (Nat'l Bureau of Econ. Research, Working Paper No. 20798, 2014), *available at* www.nber.org/papers/w20798.

[54] *See* STEVE KRUG, DON'T MAKE ME THINK REVISITED: A COMMON SENSE APPROACH TO WEB AND MOBILE USABILITY (2014).

It would be possible, of course, to define choice architecture in a narrower way, and to limit it to intentional designs by human beings. There is nothing intrinsic to human language that rules out that definition, and for most purposes, I will be emphasizing intentional design, because that is what raises ethical issues. But if the goal is to see how and when people are influenced, the broader definition is preferable. It shows that our choices are often an artifact of an architecture for which no human being may have responsibility – a sunny day, an unexpected chill, a gust of wind, a steep hill, a full (and romantic) moon.

On any plausible definition, it will not be possible for the state to avoid nudging. For many tasks, nudging itself will be literally unavoidable; recall the design of offices and websites. Any government, even one that is or purports to be firmly committed to laissez-faire, has to establish a set of prohibitions and permissions, including a set of default entitlements, establishing who has what before bargaining begins. The legal system's default settings will nudge. Even the most humble state will do a lot of nudging. Here as well, we might emphasize that some nudges are intentional, whereas others are not, and insofar as we are speaking of ethical concerns, intentional nudges on the part of the state are the right focus.

True, a government can aspire to relevant kinds of neutrality. Some forms of choice architecture will refrain from certain kind of nudging. A free society will allow people to choose their religious beliefs, free from nudging. A political system might embrace the idea that voters can select the leaders they prefer, and it might operate its electoral process in such a way as to avoid any kind of favoritism. With respect to intimate choices – about marriage and sex – public officials could well decide not to nudge.

In some settings, moreover, randomization is appropriate. Randomization is a form of choice architecture, one that might be favored on ethical grounds. Consider randomly generated orders on ballots. One goal of randomization is specifically to prevent the intentional use of choice architecture to promote certain kinds of ends. The prevention of that intentional use might be an important virtue, at least if we care about a certain kind of neutrality.

The defense of spontaneous orders

We can easily imagine the following view, which motivates ethical objections to a great deal of government action: Choice architecture is unavoidable, to be sure, but it is important if it is the product of nature or some kind of spontaneous order, rather than of conscious design, or of the action of any designer. Perhaps the law can build on that order; perhaps the law of contract, property, and tort does exactly that. For better or for worse, invisible-hand mechanisms often produce choice architecture.[55] Many social practices that appear to be a product of conscious design lack any kind of human designer. One example is the story of money,[56] which:

> begins with the early goldsmiths who used to be paid a small fee for the safekeeping of people's gold and valuables. It proceeds with those intelligent goldsmiths who came to realize, first, that they don't necessarily have to give back to the customer exactly the same piece of gold that he had deposited, and, later, that since not all deposits are withdrawn together and new deposits tend to balance withdrawals, only a small percentage of the cash entrusted to them is needed in the form of vault cash. The rest of the story has to do with these shrewd bankers' investment in securities and loans of most of the money deposited with them, leading to the account of the actual creation of money through the consideration of the overall impact of this newly-developed banking system as a whole rather than of each small establishment taken in isolation.

The basic idea here is that many practices, and many institutions, may be "the product neither of centralized decisions nor of explicit agreements to bring it about; rather, [they are] presented as the end result of a certain process that aggregates the separate and 'innocent' actions of numerous and dispersed individuals into an overall pattern."[57] We might think that if no centralized decisions and explicit agreements are involved, and if practices emerge from individual judgments of many people, we have safeguards of an important kind. Of course there are no guarantees here;[58] dispersed individuals need not always produce good things. But perhaps the process of aggregation, alongside evolutionary and market pressures, usually works pretty well. And perhaps a lot of law has emerged in that way. On a time-honored view, much of law, including default rules, is in fact "customary law." It codifies the actual practices of numerous people; it does not reflect any kind of dictation by public authorities. That might be a significant safeguard.

It is true and important that some default rules are a product not of government decree, but of traditions, customs, spontaneous orders, and

---

[55] For a superb discussion, *see* Edna Ullmann-Margalit, *The Invisible Hand and the Cunning of Reason,* 64 Social Research 181 (1997).

[56] Edna Ullmann-Margalit, *Invisible Hand Explanations,* 39 Synthese 263, 264 (1978).

[57] *Id.* at 265.

[58] *See* Ullmann-Margalit, *The Invisible Hand and the Cunning of Reason* (1997), at 184–189.

invisible hands. By tradition, for example, employers and employees might work together to produce some default rules about overtime work, week-end work, and civil behavior. A great deal of research shows that traditions, embodying the wisdom of crowds, can in fact produce practices that work well.[59] If traditions are responsible for default rules, those who especially distrust public officials might feel greatly comforted. Perhaps traditions and customs are reliable; if they have managed to survive over time, it might be because they are sensible and helpful and really do make people's lives better. Perhaps public officials, or law, can build on traditions and avoid any kind of top-down dictation. Even if traditions are a form of choice architecture, and even if they nudge, they might be trustworthy by virtue of their longevity. Social norms can be understood in this way.

With these ideas in mind, many people celebrate what they call "spon-taneous orders."[60] Suppose, for example, that people have produced some kind of organization, containing social norms that permit and prohibit, without any kind of official dictation. They might have figured out a way to solve coordination problems, or to ensure that people treat each other courteously and considerately, and in ways that contribute to the public good.[61] If an order is genuinely spontaneous, there is some reason to think that it reflects the judgments of many people about how it makes sense to proceed. On certain assumptions, spontaneous orders can promote people's welfare, and we have good reason to trust and not to disrupt them.

Consider Friedrich Hayek's celebration of the "empiricist, evolutionary tradition," for which "the value of freedom consists mainly in the opportunity it provides for the growth of the undesigned, and the beneficial functioning of a free society rests largely on the existence of such freely grown institutions. There probably never has existed a genuine belief in freedom, and there certainly has been no successful attempt to operate a free society, without a genuine reverence for grown institutions, for customs and habits."[62]

This is a provocative claim, and it might be true. Nonetheless, what Hayek celebrates are forms of choice architecture no less than intentional designs, and they will include a measure of nudging – not least if they create, embed, and perpetuate social norms.[63] If invisible hands create

---

[59] *See* Elinor Ostrom, Governing the Commons (1990); Robert Ellickson, Order without Law (1994).

[60] *See* Friedrich Hayek, Freedom, Reason, and Tradition 229 (1958); Friedrich Hayek, The Market and Other Orders (2014).

[61] *See* Edna Ullmann-Margalit, The Emergence of Norms (1976).

[62] Hayek, Freedom, Reason, and Tradition 234.

[63] *See* Ullmann-Margalit, The Emergence of Norms.

norms, they will nudge every bit as much as the most visible ones. To be sure, spontaneous orders and invisible hands may be less dangerous than intentional designs, and on certain assumptions[64] they are likely to be benign (or better). But they are nonetheless forms of choice architecture – and as behavioral economists have shown, we should be quite careful before accepting the assumptions on which they should be accepted as likely to be benign.[65]

On Hayek's view, there is special reason, from the standpoint of freedom itself, to value forms of choice architecture that reflect the work of "grown institutions," rather than designed ones. We might be comfortable with any nudging that reflects "customs and habits" but deeply suspicious of any nudging that displays no reverence for them. Here, then, is a foundation for skepticism about any kind of social engineering, and the skepticism might be applied to nudges as well as to mandates and bans. If we believe that when government requires disclosure of information, it might well get things wrong, then we might not want government to require disclosure of information. If we think that if government devises or promotes default rules, it will steer people in bad directions, then we will not want government to devise or promote default rules.

Even if the law of contract, property, and tort constitutes forms of choice architecture, and even if it is not quite customary (and involves a degree of dictation and design), the relevant architecture can be made as flexible as possible and maintain a great deal of room for private ordering – and thus for freedom. To summarize a lengthy argument[66]: the state, and the law, can provide the background rules for private interaction and decline to specify outcomes. Even if those rules turn out to nudge (as in the case of default rules), they are very different from social planning – on one view, far more modest and less dangerous.

To be sure, the criminal law will include some dictation; we will not deal with murder, assault, and rape with mere nudges. But perhaps the criminal law can restrict itself to prohibitions on force and fraud (and also play a role in correcting the standard market failures). If it does so, perhaps it can copy what emerges from spontaneous order and the norms that develop from them. A nation can certainly minimize the number of activities that it criminalizes. It might adopt a narrow account of the scope of the criminal law, perhaps focused on harm to others. And it might

---

[64] Ullmann-Margalit, *The Invisible Hand and the Cunning of Reason* (1997).
[65] *See* GEORGE AKERLOF AND ROBERT SHILLER, PHISHING FOR PHOOLS (2015).
[66] *See* FRIEDRICH HAYEK, THE CONSTITUTION OF LIBERTY (1976).

restrict any nudging to initiatives that operate in the service of the criminal law, narrowly conceived.

Dangers and risks

Why and exactly when would spontaneous orders be benign? Is there some kind of social Darwinism here[67]? We might be able to agree that action by government poses dangers and risks while insisting that efforts to defend the results of all spontaneous orders and invisible hands run into serious problems and objections.[68] For example, spontaneous orders can leave a lot of poverty and distress; invisible hands might not do nearly enough to help people with physical or mental handicaps. A government that forbids racial discrimination, or that takes steps to ensure reasonable accommodation of disabled people, is not relying on an invisible hand.

Moreover, it would be extravagant, and quite foolish, to say that survival over time is a guarantee of goodness.[69] Survival might reflect any number of things – inertia, habit, inattention, adaptation, or sheer disparities in power. With respect to relationships between men and women, tradition has created a number of default rules, which operate through norms if not through law (as in, women do most of the household work), and it would be not be easy to show that those rules are fair. And even if traditions are both fair and good, they will nudge individuals who live with them, and it takes a lot of work to transform them into law, where they will have significant effects on people's lives.

Even when a default rule is chosen on the ground that it captures what most people will do, and is in that sense "market-mimicking," it may affect people's preferences and hence social outcomes. Recall that a default rule establishes initial entitlements – that is, who owns what – before bargaining begins, and it can be important for that reason, affecting what people like and prefer. The influence of default rules raises ethical issues of its own, to which we shall turn in due course. For present purposes, the point is that default rules of one or another kind are sometimes unavoidable.

What is so great about randomness? We should agree that a malevolent choice architect, aware of the power of nudges, could produce a great deal of harm. We should agree that by assigning outcomes to chance, randomness can reflect an understanding of fairness. But by definition, random processes have the vice of arbitrariness, in the sense that winners and losers

---

[67] *See id.*   [68] Ullmann-Margalit, *The Invisible Hand and the Cunning of Reason* (1997).
[69] For a superb discussion, *see id.* at 181.

win and lose because of chance or fate, not because of merit or desert.[70] In any case, the argument for spontaneous orders seeks to restrict, above all, the coercive power of the state, not nudges as such. Whatever our theory of the legitimate domain of government, the most serious harms tend to come from mandates and bans (from genuine coercion), and not from nudges, which maintain freedom of choice.

It is true that spontaneous orders, invisible hands, and randomness can avoid some of the serious dangers, and some of the distinctive biases, that come from self-conscious nudging on the part of government. If we are especially fearful of official mistakes – coming from incompetence or bad motivations – we will want to minimize the occasions for nudging. And if we believe that invisible hand mechanisms promote welfare or freedom, we will not want to disturb their products, even if those products include nudges.

In my view, the strongest position in favor of spontaneous orders and invisible hands cannot, in the end, be defended, because such orders and such hands do not promote welfare, autonomy, dignity, or self-government. But the minimal point is that a degree of official nudging cannot be avoided. If we are committed to spontaneous orders and invisible hands, we will be committed to a particular role for government, one that will include a specified choice architecture and specified nudges.

Illicit Reasons and Transparency

It must be emphasized that choice architecture can be altered, and that new nudges can be introduced, for illicit reasons. Indeed, many of the most powerful objections to nudges, and to changes in choice architecture, are based on a fear that the underlying motivations will be illicit.[71] With these points, there is no objection to nudges as such; the objection is to the grounds for the particular nudges.

For example, an imaginable default rule might skew the democratic process by saying that voters are presumed to vote for the incumbent politician, unless they specify otherwise. Such a rule would violate principles of neutrality that are implicit in democratic norms; it would be unacceptable for that reason. As we shall see in Chapter 6, Americans are

---

[70] To be sure, arbitrariness can be a virtue, in part because it eliminates the role of human agency and potentially bias. A lottery can embody a form of neutrality. *See* Jon Elster, Solomonic Judgments (1989).

[71] *See* Edward L. Glaeser, *Paternalism and Psychology*, 73 U. Chi. L. Rev. 133 (2006); Riccardo Rebonato, Taking Liberties: A Critical Examination of Libertarian Paternalism (2012).

generally unenthusiastic about a default rule that assumes, for purposes of the census, that people are Christians, or that assumes, for purposes of voter registration, that people are Democrats. Alternatively, a warning might try to frighten people by fabricating stories about the supposedly nefarious plans of members of a minority group. Social norms might be invoked to encourage people to buy unhealthy products ("most people are buying these products; you should too!"). In extreme cases, private or public institutions might try to nudge people toward violence.

It must also be acknowledged that the best choice architecture often calls for active choosing. Sometimes the right approach is to *require* people to choose, so as to ensure that their will is actually expressed. Sometimes it is best to *prompt* choice, by asking people what they want, without imposing any requirement that they do so. A prompt is emphatically a nudge, designed to get people to express their will, and it might be unaccompanied by any effort to steer people in a preferred direction – except in the direction of choosing.

Choice architecture should be transparent and subject to public scrutiny, certainly if public officials are responsible for it. At a minimum, this proposition means that when such officials institute some kind of reform, they must not hide it from the public. If officials alter a default rule so as to promote clean energy or conservation, they should disclose what they are doing. Self-government itself requires public scrutiny of nudges. Such scrutiny is an important ex post safeguard against harmful nudges; it is also an important ex post corrective. Transparency and public scrutiny can reduce the likelihood of welfare-reducing choice architecture. Nations should also treat their citizens with respect, and allowing public scrutiny shows a measure of respect at the same time that it reduces the risk that nudges will reduce welfare or intrude on autonomy or dignity.

There is a question whether transparency and public scrutiny are sufficient rather than merely necessary. The answer is that they are not sufficient. We could imagine forms of choice architecture that would be unacceptable even if they were fully transparent; consider (transparent) architecture designed to entrench inequality on the basis of sex. Here again, the problem is that the goals of the relevant nudge are illicit. As we shall see, it is also possible to imagine cases of manipulation, in which the goals are not illicit, but in which the fact of transparency might not be sufficient to justify a nudge. A transparent nudge, announced in advance but taking the form of subliminal advertising of one or another kind, would run into legitimate objections about manipulation. I will explore this point in some detail in Chapter 5.

CHAPTER 3

"As Judged by Themselves"

Some of the most vexing questions about the exercise of official power arise when third parties are not at risk and when the welfare of choosers is all that is involved. In such cases, the objective of nudging is to "influence choices in a way that will make choosers better off, *as judged by themselves*"[1] (italics in original).

It is important to underline the fact that many nudges are designed to reduce harms to others. In the environmental context, for example, that is a major goal of choice architecture (see Chapter 7), and if the goal is to reduce crime, choice architecture can help a great deal. But when people's decisions will affect only their own lives, and if we are concerned about welfare, autonomy, and dignity, we should begin by asking whether a nudge would make people better off by their own lights. If people believe that they have been made worse off, there is an excellent chance that they have, in fact, been made worse off. And if people's own tastes and values suggest that the nudge has harmed them, public officials should be concerned that they have failed to respect autonomy and dignity.

In some cases, a concern with welfare might lead in a direction different from that suggested by a concern with autonomy. But happily, the "as judged by themselves" standard can command support from both standpoints. In fact we might say that ordinarily, this standard is a reasonable test for all exercises of official power, at least when third parties are not at risk. Suppose that the state is imposing a mandate designed to protect people from unsafe food or unsafe workplaces. In such cases, it is sensible to start by asking whether the mandate will meet the "as judged by themselves" standard. In fact mandates – and incentives of all kinds – can be evaluated, and sometimes defended, with that kind of test.

In most real-world cases, the standard is fairly straightforward to apply (and hence this chapter will be relatively short). At the same time, the test

---

[1] Richard H. Thaler and Cass A. Sunstein, Nudge 5 (2008).

sometimes raises reasonable concerns, both practical and conceptual. One question is whether some kind of principled analysis can be used to decide which context more reliably reflects people's real preferences, or the preferences that they would show under ideal decision-making conditions. At a minimum, we would want to make sure that people are adequately informed. Some situations, and some forms of choice architecture, produce quite unreliable measures of what people really want. Others are much better. Consider a few examples, drawn from the empirical literature:[2]

(1) People are more likely to enroll in pension plans if they are required to make active choices than if they merely have the right to opt in.

(2) People are more likely to choose a lower-cost health insurance plan when given simplified comparison information.

(3) People are less likely to buy a product when more of the cost is included in the base price instead of being "shrouded" as part of shipping and handling charges.

If we are genuinely concerned with making people better off by their own lights, we might want to see what they do when they are well-informed, when they choose actively, when their judgments are considered (in the sense that they are thinking about all relevant features of a product or activity), and when they are not being impulsive or reckless.

In many situations, the "as judged by themselves" standard raises no problems. If a GPS steers people toward a destination that is not their own, it is not working well. And if it offers them a longer and less convenient route, it will not make choosers better off by their own lights. Many nudges can be understood in precisely the same terms; consider a reminder, a warning, or disclosure of relevant information. Nudges that increase "navigability," by making social situations easier to manage, easily satisfy the standard. (Another way to think about this is that some nudges make the world more "legible.") If people are reminded of something that is irrelevant to their lives, they are not being made better off (by their own lights). If they are reminded that a bill is due, or that a doctor's appointment is coming up, the "as judged by themselves" standard is satisfied. To know whether it is, we would have to take each nudge, and every form of influence, on its own. Fortunately, most nudges can be evaluated very quickly, and so the standard will often provide sufficient guidance.

---

[2] *See* Hunt Allcott and Cass R. Sunstein, *Regulating Internalities* (2015), 34 J. POL'Y ANALYSIS & MGMT 698 (2015). *available at* http://papers.ssrn.com/sol3/papers.cfm?abstract_id=2571343.

At the same time, I have acknowledged that the standard raises some serious questions. I explore those questions in ascending order of complexity. As we will see, some of them raise serious philosophical problems, which the "as judged by themselves" standard is not always able to avoid. Some of the problems might seem a bit fussy, but to come to terms with the ethical issues, they must be engaged.

Informed Judgments?

When we ask about choosers' judgments, and say that they provide the standard, what kind of information do we expect choosers to have? For reasons just given, it makes sense to say that choice architects should be interested in choosers' informed judgments, rather than their uninformed ones. Suppose that choosers select an evidently bad retirement plan and reject one that is evidently better. Suppose that when confronted with a set of possible health insurance plans, choosers choose one that is more expensive than several others, but better along no dimension. In such cases, it is fair for choice architects to insist that actual judgments do not reflect informed choices. Whether our focus is on welfare or autonomy, respect for uninformed choices is not the best idea. Those choices are not likely make people's lives go better, and autonomous choices require a certain degree of knowledge.

As a matter of practice, these simple ideas provide a great deal of guidance. If people are not sufficiently informed, choice architects should work to provide information – to offer that kind of nudge that serves as a "boost." That work might also entail framing the information in a way that people can actually grasp. And if there is clear evidence about what informed choosers would do, then choice architects might rely on that evidence to design nudges, or perhaps even mandates and bans, in the context of (say) food safety and occupational health. True, one size does not fit all, and because of people's diverse tastes and situations, nudges have major advantages over coercion. But if a particular chemical creates serious health risks, and if informed people really would not run those risks, we have no reason for alarm if a ban is imposed.

Nonetheless, there might be a real danger if choice architects are loosened from choosers' actual judgments and asking what choosers would do if they were informed. The danger is that choice architects will be relying on their own values and beliefs, rather than choosers' own. If so, we would be defeating the whole purpose of the "as judged by themselves" standard. Unless it is really clear that choosers are uninformed, choice architects should focus on their actual choices and try to inform them – or to make more salient, or to prevent distortion of, information that choosers should want to use.

A pervasive problem is that public officials might themselves lack sufficient information to know when informed choosers would deem themselves to be better off. It might not be at all simple for outsiders to compare – from the point of view of choosers – the various outcomes that result from different nudges. Would choosers think that they are better off if the default settings on printers are changed to double-sided? If they are automatically assigned to green energy suppliers? If they are automatically enrolled in retirement plans featuring low-cost, highly diversified, passively managed funds? If their cafeteria is designed so as to make salient, and easily available, low-calorie (but not especially delicious) food? If these questions are hard to answer, the best approach is to find out – perhaps by acquiring real data, from pilot studies, from experiments, or otherwise. Of course it is true that technical specialists might know enough to say that informed choosers really would prefer a specific approach.

In some cases, the absence of reliable evidence about what informed choosers would do will raise serious challenges. Nonetheless, the idea of choosers' informed judgments serves as the lodestar, and it imposes real discipline. Certainly choice architects should be focused on the welfare of choosers, rather than their own. (In a well-functioning market system, that focus is promoted by competitive forces, at least under optimistic assumptions.)[3]

Self-Control

There are hard questions about how to handle the "as judged by themselves" standard in the face of self-control problems. Suppose that someone faces such problems and is aware of that fact – but nonetheless wishes, at Time 1, to give into his impulses. Do we look to the assessment of (1) the alcoholic, who wants that vodka, (2) the would-be former alcoholic, who wants to quit, or (3) the actual former alcoholic, who is grateful to have been nudged away from alcoholism? We might ask the same question about smokers, those who have unhealthy diets, those who fail to engage in financial planning, and those who make a lot of purchases on impulse.

---

[3] Optimistic, not realistic. *See* AKERLOF AND SHILLER, PHISHING FOR PHOOLS (2015); OREN BAR-GILL, SEDUCTION BY CONTRACT (2011).

It is reasonable to think that no former alcoholic regrets the "former" (at least in the absence of highly unusual circumstances). For that reason, there is a strong argument that the "as judged by themselves" standard should be taken to refer to *the judgment of the person who is no longer in the grip of an addiction or some other problem that is undermining the capacity for self-control.* What matters are people's considered judgments, not their assessments while they are in the heat of the moment. If people wish, on reflection, that they had started to save money, or acted in a way that promotes their long-term health goals, then their reflective judgment deserves priority. At least this is so if the question is in what direction to nudge. Because of the risk of error, choice architects should hesitate before imposing mandates and bans.

One challenge is that there can be a thin line between a self-control problem and a legitimate focus on short-term pleasure (which is not a problem at all). Cinnabon, which offers high-calorie food, is often ridiculed for its clever slogan: *Life needs frosting.* But life really does need frosting, which means that it is not always clear how to think about apparent self-control problems. Suppose that people choose unhealthy but delicious desserts and regret it the next day. Or suppose that at certain times in their lives, people have many romantic partners, but don't feel so great about that in retrospect. Or suppose that people purchase products (say, cozy, warm winter coats) that they really want in October, but in June, they regret those purchases.

True, the current self might pay too little attention to the future self. But the current self might also pay too little attention to the past self, who was able to enjoy good experiences to which the current self might be relatively indifferent (except insofar as he cares about good memories). No choice architect should engage in a program of nudging that disregards the importance of short-term pleasures, or pleasures in general, which are of course crucial parts of good lives.

Preferences about Preferences

People do not only have preferences (or first-order preferences); they also have preferences about their preferences (or second-order preferences).[4] They make judgments, but they also make judgments about their

---

[4] *See* Harry Frankfurt, *Freedom of the Will and the Concept of a Person,* 68 J. PHIL. 5 (1971). For relevant discussion, *see* Cass R. Sunstein and Edna Ullmann-Margalit, *Second-Order Decisions,* 110 ETHICS 5 (1999).

judgments (second-order judgments). People might want to buy a lot of new clothes, or to watch a lot of television, but they might want not to want those things. In applying the "as judged by themselves standard," should choice architects consult first-order or second-order preferences? Is the goal to capture what people choose, or what they think about their choices?

These questions are similar to those raised by self-control problems, and here too, the general answer is straightforward: If second-order preferences reflect System 2 – understood, in this context, as people's reflective judgments, as opposed to their impulses or their immediate intuitions – those preferences have authority. In ordinary life, we do not want our lives to be rules by our impulses if we think, on reflection, that they are moving us in harmful, bad, or otherwise wrong directions. When there is a divergence, choice architects should follow people's reflective judgments. In fact a lot of good choice architecture can be understood as responsive to those judgments, or as an effort to give them the benefit of the doubt. Such architecture makes it easier for people to make healthy decisions, and harder for them to make unhealthy or dangerous ones.

But here as well, some cases are hard. One reason is that choice architects may make mistakes: Their own judgments and values might lead them to attribute to a population a supposedly reflective judgment that its members do not actually have. For this reason, the right to go one's own way is essential.

Another reason is captured by a nice slogan, which System 2 should not be permitted to disparage: "Enjoy life now. This is not a rehearsal." A candy bar, or even two or three, can be a great pleasure. Ideally, of course, System 2 should take full account of life's pleasures, and if it wants to override first-order desires, it is only after giving them appropriate consideration. Good nudges apply the "as judged by themselves" standard with this point firmly in mind.

Ex Ante Judgments or Ex Post Judgments?

The "as judged by themselves" standard raises a tricky temporal question: Do we ask about choosers' judgments before the official intervention – or after? The question is important, because choosers' ex ante judgments might diverge from their ex post judgments. If choosers' judgments – their preferences and values – are influenced or even constructed by a nudge, then *choice architects might be engineering the very judgment from which they are claiming authority.* That can be a serious problem for the "as judged by themselves" standard.

Suppose, for example, that choice architects select a "green" default rule, one that provides an environmentally friendly energy provider, subject to opt out in favor of a cheaper but environmentally inferior provider. Suppose too that choosers are perfectly content with the green default rule, not only in the sense that they do not change it (which might reflect inertia and procrastination), but also in the sense that in surveys they support it.

But assume as well that they would also be content with the opposite default rule – and would also support that rule in surveys. The assumption is plausible, because people might well support different default rules, depending on which is in place, Consider the important finding of "status quo policy bias," which suggests that people are significantly more likely to support policies if they believe that those policies are now in effect.[5] Wherever a nudge, or other intervention, influences choosers' judgments, have we lost our anchor? How can we apply the "as judged by themselves" standard when people will tend to be enthusiastic about whatever approach the choice architect selects? For that standard, isn't there a fatal problem of circularity? We cannot defend a particular nudge by reference to the "as judged by themselves" standard if people's assessment is a product of whatever nudge has been put in place.

In many cases, of course, official action will not much affect choosers' judgments; they will be the same ex ante and ex post. Most people do not want to be cold, and if the default setting on thermometers is set very low, it will be inconsistent with their preferences. A lot of people like drinking coffee, and a nudge that discourages them from doing so is unlikely to fit with their preferences. Most people do not want to devote 40 percent of their salary to savings or to charitable contributions. Most people want to find a good way to get to their own preferred destination, and efforts to increase navigability – as, for example, with a GPS device and with accurate information – do not alter people's judgments. But when a nudge, or other official action, does affect people's judgments, the standard certainly becomes more difficult to apply.

In such cases, several reasonable options are available. One would be to use active choosing, with sufficient information, to see what people independently want. That form of choice architecture can elicit people's actual

---

[5] *See* Avital Moshinsky and Maya Bar-Hillel, *Loss Aversion and Status Quo Label Bias*, 28 Soc. Cognition 191 (2010).

judgments, without influencing them. Another option would be to explore the number of opt-outs under different default rules.[6] If a lot of people are opting out under default rule A, and very few under default rule B, we have reason to think that the default rule B is better by people's own lights.

A more complex, but possibly more accurate, approach would be to try to learn someone about the population of people who are opting out under various default rules. If those who opt out actually know something about the problem, and if those who do not are simply suffering from inertia, we might be able to draw some lessons about which approach suits informed choosers.[7] If that is the case, then the chosen default rule does not seem so good, because informed people are opting out. A final approach would be to attempt a more direct inquiry into people's welfare under different forms of choice architecture. Which approach improves their lives – for example, by making people live longer, be healthier, and show higher levels of happiness? Those might not be easy questions to answer, but some evidence might be available to help.[8]

Objectively Good Lives?

Some people believe that human lives can be objectively good or objectively bad, and that choosers can and do make objective mistakes about what makes their lives good. For those who share this belief, the "as judged by themselves" standard runs into serious trouble, because it relies on choosers' own beliefs, including their most serious errors.

Many philosophers embrace "perfectionism,"[9] which argues for approaches to government that try to increase the likelihood that people will have objectively good lives. Of course there are many different forms of perfectionism. We can imagine a form of perfectionism, liberal in character, that insists that people should be autonomous in the sense that they should be *authors of the narratives of their own lives* – whether or not they wish to be. John Stuart Mill seemed to embrace this form of perfectionism; Joseph Raz is a contemporary exponent. We could also imagine a form that stresses people's ability to develop their own faculties,

---

[6] THALER AND SUNSTEIN, NUDGE. This approach is subject to some interesting objections in Jacob Goldin, *Which Way to Nudge? Uncovering Preferences in the Behavioral Age*, 125 YALE L.J. 226 (2015).
[7] *See* Goldin, *Which Way to Nudge?* (2015), who offers a more elaborate and detailed account in this general direction; his analysis repays careful reading.
[8] *See* PAUL DOLAN, HAPPINESS BY DESIGN (2014).
[9] A form of liberal perfectionism is defended in JOSEPH RAZ, THE MORALITY OF FREEDOM (1985).

and that sees lives as less than good, and less than fully human, if they are not developing those faculties. The "capabilities approach," elaborated by Amartya Sen and Martha Nussbaum, includes a large scope for freedom of choice, but also offers guidance about what truly human lives contain.[10] The capabilities approach fits within the liberal tradition, but it can be seen to have perfectionist elements. Or we could imagine a form of perfectionism that sees human lives as good only if people are devoted to the worship of God. The unifying theme is that perfectionists insist that some lives are better than others, and that it is legitimate for societies to move lives in the direction of the better.

For people who have this belief, the "as judged by themselves" standard seems to be based on a fundamental mistake, because it is too subjective, and because it defers too readily to choosers. It allows choosers' judgments to prevail even if they are wrong. Imagine, for example, that a chooser makes decisions that ensure a life that is dull, short, and unhealthy, or that is without either meaning or pleasure,[11] or that involves a great deal of suffering. It might be asked: Why should choice architects defer to choosers in such circumstances? Shouldn't they be allowed to evaluate where the "as judged by themselves" standard actually leads people?

These questions raise serious questions within political philosophy, which I cannot adequately answer here.[12] But there are many reasons to reject perfectionism in both theory and practice. To the extent that choice architects defer to choosers, it might be because of their own moral judgment, which is that choosers should be allowed to have ultimate sovereignty over their own lives (as some religious traditions teach, as a way of respecting God's will). That moral judgment might be rooted in ideas about welfare, autonomy, or dignity. Or choice architects might defer to choosers because of their own humility. They might believe that they simply know less than those whose own lives are at stake. Insofar as choice architects adopt the "as judged by themselves" standard, they reject perfectionism, and they do so on principle.

The good news is that most examples of sensible choice architecture do not require us to take a stand either for or against the most plausible forms

---

[10] Martha C. Nussbaum, Creating Capabilities (2011); Amartya Sen, Commodities and Capabilities (1999).

[11] On the importance of purpose and pleasure, *see* Paul Dolan, Happiness by Design 34 (2014).

[12] Relevant discussion can be found in Adler, Well-Being and Fair Distribution (2011); Sen, Commodities and Capabilities (1999); Nussbaum, Creating Capabilities (2013). For a short, vivid set of objections to perfectionism, *see* Conly, Against Autonomy (2012).

of perfectionism. Suppose, for example, that choice architects nudge people to have healthy diets, to save for retirement, to avoid smoking and alcohol abuse, and not to waste money. These kinds of nudges can attract support from people with diverse theoretical positions, including those who are drawn to perfectionism. The same can be said for many more aggressive forms of regulation, such as food safety laws. For this reason, many forms of choice architecture can claim to be rooted in an *incompletely theorized agreement* – an agreement from people who do not agree on the foundational questions in moral and political philosophy, or who do not know what they think about those questions.[13]

Of course it is true that for some problems, disagreements about foundational questions might end up mattering for particular controversies. My hope is that if we apply the "as judged by themselves" standard, those disagreements will not arise often. Let us now see to what extent that might be so.

---

[13] *See* CASS R. SUNSTEIN, LEGAL REASONING AND POLITICAL CONFLICT (1996).

CHAPTER 4

Values

I have said that government action might be evaluated by asking whether it increases welfare, promotes autonomy, respects dignity, and promotes self-government. I have also noted that the four values might conflict with one another. In many of the most important cases, however, they do not. Let us explore the relationship between choice architecture and each of the values, focusing in particular on the role of nudges.

Welfare

If we care about human welfare, the guidance for public officials is simple and straightforward: Act to promote social welfare.[1] But the idea of welfare can be specified in many different ways, and it is not clear how to measure or to promote it. One idea, associated with F. A. Hayek, is that government should create a basic structure, featuring property rights, freedom of contract, and free markets, and expect that the structure will generally promote social welfare.[2] But as Hayek himself acknowledged, that framework is too simple. A government that wants to promote social welfare, however specified, will do other things as well. Above all, it will have to correct market failures, and that will require it to do a great deal, especially (but not only) if behavioral market failures count.

Some form of cost-benefit analysis, meant to capture the consequences of various possible interventions (including none at all), is the most administrable way of measuring the welfare effects of government action. If welfare is the guide, there is no prohibition on mandates and bans, because they can be amply justified on that ground. Air pollution

---

[1] For a helpful, brief discussion, *see* Jonathan Baron, *A Welfarist Approach to Manipulation,* J. BEHAV. MARKETING (forthcoming); for more elaborate ones, *see* LOUIS KAPLOW AND STEVEN SHAVELL, FAIRNESS VERSUS WELFARE (2011); MATTHEW ADLER, WELL-BEING AND FAIR DISTRIBUTION (2011).
[2] *See* F. A. HAYEK, THE ROAD TO SERFDOM (1944).

regulations often have health and other benefits that dwarf the costs. Occupational safety and health regulations can save significant numbers of lives without imposing unjustified burdens. Of course it is true that environmental and occupational safety regulations can reduce rather than increase social welfare. What is needed is an accounting of their human consequences, not a celebration of regulation as such. And in some cases, mandates will have far higher costs than choice-preserving approaches, and their benefits will not justify those higher costs. The only point is that if welfare is our guide, our analysis of what government should do will be informed and guided by some form of cost-benefit analysis, and everything will depend on the details.

The air pollution problem should not be controversial, at least in principle. Air pollution is an externality, and some kind of government action is justified in response. For present purposes, the hardest questions, and the most interesting ones, involve harms to self, and hence the relationship between welfare and paternalism. If we care about welfare, will we favor nudges that are designed to reduce the risk that people will make bad choices for themselves?

Choice architecture, taken as such, may or may not be paternalistic. If the government makes things simple rather than complex, it is not clear that we need to speak of paternalism at all. But it is true that many nudges can be seen as a form of "libertarian paternalism" insofar as they attempt to use choice architecture to steer choosers in directions that will promote their welfare (again, as judged by choosers themselves). If we believe that choosers know best, any such effort at steering might seem misguided, at least if welfare is the lodestar.

Means paternalism

To evaluate this objection, it is important to see that with nudges, we are speaking of a form of paternalism that it is at once (a) soft and (b) means-oriented.[3] It is soft insofar as it avoids coercion or material incentives and thus preserves freedom of choice.[4] It is means-oriented insofar as it does not attempt to question or alter people's ends. Like a GPS, it respects those ends. To those who object to paternalism on welfare grounds, the most serious concerns arise in the face of coercion (where freedom of choice is blocked) and when social planners, or choice architects, do not respect

---

[3] *See* Cass R. Sunstein, Why Nudge? 1–20 (2015).   [4] On some of the complexities here, *see id.*

people's ends.[5] To this extent, nudges aspire to avoid some of the standard welfarist objections to paternalism.

Nonetheless, some skeptics, concerned about welfare, object to paternalism as such.[6] Perhaps people are the best judges not only of their ends, but also of the best means of achieving those ends, given their own tastes and values. People might reject the route suggested by the GPS on the ground that they prefer the scenic alternative; the GPS might not easily capture or serve their ends. People might want to be healthy, but their own means to that end might involve a complex trade-off among various routes, including diet, exercise, sleep, and emotional well-being. A choice architect, focusing on one aspect of the trade-off (diet?), might not be in the best position to identify the best means to the chooser's ends.

Moreover, the distinction between means and ends is not always simple and straightforward. One question is the level of abstraction at which we describe people's ends. If we describe people's ends at a level of great specificity – eating that brownie, having that cigarette, texting while driving – then people's means effectively *are* their ends. The brownie is exactly what they want; it is not a means to anything at all (except the experience of eating it). If, by contrast, we describe people's ends at a level of high abstraction – "having a good life" – then nearly everything is a means to those ends. But if we do that, then we will not be capturing people's actual concerns; we will be disregarding what matters to them. These points do raise some problems for those who favor a solely means-oriented form of paternalism. They must be careful to ensure that they are not describing people's ends at such a high level of abstraction that they are mischaracterizing what people care about.

But insofar as a GPS is a guiding analogy, it is not easy to see nudges as objectionably paternalistic. Many nudges are entirely focused on helping people to identify the best means for achieving their preferred ends. Consider cases in which people are *mistaken about facts* (with respect to the characteristics of, say, a consumer product or an investment). If a nudge informs them, then it is respecting their ends. Or suppose that certain product characteristics are in some sense shrouded, and the nudge helps people to see them for what they are (such as the cost of operating an

---

[5] This is the fundamental concern in John Stuart Mill, *On Liberty* in THE BASIC WRITINGS OF JOHN STUART MILL: ON LIBERTY, THE SUBJECTION OF WOMEN, AND UTILITARIANISM 3, 11–12 (2002) (1863).

[6] *See, e.g.*, RICCARDO REBONATO, TAKING LIBERTIES: A CRITICAL EXAMINATION OF LIBERTARIAN PATERNALISM (2012); Joshua D. Wright and Douglas H. Ginsburg, *Behavioral Law and Economics: Its Origins, Fatal Flaws, and Implications for Liberty*, 106 Nw. U. L. REV. 1033 (2012).

energy-inefficient refrigerator). Or suppose that people suffer from a behavioral bias – perhaps because they use the availability heuristic, perhaps because of unrealistic optimism. A nudge that corrects their mistake can help them to achieve their ends.

To be sure, some behavioral biases are not so easy to analyze in these terms. If people suffer from present bias, is a nudge a form of paternalism about means? Suppose that people gamble or drink a great deal, or fail to exercise, because they value today and tomorrow, and not so much next year or next decade. If a nudge succeeds in getting people to focus on their long-term interests, it might increase their aggregate welfare over time. But is such a nudge focused solely on means? If a person is seen as a series of selves extending over time, the choice architect is effectively redistributing welfare from people's earlier selves to their later ones (and by hypothesis maximizing welfare as well). Maybe that is a good idea, at least if the later selves gain a lot more than the earlier selves lose. But it is not clear that we can fairly speak, in such cases, of means paternalism. Efforts to counteract present bias may well be undermining the ends of the chooser at the time of choice.

Mill's argument

Let us bracket the most difficult issues and acknowledge that some forms of choice architecture count as paternalistic. If welfare is our concern, is that a problem? "Paternalistic" is a description, not an epithet, and to know whether we should object to paternalism, we need to give some account of why and when it is wrong or bad. Perhaps people are the best judges of what will promote their interests, and perhaps outsiders will blunder. John Stuart Mill famously so believed.[7] In a great passage in his essay *On Liberty*, Mill insisted,

> The only purpose for which power can be rightfully exercised over any member of a civilized community, against his will, is to prevent harm to others. His own good, either physical or moral, is not a sufficient warrant. He cannot rightfully be compelled to do or forbear because it will be better for him to do so, because it will make him happier, because, in the opinion of others, to do so would be wise, or even right.[8]

Mill offered a number of separate justifications for his famous Harm Principle, but one of his most important, and the most relevant here, is

---

[7] JOHN STUART MILL, ON LIBERTY 8 (Kathy Casey ed., 2002) (1859).
[8] John Stuart Mill, *On Liberty* (2d ed. 1863), in THE BASIC WRITINGS OF JOHN STUART MILL: ON LIBERTY, THE SUBJECTION OF WOMEN, AND UTILITARIANISM 3, 11–12 (Dale E. Miller ed., 2002).

that individuals are in the best position to know what is good for them. In Mill's view, the problem with outsiders, including government officials, is that they lack the necessary information. Mill insists that the individual "is the person most interested in his own well-being," and the "ordinary man or woman has means of knowledge immeasurably surpassing those that can be possessed by any one else." When society seeks to overrule the individual's judgment, it does so on the basis of "general presumptions," and these "may be altogether wrong, and even if right, are as likely as not to be misapplied to individual cases." If the goal is to ensure that people's lives go well, Mill concludes that the best solution is for public officials to allow people to find their own path. Consider in the same vein F. A. Hayek's remarkable suggestion that "the awareness of our irremediable ignorance of most of what is known to somebody [who is a planner] is *the chief basis of the argument for liberty.*"[9]

It is true and important that Mill and Hayek were focused on coercion, not nudges. For that reason, it would seem odd to enlist their arguments as an objection to such nudges as disclosure of information, warnings, and reminders. But if we really think that people are the best judges of what suits their situations, then we might question even those very mild interventions. Perhaps public officials will require disclosure of the wrong information, or remind people of the wrong things, or impose costs without sufficient benefits. In general, Mill and Hayek might be invoked to reject nudging as well (at least when nudging is optional). No one should question that their objections to paternalism have a great deal of intuitive appeal. But are they right?

That is largely an empirical question, and it cannot be adequately answered by introspection and intuition. We have seen that behavioral findings are cutting away at some of the foundations of Mill's harm principle, because they show that people make a lot of mistakes, and that those mistakes can prove extremely damaging. In light of these findings, it is even possible that those who are focused on human welfare should ultimately embrace *coercive* paternalism, at least in the face of behavioral biases. Some people have made vigorous arguments to this effect.[10]

Here is one way to understand those arguments. When public officials impose mandates, they are in effect responding to a delegation of authority

---

[9] Friedrich Hayek, *The Market and Other Orders,* in THE COLLECTED WORKS OF F. A. HAYEK 384 (Bruce Caldwell ed., 2013).
[10] *See generally* SARAH CONLY, AGAINST AUTONOMY (2012).

from the public.[11] People are well aware that there is a great deal that they do not know – about carcinogens, about food safety, about financial products – and they may well be willing to grant authority to public officials to make up for their own lack of information. Of course that authority might take the form of nudges, but it might also support mandates. Indeed, there is evidence that people want to make such delegations.[12] The more general point is that if welfare is our concern, paternalism should be evaluated on a case-by-case basis – unless there is some systematic reason to support a principle or presumption against paternalism.

In Chapter 8, we shall explore the grounds for a presumption, rooted in a judgment that in general, and notwithstanding the behavioral findings, choosers are likely to have better information than choice architects. For the moment, consider a suggestive and also remarkable finding: When giving people gifts during the holiday season, family members and close friends make systematic mistakes: *They typically give people things that are worth far less than their cash value.*[13] If family members and close friends make such mistakes, and give people things that they do not much want, we might conclude that in the end, choosers really are likely to be in the best position to know what suits their values and tastes – and that outsiders, and particularly those who work for government, will not.

In identifiable cases, however, that judgment is wrong, because choosers lack knowledge of facts. At the very least, educative nudges are a natural corrective. In some cases, a good default rule – say, automatic enrollment in pension programs – is hard to reject on welfarist grounds. To be sure, active choosing might be better, but that conclusion is not obvious. If we care about welfare, we might well be inclined to favor choice-preserving approaches, on the theory that individuals usually well know what best fits their circumstances, but the fact that a default rule has a paternalistic dimension should not be decisive against it.

In short, paternalism is often (not always) objectionable on the ground that it will reduce rather than increase human welfare, but that possibility is not a convincing argument against paternalistic nudges. Because they are mere nudges, they preserve freedom of choice, which reduces (without eliminating) the risks to welfare. And because choosers err, nudges might well increase welfare. If welfare is our guide, there is no good reason for an

---

[11] *See* Oren Bar-Gill and Cass R. Sunstein, *Regulation as Delegation*, 7 J. LEGAL ANALYSIS 1 (2015).
[12] *Id.*   [13] *See* JOEL WALDFOGEL, SCROOGENOMICS 71–77 (2012).

across-the-board objection to nudging, and indeed, much nudging emerges as morally required, not morally forbidden.

One qualification is necessary. Suppose that we are speaking about optional nudges. Suppose too that public officials are systematically unreliable – ignorant, biased, or both – and that most markets are highly competitive and also operate as excellent safeguards for both consumers and investors. If we add that people choose pretty well, most of the time, we might well end up adopting a rule or presumption against (optional) nudging. Instead of making case-by-case judgments, we might conclude that on welfare grounds, such a rule or presumption is an excellent idea.

In theory, that conclusion can hardly be ruled out of bounds. But it does depend on some extreme assumptions. With respect to smoking, drinking, seatbelt buckling, drug abuse, and obesity, government information campaigns have done a great deal of good, saving many lives in the process. We have encountered many recent examples of nudges that have had profoundly beneficial effects.[14] With respect to markets, there is good reason, in both theory and practice, to believe that competitors will target or exploit people's ignorance or behavioral biases, and that such targeting or exploitation can cost both lives and money.[15] The invisible hand sometimes ensures exploitation of human errors, because competitors who fail to engage in that exploitation will lose out to those who do.

True, we should avoid an unrealistically rosy view of government or an unremittingly skeptical picture of markets. But unremitting skepticism also makes no sense for governments, and for all the wonders of markets, there is a serious risk of unrealistic rosiness there as well. It is not easy to defend, except in very abstract theoretical terms, the assumptions that would justify a rule or presumption against nudges.

Learning

But consider a different kind of concern, one that also grows from a focus on welfare: *Choice-making is a muscle, and the ability to choose well is strengthened through exercise.* If nudges would make the muscle atrophy, we would have an argument against them, because people's welfare depends on strengthening that muscle. We could imagine an ethical objection that would contend that some nudges do not allow people to

---

[14] *See* CASS R. SUNSTEIN, SIMPLER (2013); DAVID HALPERN, INSIDE THE NUDGE UNIT (2015).
[15] *See* AKERLOF AND SHILLER, PHISHING FOR PHOOLS (2015).

build up their own capacities and might even undermine their incentive to do so. If so, people's welfare is reduced.

Return to the example of the GPS. I have suggested that the GPS should be seen as a prime nudge, because it helps people to find the right route while also allowing them to go their own way.[16] But there is a serious downside, which is that use of the GPS can make it harder for people to know how to navigate the roads. Indeed, London taxi drivers, not relying on the GPS, have been found to experience an alteration of their neurological functioning as they learn more about navigation, with actual changes in physical regions of the brain.[17] As the GPS becomes widespread, that kind of alteration will not occur, thus ensuring that people cannot navigate on their own.

This is an unusually dramatic finding, but it should be taken as a metaphor for a wide range of actual and potential effects of certain nudges. It raises the possibility that when people rely on some nudges (such as defaults), rather than on their own active choices, important capacities will fail to develop or may atrophy. This is the anti-developmental consequence of some helpful nudges, including the GPS itself.

We could easily imagine a kind of science fiction tale, envisioning a Brave New World in which people are defaulted into a large number of good outcomes, or even choose to be so defaulted, and are made comfortable but thereby deprived of agency and learning. In Huxley's own words: "A really efficient totalitarian state would be one in which the all-powerful executive of political bosses and their army of managers control a population of slaves who do not have to be coerced, because they love their servitude."[18] If some people fear that default rules threaten to infantilize people, the underlying concern lies here. Consider the pleas of Huxley's hero, the Savage, surrounded by a world of comfortable defaults: "But I don't want comfort. I want God, I want poetry, I want real danger, I want freedom, I want goodness. I want sin."[19] Or consider this passage[20]:

> "All right then," said the Savage defiantly, "I'm claiming the right to be unhappy."
>
> "Not to mention the right to grow old and ugly and impotent; the right to have syphilis and cancer; the right to have too little to eat, the right to be lousy; the right to live in constant apprehension of what may happen

---

[16] I borrow here and in the next few paragraphs FROM CASS R. SUNSTEIN, CHOOSING NOT TO CHOOSE (2015).

[17] Eleanor A. Maguire et al., *Navigation-Related Structural Changes in the Hippocampi of Taxi Drivers*, 97 PROC. NAT'L ACAD. SCI. 4398 (2000).

[18] ALDOUS HUXLEY, BRAVE NEW WORLD xii (1931).   [19] *Id.* at 163.   [20] *Id.*

tomorrow; the right to catch typhoid; the right to be tortured by unspeakable pains of every kind."

There was a long silence.

"I claim them all," said the Savage at last.

Such objections should not be romanticized (as Huxley tended to do) or overstated. Syphilis and cancer, typhoid and torture, and having too little to eat are likely to be "claimed" by those who have never suffered from those things. Human beings have lost the capacity to memorize pages and pages of text, but that isn't exactly a serious loss. Nonetheless, there are important domains in which learning is important, and active choosing is necessary to promote it.

Here too, it is necessary to investigate the particulars – the kinds of nudges and choice architecture that are involved. Active choosing and prompted choice hardly impede learning. Nor do information and reminders. On the contrary, they promote learning. Nudges of this kind exercise the choice-making muscle, rather than the opposite.[21]

With respect to learning, a potential problem does come from default rules. It is possible to say that active choosing is far better than defaults, simply because choosing may promote learning. Consider, for example, the question whether employers should ask employees to make active choices about their retirement plans, or whether they should instead default people into plans that fit their situations. The potential for learning might well count in favor of active choosing; if employees must choose, and if they are helped or encouraged to learn, the resulting knowledge might help them for the rest of their lives. If people are defaulted into certain outcomes, they do not add to their stock of knowledge, and that may be a significant lost opportunity.

But the strength of the argument for learning depends on the setting. (Recall the earlier discussion of educative nudges.) In many areas, what the choice-making muscle needs is rest, not exercise. Consider the words of President Barack Obama: "You'll see I wear only gray or blue suits. I'm trying to pare down decisions. I don't want to make decisions about what I'm eating or wearing. Because I have too many other decisions to make."[22]

---

[21] *See* Benjamin York and Susanna Loeb, *One Step at a Time: The Effects of an Early Literacy Text Messaging Program for Parents of Preschoolers* 31 (Nat'l Bureau of Econ. Research, Working Paper No. 20659, 2014), *available at* www.nber.org/papers/w20659.

[22] *Quoted in* Michael Lewis, *Obama's Way* (Oct. 12, 2012), *available at* www.vanityfair.com/news/2012/10/michael-lewis-profile-barack-obama.

For most people, it is not important to become experts in the numerous decisions that lead to default settings on cell phones, and hence the use of such settings is not objectionable. The same point holds in many other contexts in which institutions rely on defaults rather than active choosing. To know whether choice architects should opt for active choosing, it is helpful to explore whether the context is one in which it is valuable, all things considered, for choosers to acquire a stock of knowledge. It is not necessarily terrible if employers create default allocations for retirement plans, so long as those allocations are in the interest of all or most employees.

I have emphasized that if people are likely to make mistakes, because they lack information or because of some kind of behavioral bias, education well might be the appropriate response. Invoking this point, Jeremy Waldron writes: "I wish, though, that I could be made a better chooser rather than having someone on high take advantage (even for my own benefit) of my current thoughtlessness and my shabby intuitions."[23] But if people had to obtain sufficient education on all of the issues that affect their lives, they would quickly run out of time. On welfare grounds, a default rule is often the best approach, because it would preserve desirable outcomes (again, from the standpoint of choosers themselves) without requiring people to take the functional equivalent of a course in (say) statistics or finance. If we care about welfare, there is a recurring question whether, in particular circumstances, the costs of education justify the benefits. For those who are engaged in many activities, it would be impossibly demanding to insist on the kind of education that would allow active choices about all relevant features. Default rules may well be best.

Autonomy

Many people focus on autonomy rather than welfare. Insofar as official paternalism is involved, the most natural objection may well be that the government is not showing respect for persons. Nudges might well run into this objection. Stephen Darwall writes that the "objectionable character of paternalism of this sort is not that those who seek to benefit us against our wishes are likely to be wrong about what really benefits us. . . . It is, rather, primarily a failure of respect, a failure to recognize the

---

[23] *See* Jeremy Waldron, *It's All for Your Own Good*, NY REVIEW OF BOOKS (2014), *available at* www.nybooks.com/articles/archives/2014/oct/09/cass-sunstein-its-all-your-own-good/.

authority that persons have to demand, within certain limits, that they be allowed to make their own choices for themselves."[24]

We should be able to see the force of this objection most clearly in the context of mandates and bans. If people want to engage in risky behavior, so be it; perhaps they have the right to run their own lives as they see fit. Mill emphasized the value of "experiments of living," and while his own focus is on welfare, we might want to insist that on grounds of autonomy, diverse people, with their different values and tastes, should be allowed to construct the narratives of their lives. This point might seem to hold most strongly for intimate or highly personal choices – whom to marry, whom to love, whether and how to worship, what career path to follow. Officials who forbid such choices are failing to treat people with respect. But that conclusion might hold for a wide range of choices, not merely those that are intimate or highly personal.

Even with respect to mandates and bans, however, the idea of autonomy must be used with care. Suppose that if informed, people would not engage in certain behavior, and that they do so only because they lack important information. Respect for their autonomy does not entail respect for whatever people choose. To be sure, public officials should usually respond with information rather than with coercion. But as we have seen, there are circumstances in which informed people would clearly refrain from certain courses of action, and if so, coercion cannot be ruled out of bounds. And if autonomous citizens really do want to delegate certain decisions to public officials, there is a good argument for respecting their delegation.

Do nudges intrude on autonomy? Darwall emphasizes people's right to make their own choices for themselves, and nudges preserve that right. But in speaking of autonomy, philosophers could learn a great deal from economists, who know that the real question is usually not whether people are going to be *allowed* to make choices, but whether someone (such as government) will or should *impose costs on* people who make choices. A small tax on smoking "allows" people to choose to smoke; the same is true of a small fee for eating pizza or for drinking soda, or of a requirement that before you drink two beers, you have to give $100 to an organization that helps recovering alcoholics. Even a large economic penalty "allows" you make your own choices; it simply increases the cost of making them. A better way to make Darwall's point would be to drop the idea of

---

[24] *See* Stephen Darwall, *The Value of Autonomy and the Autonomy of the Will*, 116 ETHICS 263, 269 (2006).

"allowing" choices and instead to say that the problem of autonomy arises when third parties "impose significant costs on" those who seek to make their own choices for themselves. So adjusted, Darwall's objection remains intact. Why – it might be asked – should officials impose significant costs on people who are seeking to run their own lives as they see fit?

We have already seen some possible answers. If people lack information, those costs might be a way of promoting their autonomy, by leading them in the direction that they would go if they were informed. If people suffer from behavioral biases, those costs might well be welcomed, or at least they might well be welcomed under ideal conditions. If people are being deceived or manipulated by clever sellers exploiting their ignorance or their biases, those costs might a solution, not a problem. The imposition of costs might be seen as a product of a delegation from citizens to their government. Of course that delegation might turn out to be a fiction – a rationalization rather than a fact. But there is evidence that people do, in fact, want to delegate at least some such power to public officials.[25] If so, the objection from the standpoint of autonomy is severely weakened.

For nudges, moreover, the issue of autonomy might seem to drop away, because they are specifically designed not to impose significant costs on choosers – at least not of the material sort. If taxes or subsidies are involved, we are not dealing with nudges. If a friend tries to influence you to stop smoking, or to move to another city, or to quit your job, you might not be thrilled with your friend, but it would not be easy to say that your autonomy has been invaded. True, social influences can cross certain lines. If a friend threatens to impose certain losses on you, you might see a risk to your autonomy. But information, warnings, reminders, and strongly worded advice do not seem to create that kind of risk.

But we should be careful here. It must be acknowledged that some nudges impose at least burdens, or some kinds of cost, on choosers. A GPS device is talking to you and telling you where to go; you will not be fined if you ignore it, but so long as it is turned on, it is imposing psychic or cognitive costs on you if you deviate from the suggested route. A warning can be analyzed in exactly the same way. If it is graphic, the cognitive costs of seeing it, and acting as you like in the face of it, might be high. If a default rule is a nudge, and nothing more, it should be easy to deviate from it. But because of the power of inertia, some kind of "effort cost" is involved in any such deviation, and it operates a bit like a tax on people's cognitive capacities. (Whenever someone sends you an email that requires a response, you face a bit of a tax on your time and attention.) For this reason, it would be too simple – and conclude the argument far too quickly – to insist that because nudges impose no significant (material) costs, they raise no problem from the standpoint of autonomy.

I have said that autonomy requires informed choices. If you enter into a mortgage agreement without a sense of its terms, it is fair to question whether you have acted autonomously. If you have received valuable assistance in filling out complicated forms for attending college, or receiving financial aid, you might have been nudged, but it would be hard to argue that your autonomy has been reduced. Many nudges are specifically designed to ensure that choices are informed and that relevant information is salient and easy to process. In the face of a behavioral bias, or some kind of systematic mistake (by the actor's own reflective lights), it is hardly clear that a nudge infringes on autonomy, rightly understood. When they help correct some kind of bias, nudges might well promote people's autonomy. We might identify autonomy with people's reflective judgments rather than their impulses, and many nudges operate in the interest of autonomy, so understood.

It is also important to underline the fact that autonomy does not require choices everywhere; it does not justify an insistence on active choosing in all contexts. There is a close relationship between time management and autonomy. People should be allowed to devote their attention to the questions that, in their view, deserve that attention. If people have to make choices everywhere, their autonomy is reduced, if only because they cannot focus on those activities that seem to them most worthy of their time. To the extent that default rules relieve people of unwanted burdens, and do not force them to make choices, they increase autonomy and do not compromise it.

It is nonetheless true that on grounds of autonomy, the best choice architecture often calls for active choosing. Even though they preserve freedom of choice, default rules might raise questions from the standpoint of autonomy, certainly if they do not track people's likely choices. We have seen the central problem: Because of the force of inertia, people might not reject harmful defaults. If so, there is arguably an intrusion on their autonomy, because they will end up with outcomes that they did not specifically select. Consider, for example, a default rule that says that if you do not indicate otherwise, you are presumed to to want your estate to go to Catholic Church, or prefer your organs to go to people with the right skin color. Even though people can opt out, default rules can intrude on autonomy insofar as they impose that burden on people – and insofar as the particular rules (a) might stick because of that very burden and (b) do not reflect what informed people would like. (We will encounter relevant examples, and survey evidence, in Chapter 6.)

There is a further point, captured in the philosophical claim that autonomy requires that people must be, in some strong sense, the authority behind their actions. If you affirmatively decide to save money or to diet, because saving money or dieting seems to you the right thing to do, then there is no problem from the standpoint of autonomy. Some people go further and suggest that in order to be autonomous, people must be the authority not only behind their actions, but also behind the reasons that account for their actions. If so, then those reasons must square with their own attitudes or standards. If you diet because you want to be healthier, the interest in autonomy is preserved. How do these ideas square with nudges and choice architecture? Maybe not at all, or not well enough, if people's own attitudes are not responsible for outcomes that affect them. At least some nudges produce results that people do not necessarily endorse. When they fail to alter default rules, or are influenced by the order of items in a cafeteria, inertia may be the important factor, and perhaps that is a problem from the standpoint of autonomy.

It is important not be too fussy here. It is excessive to say that in order to be autonomous, people must always act for reasons. They might flip a coin, or do the equivalent, thus "picking" rather than "choosing" (acting for reasons).[26] When the stakes are low, or when we really do not know what to do, we pick. From the standpoint of autonomy, nothing is wrong with that. People might do things, even important things, simply because they "felt like it" – an idea that might refer to reasons (in highly compressed form) but that might not. If we thought that people lacked autonomy whenever they did not act on the basis of reasons that square with their own standards, we would find a lot of situations in which people were not autonomous. But some people do insist that autonomy is not so much a right as a *state*, and that when people are being nudged, they are not autonomous, because they do not have that state.

It should be clear that in order to evaluate this concern, we need to specify the nudge. Educative nudges do not compromise autonomy, even if it is understood in this way. From the standpoint of autonomy, warnings and reminders do not run into problems. The real problem would seem to lie with default rules. But again, it is important not to be too fussy. A view

---

[26] For an important discussion, *see* Edna Ullmann-Margalit and Sidney Morgenbesser, *Picking and Choosing*, 44 SOCIAL RESEARCH 757 (1977).

of autonomy that condemns default rules is a view of autonomy that is unfit for human beings. In some domains, to be sure, people should be deeply responsible for outcomes that affect them. Spouses, friends, and political convictions are three examples – though even there, choice architecture plays an inevitable (and large) role. But with respect to cell phone and printer settings, or mortgage and rental card agreements, or even heath and savings plans, default rules are nothing to get distressed about – and we should not accept a conception of autonomy that would cause such distress.

Whether the interest in autonomy calls for active choosing, as opposed to reliance on a default rule, depends on the choice at issue and on the circumstances. Intimate choices should not be made by default. But along some dimensions, default rules are actually superior to active choosing on autonomy grounds, and so the interest in autonomy calls for them. If people choose not to choose, or if they would make that choice if asked, it is an insult to their autonomy, and a form of paternalism, to force them to choose.[27] And if people would actually like to choose, a default rule does not deprive them of that choice; they can reject the default. Even in the face of inertia, many people will do so, at least if the default really does not fit their situations.

Preservation of freedom of choice is not sufficient to meet all imaginable concerns from the standpoint of autonomy, but it does go some distance toward ensuring that people's autonomy is respected. So does a requirement that any paternalistic nudges focus on people's own ends and otherwise have legitimate goals. But with respect to autonomy, a continuing problem lies in the possibility of manipulation; I will turn to that problem in Chapter 5.

Dignity

The idea of "dignity" is complex and contested. We might begin by suggesting that, in ordinary language, the antonym of autonomy is coercion; the antonym of dignity is humiliation.[28] Of course the two concepts overlap. An infringement on autonomy might also be an insult to dignity. Consider slavery, or a requirement that you get official permission before you can buy certain products or engage in certain activities. But some infringements on autonomy do not insult dignity, and some insults to

---

[27] *See* SUNSTEIN, CHOOSING NOT TO CHOOSE (2015)
[28] *See* AVISHAI MARGALIT, THE DECENT SOCIETY 9–27 (1998).

dignity do not really endanger autonomy. If people are treated disrespect-fully, as if they were children, they might nonetheless retain their auton-omy, in the sense that they are ultimately free to select their own path. We might think that the wrongness of paternalism lies in this kind of insult.

As Nicholas Cornell has powerfully argued, paternalism can be taken to suggest that the choice architect knows better than the chooser, who is thought to be incapable of making the right judgments for herself.[29] Cornell urges that it is a presumptive wrong, and an insult to dignity, to express a disrespectful attitude of that kind. The problem lies in what paternalism, even of the soft variety, tends to *express*.

Do nudges threaten dignity? Jeremy Waldron captures the concern: "What becomes of the self-respect we invest in our own willed actions, flawed and misguided though they often are, when so many of our choices are manipulated to promote what someone else sees (perhaps rightly) as our best interest?"[30] Let's bracket, for now, the charge of manipulation, and focus on Waldron's emphasis on the importance of "dignity in the sense of self-respect, an individual's awareness of her own worth as a chooser." In his view, there is a serious problem if "my choosing is being made a mere means to my ends by somebody else," which points to "what the concern about dignity is all about." Waldron puts the concern well. With certain kinds of nudges, someone's choosing seems to be used as a means to that someone's ends – with choosing itself being influenced by "somebody else." From the standpoint of dignity, isn't that a problem?

There are of course large questions about the place of dignity in ethics and about the appropriate specification of the basic idea.[31] On one (admit-tedly unconventional) view, dignity is properly part of an assessment of welfare. If people feel humiliated, they suffer a welfare loss. That loss might be extremely serious; it is horrible to feel humiliated. In any assessment of welfare consequences, that feeling must be considered. It might turn out to be exceedingly important – and to argue against particular nudges.

A good welfarist should also acknowledge that an offense to dignity is qualitatively distinct; by its very nature, it is a special sort of harm, a different kind of loss from the loss of (say) money or an opportunity to visit a beach. But on the welfarist view, a dignity loss must be weighed

---

[29] *See* Nicolas Cornell, *A Third Theory of Paternalism*, 113 MICH. L. REV. 1295 (2015).

[30] *See* WALDRON, IT'S ALL FOR YOUR OWN GOOD (2014).

[31] *See* AVISHAI MARGALIT, THE DECENT SOCIETY (1998) at 9–27; MICHAEL ROSEN, DIGNITY: ITS HISTORY AND MEANING (2012); Charles Beitz, *Human Dignity in the Theory of Human Rights*, 41 PHIL & PUB. AFFAIRS 259 (2013); THOMAS CHRISTIANO, TWO CONCEPTIONS OF HUMAN DIGNITY AS PERSONS (UNPUBLISHED MANUSCRIPT 2008).

against the other goods that are at stake. Suppose, for purposes of argument, that a graphic and highly emotional appeal, triggering strong emotions (System 1) in order to discourage people from smoking, is plausibly
seen as an offense to dignity – as a way of treating smokers disrespectfully
(and perhaps infantilizing them). Some smokers might so regard such an
appeal and object for that reason. They want to be treated as adults, and
not to be frightened by their government. Fair enough. A welfarist might
still be willing to support the emotional appeal, notwithstanding the
relevant loss, if it saves a significant number of lives.

On another view, fitting much better with Waldron's concern, an insult
to dignity is not merely a part of a welfarist calculus. Such an insult does
not depend on people's subjective feelings, and it is a grave act, perhaps
especially if it comes from government. An insult to dignity should not be
permitted unless (perhaps) it has an overwhelmingly strong justification. If
we endorse this view, it is especially important to ask whether nudges do in
fact offend human dignity. In ordinary life, people sometimes do feel that
certain influences, imposed by family or friends, fail to treat them as adults
and are ethically questionable for that reason. If family members want you
to change your behavior, they should treat you with respect. The same can
certainly be demanded of the state.

To return to my general plea: The force of the objection depends on the
particular nudge. A GPS insults no one's dignity. If application forms are
made easier to navigate, dignity is not at risk. Disclosure of factual information can hardly be seen as an offense to dignity – certainly if the
information is useful and not based on a false and demeaning belief that
people need it. If people are reminded that a bill is due or that a doctor's
appointment is scheduled for tomorrow, it would be pretty odd to raise a
question about dignity.

But we can easily imagine nudges that would offend one or another
conception of dignity. Consider a public health campaign, directed at the
prevention of obesity, that stigmatized and humiliated people who are
overweight by portraying them in a demeaning light.[32] (In Chapter 6,
however, we will see that most people seem willing to support a campaign
of that kind.) Or consider, as a somewhat more difficult case, an antismoking campaign that did the same for smokers. Here again, the fact that
nudges preserve freedom of choice, and do not impose any kind of
mandate, should not be taken as a license to do anything at all. It is
possible to imagine public education campaigns that offend people's

---

[32] I am grateful to Gertrude Lubbe-Wolff for this example.

dignity, though admittedly the more familiar real-world campaigns do not have anything approaching that vice.

We can find historical examples in the ugliest forms of propaganda, including the sophisticated Nazi propaganda machinery attacking the dignity of Jews.[33] If public education campaigns count as nudges, then the same must be said of propaganda campaigns, however despicable their motives. Such campaigns often play on System 1, portraying adversaries (including enemies and despised minorities) as malformed, grotesque, and highly threatening. To the extent that they do so, they offend the dignity of those whom they attempt to dehumanize. It is fair to ask whether propaganda of certain kinds is insulting not only to the groups against which they are directed, but also to the target audience, which is itself being treated disrespectfully and as objects for official control. I have noted that the German constitution explicitly safeguards human dignity, and some forms of propaganda cross the line not only because of their ignoble goals, but also because of the ignoble methods used to achieve those goals.

To turn to more prosaic matters: It might also count as an insult to dignity, and a form of infantilization, if the government constantly reminds people of things that they already know. Every child, and everyone who was once a child, can recall this form of infantilization, and it is not always absent from adult life either. If people are informed of the same thing every hour or even every day (say, by their spouse, by their doctor, or by some public official), they might legitimately feel that their dignity is not being respected.

The same things can be said about reminders, warnings, and uses of social norms. If, for example, choice architects refer to norms, to let people know what most people do, they are not likely to be humiliating anyone. In some cases, however, the concern about dignity might become a bit more serious. If people are constantly reminded that a due date is coming, they might feel as if they are being treated like children. Warnings can run into the same concern insofar as they are repetitious or condescending, or (are meant to) trigger strong emotions instead of merely giving people a sense of factual realities. Repetitive advertising infantilizes people, as does repetitive sloganeering. Both work in large part because of the availability heuristic: The very repetition makes certain messages available. In political campaigns, some forms of sloganeering do not exactly treat citizens with dignity. These are examples of infantilization that we all live with as adults,

---

[33] Steven Luckert and Susan Bachrach, State of Deception: The Power of Nazi Propaganda (2009).

but they are not exactly welcome, and they might be particularly unwelcome if they come from those who work for government.

Here as well, there is no objection to the relevant nudges in the abstract, but there is an objection to imaginable nudging. At the same time, it must be emphasized that any offense to dignity – coming, for example, from unwelcome and numerous reminders – are usually pretty minor. From the standpoint of the concerns that have produced the focus on dignity in the Western political tradition, they are laughably modest.

What is the relationship between dignity and default rules? Recall Waldron's words: "What becomes of the self-respect we invest in our own willed actions, flawed and misguided though they often are, when so many of our choices are manipulated to promote what someone else sees (perhaps rightly) as our best interest?" That's an important question in the abstract, but it is best to bring it into contact with concrete practices. If an employer automatically enrolls employees in retirement and health care plans, dignity is hardly at risk. If a cell phone company adopts a series of defaults for the phone and the contractual arrangement, nothing need be amiss in terms of dignity.

But we could imagine harder cases. Suppose that the government insisted on "default meals" in various restaurants, so that people would be given certain healthy choices unless they specifically chose otherwise. Put to one side the fact that with respect to restaurants, this approach is a mandate, not a mere nudge. In terms of dignity, a reasonable response is: Why shouldn't free people be asked to select the meals they want?

That response raises a more general question. From the standpoint of dignity, is it enough if the government, or a private institution, gives people the option of going their own way? Or is it particularly important to get people to say precisely what they want? John Stuart Mill made the essential point, emphasizing that "the free development of individuality is one of the leading essentials of well-being" and indeed that such free development "is not only a coordinate element with all that is designated by the terms civilization, instruction, education, culture, but is itself a necessary part and condition of all those things."[34] Mill noted that conformity to custom (a pervasive influence, which operates very much as a series of nudges or default settings) "does not educate or develop . . . any of the qualities which are the distinctive endowment of a human being. The human faculties of perception, judgment, discriminative feeling, mental

---

[34] John Stuart Mill, *On Liberty* in THE BASIC WRITINGS OF JOHN STUART MILL: ON LIBERTY, THE SUBJECTION OF WOMEN, AND UTILITARIANISM 3 (2002) (1863).

activity, are exercised only in making a choice. . . . The mental and moral, like the muscular powers, are improved only by being used."[35] We can understand this as a point not only about learning, taken up above, but also about the dignity of exercising one's own personal agency.

In extreme situations, default rules could indeed be a serious affront to dignity. If so, there should be a strong presumption against them (whatever our foundational commitments).[36] But it would be a mistake to use extreme situations, or imaginable cases, as a reason to challenge default rules in general. People are not treated disrespectfully if an institution adopts a double-sided default for printing, or if they are automatically enrolled in health insurance or retirement plans. The objection from dignity has far more force in the abstract than in the context of all, or nearly all, real-world cases in which default rules are actually at work.

Self-Government

Ideas about autonomy and dignity emphasize the importance of a kind of self-government for individuals in their own lives. Those same ideas seem to lie at the heart of democratic theory insofar as it emphasizes the importance of self-rule. Indeed, the very concept of self-government is closely connected with the values of autonomy and dignity – and if we want to promote welfare, there is a good argument that self-government is the best instrument. Self-governing societies are in a far better position to anticipate, to prevent, and to correct serious problems that reduce people's welfare.[37] But whatever its foundations, the commitment of self-government must be kept in mind by those who devise various forms of choice architecture.

It is obvious that if self-government is a fundamental value, public officials must be accountable to the public. Those who impose mandates or fines, those who give out subsidies, and those who nudge should be subject to the electorate – a central goal of democratic design. But elections are not sufficient. The American Supreme Court Justice Louis Brandeis wrote that "sunlight is said to be the best of disinfectants,"[38] and whether mandates or nudges are involved, they should not be hidden or covert.

---

[35] *Id.*
[36] The presumption could be rebutted with a sufficiently strong consequentialist justification – as, for example, by showing that many lives would be saved with the appropriate default.
[37] *See* AMARTYA SEN, DEVELOPMENT AS FREEDOM (2000).
[38] LOUIS BRANDEIS, OTHER PEOPLE'S MONEY 65 (1914).

We have seen that transparency is a safeguard against ill-motivated or foolish action, including nudging.

Many nudges are specifically designed to promote self-government, and they are undertaken in its name. I have mentioned the idea of automatic voter registration, which is used in many nations in Europe (and was adopted in 2014 in Oregon). Efforts to encourage people to vote, and to educate people about the candidates and their positions, are democracy-reinforcing nudges. Many of these efforts are undertaken by the private sector. Political campaigns have used a range of behaviorally informed strategies to nudge people to vote,[39] and those strategies enhance, rather than compromise, democratic goals. It is legitimate for public officials to nudge for the same purpose. They can offer reminders. They can simplify both registration and the process of voting. The can make it easy for people to vote.

Insofar as government action has a democratic pedigree and is fully transparent, objections from the standpoint of self-government are harder to sustain. Of course a self-governing society constrains what governments can do, and nudges, no less than mandates, can run afoul of those constraints. Rights-based restrictions on religious favoritism impose important limits on some kinds of nudging. (We shall encounter an example in Chapter 6.) And if government action is illegitimately motivated – say, by an effort to skew the political process itself – it is not sufficient to say that a majority supports that action. (Here too, we shall encounter an example in Chapter 6.) All forms of choice architecture are subject to the constraints that are built into the very idea of self-government and that restrict what self-governing societies can do to their citizens.

But these points leave some important questions open. For example, what form does transparency take? In many societies, legislatures have explicitly required or authorized nudges, as in the cases of automatic enrollment in savings plans, calorie labels, energy efficiency labels, automatic voter registration, and graphic warning labels for cigarettes. In many cases, nudges of this kind have come from executive officials, who have typically given the public advance notice about the potential nudge, treating it as a proposal for public comment. In general, advance notice is an excellent idea. It subjects the proposal to a focused process of public scrutiny and review. If the nudge is not a good idea – if it intrudes on some

---

[39] *See, e.g.,* David Nickerson and Todd Rogers, *Do You Have a Voting Plan? Implementation Intentions, Voter Turnout and Organic Plan-Making,* 21 Psychological Science 194 (2010).

important interest, will not work, or will have unintended bad consequences – there is a good chance that public officials will hear about the problem.

If government is changing a default rule, or using graphic warnings to reduce smoking, it should never hide what is doing, and in the nature of things, it is most unlikely to do that. Graphic warnings are conspicuous by their very nature, and default rules should not be kept secret. But is government also obliged to disclose the reasons for its nudge? Is it required to divulge the behavioral justification? At least in general, the answer is to both questions is "yes."

We have encountered many examples. When the Federal Reserve Board banned banks from enrolling people automatically in "overdraft protection" programs, it was explicit about the behavioral rationale. When the Food and Drug Administration proposed to change its "nutrition facts" panel, it referred to behavioral findings. The same is true of American efforts to promote automatic enrollment in pension programs and to use "direct certification" to make children eligible for school meals. Fuel economy standards have been explained and defended in large part by reference to behavioral findings (see Chapter 8).

There is no good reason for public officials to fail to disclose the reasons for their actions. Indeed, any such hiding shows a failure of respect – and it compromises the process of self-government. Of course it is reasonable to wonder whether and when such disclosures might make a nudge less effective. I will turn to that question in Chapter 6.

Ignorant or Biased Officials

Why should we trust public officials? As I have noted, they might have improper motivations. Perhaps they are influenced by powerful private groups with a stake in the outcome and hence will mandate, impose costs, or nudge in a way that serves the interests of those groups.[40] Public choice theory draws attention to such risks, and it has shown the significant role of private interests in numerous areas, including environmental protection and financial regulation. It would be surprising if private interests did not try to influence any effort to revise choice architecture – and they will sometimes succeed. Automatic enrollment in pension plans is a good idea, but it must be acknowledged that those who operate such plans have a lot to gain from automatic enrollment, and they have vigorously promoted it.

[40] *See generally* PREVENTING REGULATORY CAPTURE (Daniel Carpenter and David Moss eds., 2013).

We have also seen that even if they are well-motivated, public officials might not know what is best. As Hayek and his followers emphasize, governments planners cannot possibly know what individuals know, simply because they lack that dispersed knowledge. In Hayek's words, "the 'data' from which the economic calculus starts are never for the whole society 'given' to a single mind which could work out the implications and can never be so given."[41] Thus his plea for decentralized markets: "If we can agree that the economic problem of society is mainly one of rapid adaptation to changes in the particular circumstances of time and place, it would seem to follow that the ultimate decisions must be left to the people who are familiar with these circumstances, who know directly of the relevant changes and of the resources immediately available to meet them."[42]

Hayek celebrated the price system as a "marvel," not for any mystical reason, but because it can aggregate dispersed information and do so in a way that permits rapid adjustment to changing circumstances, values, and tastes. As he put it, "We must look at the price system as such a mechanism for communicating information if we want to understand its real function."[43] The multiple failures of top-down design, and the omnipresence of unintended consequences, can be attributed, in large part, to the absence of relevant information.

Hayek was particularly concerned about socialist-style planning. He contended that even if socialist planners are well-motivated and if the public interest is their true concern, they will fail, because they will not know enough to succeed. But Hayek's concern offers a broader cautionary note for choice architects of all kinds, including contemporary regulators who are committed, at least as a general rule, to free markets and freedom of contract. Even if they despise socialism and are simply correcting market failures (as, e.g., in the domains of pollution, health care, or occupational safety), they might well lack indispensable information.

There is a further point. Choice architects are emphatically human and fully subject to behavioral biases; they may be unreliable for that reason. The field of *behavioral public choice* draws on this point to offer an account of official error.[44] The field is rapidly growing, and it is likely to

---

[41] Friedrich Hayek, *The Use of Knowledge in Society*, 35 Am. Econ. Rev. 519, 520 (1945).
[42] *Id.* at 525.   [43] *Id.*
[44] For one example, *see* Timur Kuran and Cass R. Sunstein, *Availability Cascades and Risk Regulation*, 51 Stan. L. Rev. 683 (1999); for an overview, *see* Jan Schnellenbach and Christian Schubert, *Behavioral Public Choice: A Survey* (2014), *available at* http://papers.ssrn.com/sol3/papers.cfm?

prove highly productive. Many historical mistakes on the part of public officials can be illuminated by pointing to behavioral findings. If human beings suffer from present bias or unrealistic optimism, or if they are unduly affected by memorable or recent events (the availability heuristic), then those in government are likely to show the same kinds of biases, and to blunder for that very reason. Public officials are subject to both loss aversion and overconfidence; regulations, including those that try to maintain freedom of choice, may be designed accordingly.

Here, then, is an important pragmatic concern. We might object to some nudges, and to some efforts to intervene in existing choice architecture, on the ground that choice architects are unreliable and likely to blunder. They might be biased, perhaps because their own parochial interests are at stake. They might lack important information. They might themselves display behavioral biases. In a democratic society, public officials are responsive to public opinion, and if the public is mistaken, officials might be mistaken as well.

It is unclear whether and to what extent this objection is a distinctly ethical one, but it does identify a serious cautionary note. And in fact, that cautionary note is itself a central motivation for nudges. One reason for nudges, as opposed to mandates and bans, is that choice architects may err (see Chapter 8). No one should deny that proposition, which argues in favor of choice-preserving approaches. If choice architects blunder, at least it can be said that people remain entitled to go their own way. But if we emphasize the risk of official error, we might object that public officials should avoid nudges and choice architecture as well.

The initial response to this objection should be familiar (but because it is so often neglected, we will put it in italics): *Choice architecture is inevitable.* When choice architects act, they alter the architecture; they do not create an architecture where it did not exist before. We have seen that a certain degree of nudging from the public sector cannot be avoided, and there is no use in wishing it away. To be sure, choice architects who work for government might decide that it is best to rely on free markets and to trust in invisible hand mechanisms. If so, they would select (or accept) choice architecture that reflects those mechanisms.

abstract_id=2390290. For an especially pointed discussion, *see* Ted Gayer and W. Kip Viscusi, *Behavioral Public Choice: The Behavioral Paradox of Government Policy* (2015), *available at* http://mercatus.org/publication/behavioral-public-choice-behavioral-paradox-government-policy.

No one should doubt that free markets have many virtues. But disclosure, warnings, and reminders can do far more good than harm. As we have seen, active choosing is sometimes inferior to default rules. Someone has to decide in favor of one or another, and in some cases, that someone is inevitably the government. It is true that distrust of public officials will argue against nudging, at least where it is avoidable, but if it is dogmatic and generalized, such distrust will likely produce serious losses in terms of both welfare and autonomy – and dignity and self-government as well.

CHAPTER 5

Fifty Shades of Manipulation

It ranks among the most powerful scenes in the history of American television. Don Draper, the star of the series *Mad Men*, is charged with producing an advertising campaign for Kodak, which has just invented a new slide projector, with continuous viewing. It operates like a wheel. Using the device to display scenes from a once-happy family (as it happens, his own, which is now broken), Draper tells his potential clients[1]:

> *In Greek, "nostalgia" literally means, "the pain from an old wound." It's a twinge in your heart, far more powerful than memory alone. This device isn't a spaceship. It's a time machine. It goes backwards, forwards. It takes us to a place where we ache to go again. It's not called the Wheel. It's called a Carousel. It lets us travel the way a child travels. Around and around, and back home again . . . to a place where we know we are loved.*[2]

The Kodak clients are sold; they cancel their meetings with other companies. Now consider the following cases:

1. A parent tries to convince an adult child to visit him in a remote town in Nebraska, saying, "After all, I'm your father, and I raised you for all those years, and it wasn't always a lot of fun for me – and who knows whether I'm going to live a lot longer?"
2. An automobile company advertises its new vehicle by showing a sleek, attractive couple exiting from it before going to a glamorous party.
3. In an effort to discourage people from smoking, a government requires cigarette packages to contain graphic, frightening, even gruesome health warnings, depicting people with life-threatening illnesses.[3]

---

[1] See Mad Men Quotes, Internet Movie Database, *available at* www.imdb.com/title/tt1105057/quotes.

[2] Revealingly, nostalgia actually means "longing for a return home," rather than "pain from an old wound."

[3] On the FDA's effort to require graphic warnings on packages, *see* R. J. Reynolds Tobacco Co. v. FDA, 823 F. Supp. 2d 36 (D.D.C. 2011), *aff'd*, 696 F.3d 1205 (D.C. Cir. 2012). For the government's own graphic campaign, *see* CDC, *Tips for Former Smokers, available at* www.cdc.gov/tobacco/

4. In a campaign advertisement, a political candidate displays highly unflattering photographs of his opponent, set against the background of frightening music, suitable for a horror movie. An announcer reads quotations that, while accurate and not misleading, are taken out of context to make the opponent look at once ridiculous and scary.

5. In an effort to convince consumers to switch to its new, high-cost credit card, a company emphasizes its very low "teaser rate," by which consumers can enjoy low-cost borrowing for a short period. In its advertisement, it depicts happy, elegant, energized people, displaying their card and their new purchases.

6. To reduce pollution (including greenhouse gas emissions), a city requires public utilities to offer clean energy sources as the default providers, subject to opt-out if customers want to save money.

Both public and private law are pervasively concerned with the problem of coercion, arising from the literal use of force. Under the U.S. Constitution, the Due Process Clause is designed to impose procedural safeguards in the event of actual or threatened coercion on the part of government. If private actors plan to resort to force, both criminal law and the law of tort will stand in their way. There are also legal constraints on lying and deception.[4] The First Amendment protects commercial advertising, but it does not ban regulation of false or deceptive commercial speech.[5] The Federal Trade Commission is explicitly authorized to control "unfair and deceptive" trade practices.[6]

But what of manipulation, undertaken by either private or public institutions? There is surprisingly little sustained analysis of the topic, at least within social science and law.[7] To be sure, there is a great deal of work

---

campaign/tips/resources/videos/. For evidence of success from graphic warnings, *see* Press Release, CDC, *Report Finds Global Smokers Consider Quitting Due to Graphic Health Warnings on Packages* (May 26, 2011), *available at* www.cdc.gov/media/releases/2011/p0526_cigarettewarnings.html.

[4] Within Anglo-American law, deceit has long been tortious. *See* Derry v. Peek, L.R. 14 App. Cas. 337 (1889); John Hannigan, *Measure of Damages in Tort for Deceit*, 18 B.U. L. Rev. 681 (1938). An extensive body of law deals with the related issue of misrepresentation. *See* John Cartwright, Misrepresentation, Mistake and Non-disclosure (3d ed. 2012). On the ethical issues associated with lying, *see* Sissela Bok, Lying (2011).

[5] *See* Va. State Pharmacy Bd. v. Va. Citizens Consumer Council, 425 U.S. 748 (1976).

[6] 15 U.S.C. §57a (a)(1)(B).

[7] The most valuable treatment involves the analogous problem of deception. Richard Craswell, *Interpreting Deceptive Advertising*, 65 B.U. L. Rev. 657 (1985); *Regulating Deceptive Advertising: The Role of Cost-Benefit Analysis*, 64 S. Cal. L. Rev. 549 (1991). As we shall see, manipulation is a different concept, and it is much harder to define and police. Craswell's superb discussions nonetheless bear on the question of regulating manipulation and indeed help show why regulation is so difficult.

on lies and deception,[8] and we can identify an overlap among lying, deceiving, and manipulating. We could even see manipulation as a master concept that includes lying and deceiving, or understand the three to be on some kind of continuum. Certainly this is so if our master principle is autonomy; if so, the three violate that principle, though for somewhat different reasons. (I shall have something to say about the extent to which this is so.) But in ordinary usage, it is reasonable to think that the concept of manipulation is distinctive, certainly in the sense that it can occur (as in the mythical Kodak commercial) without lies or deception (at least in their standard forms).

What does manipulation entail, and what is wrong with it? How, if at all, should the law respond to it – for example, in the context of consumer protection or in constraining government itself? When is influence manipulative, or unacceptably so? Are nudges manipulative, and ethically objectionable for that reason?

It should be clear that an action does not count as manipulative merely because it is an effort to influence people's behavior. If you are a passenger in a car, and you warn the driver that he is about to get into a crash, you are not engaged in manipulation. The same is true if you remind someone that a bill is due. A calorie label and an energy efficiency label are classic nudges, but they are not ordinarily counted as forms of manipulation. So long as a private or public institution is informing people, or "just providing the facts," it is hard to complain of manipulation.[9] There is also a large difference between persuading people and manipulating them. With (nonmanipulative) persuasion, people are given facts and reasons, presented in a sufficiently fair and neutral way; manipulation is something different.

It is often thought that when people are being manipulated, they are treated as "puppets on a string."[10] Almost no one wants to be someone else's puppet (at least without consent), and in some respects, it is

---

[8] *See* Craswell, *Interpreting Deceptive Advertising* (1985), for the seminal discussion.

[9] A qualification is necessary. If a disclosure requirement focuses on one of many aspects of a situation, and fixes people's attention on that aspect, a charge of manipulation would not be unreasonable. Consider the controversy over the idea that sellers should have to disclose that food has genetically modified organisms (GMOs). *See* Charles Noussair et al., *Do Consumers Really Refuse to Buy Genetically Modified Food?*, 114 ECON. J. 102 (2004). For those who object to compulsory labeling about GMOs, there is a plausible claim that labels are a form of manipulation, activating public concern where there is no objective reason for that concern. Of course those in the private sector might engage in similar forms of manipulation, drawing people's attention to a feature of a product that, while real, appears far more important than it actually is.

[10] *See* T. M. Wilkinson, *Nudging and Manipulation*, 61 POLITICAL STUDIES 341, 342 (2013).

especially bad to be a puppet of government. Many of the worst govern-ments in history have attempted to turn their citizens into puppets.[11] If we keep the puppet metaphor is mind, the idea of "manipulation" can be applied to many kinds of behavior; but it is not entirely clear that it is a unitary concept, or that we can identity necessary and sufficient condi-tions.[12] Manipulation takes multiple forms. It has at least fifty shades, and it is reasonable to wonder if they are tightly identified with one another.

The principal goal of this chapter is to make progress in understanding what manipulation is and what is wrong with it. If we can make progress on those tasks, we should be better equipped to assess a wide range of problems in ethics, policy, and law. For example, plausible objections might be made to acts of government that can be counted as manipulative; such objections might not treat citizens with respect. There are also free speech questions. When the government compels speech, is there a differ-ence between mandating a purely factual disclosure and mandating one that has arguably manipulative features? Are there circumstances in which manipulative speech, on the part of government, raises constitutional problems[13] or otherwise runs afoul of existing law[14]? When is advertising manipulative, and if it is, what, if anything, should be done about it? How, if at all, should government respond to manipulative behavior by the private sector – for example, in the context of financial products (such as credit cards or mortgages)? In the United States, an understanding of manipulation bears directly on the work of the Consumer Financial Protection Bureau (CFPB) and might help to orient some of its work,[15] which is unquestionably concerned with the problem.

---

[11] *See* FRANK WESTERMAN, ENGINEERS OF THE SOUL: THE GRANDIOSE PROPAGANDA OF STALIN'S RUSSIA (2012); SUSAN BACHRACH, STATE OF DECEPTION: THE POWER OF NAZI PROPAGANDA (2009).

[12] For a number of instructive treatments, see MANIPULATION: THEORY AND PRACTICE (Christian Coons and Michael Weber eds., 2014).

[13] A possible "yes" answer is provided in Wickard v. Filburn, 317 U.S. 111 (1942), though the Court ruled "no" on the particular facts, where the Secretary of Agriculture gave an arguably manipulative speech on behalf of a referendum: "There is no evidence that any voter put upon the Secretary's words the interpretation that impressed the court below or was in any way misled. There is no showing that the speech influenced the outcome of the referendum." *Id.* at 116.

[14] Labor law has an important pocket of doctrine that raises this question, though the fundamental problem is coercion (in the form of threats) rather than manipulation. *See* NLRB v. Gissel Packing Co., 395 U.S. 575 (1969).

[15] *See* the discussion of potential regulation of payday loans in Alan Zibel, *CFPB Sets Sights on Payday Loans*, WALL ST. J., Jan. 4, 2015, available at www.wsj.com/articles/cfpb-sets-sights-on-payday-loans-1420410479.

A Definition

Unfortunately, it is not easy to give a simple definition of manipulation, and I shall spend some time explaining why. The best account, I suggest, counts an effort to influence people's choices as manipulative *to the extent that it does not sufficiently engage or appeal to their capacity for reflection and deliberation*. The word "sufficiently" leaves a degree of ambiguity and openness, and properly so. It is not possible to know whether manipulation is involved without asking about the sufficiency of people's capacity to deliberate on the question at hand.[16] We can imagine clear cases of manipulation (subliminal advertising[17]), cases that clearly fall outside of the category (a warning about deer crossings in a remote area), and cases that can be taken as borderline (a vivid account of the advantages of a particular mortgage or a redesign of a website to attract customers to the most expensive products).[18]

If this is our account of manipulation, or indeed if we adopt any vaguely similar account, it should be clear that most nudges do not fall within the category. At least in general, information disclosure does not manipulate people; it is an effort to appeal to their deliberative capacities. The same is true of reminders, which may counteract the unfortunate effects of selective attention or procrastination. Warnings might cross the line into manipulation, and I shall devote some attention to that topic, but most do not; they simply give people an understanding of risks. It is hardly clear that the charge of manipulation is fairly made against an accurate statement about existing social norms: "most people pay their taxes on time" or "most people who attend this college do not abuse alcohol" or "most people in your community use less energy than you do." I shall bring the discussion of manipulation in direct contact with various nudges at multiple points.

It is important to emphasize that countless choices are at least partly a product of variables that do not involve reflective deliberation – and choosers tend to be unaware of that fact. Do you really know about all

---

[16] Compare the related discussion in Anne Barnhill, *What Is Manipulation?* in MANIPULATION: THEORY AND PRACTICE 50, 72 (Christian Coons and Michael Weber eds., 2014).

[17] *See* AUGUSTUS BULLOCK, THE SECRET SALES PITCH: AN OVERVIEW OF SUBLIMINAL ADVERTISING (2004).

[18] Importantly, the word "sufficiently" applies to the degree of reflection and deliberation that are involved; it does not speak to the issue of justification. For example, would-be kidnappers might be manipulated (in the sense that their deliberative capacities are bypassed) by police officers who are trying to stop a kidnapping, and a terrorist might similarly be subject to (justified) manipulation.

the variables that have affected your decisions this week? The cold weather? A delicious lunch? The fact that a friend was very kind to you, or perhaps a bit cruel? The success of your favorite sports teams? A minor headache? A smile from a salesperson, or a frown? The color of the wrapper that contains the candy bar? The music that is playing in the background? The fact that the salesperson is male or female? The fact that a product was at eye level or on the right-hand side?

It is also true that manipulation can occur when manipulators overload, and do not bypass, people's deliberative capacities. You can easily imagine long, complex forms, requiring calculations that strain people's abilities, and that are devised to do exactly that. In a way, complexity targets people's capacity to deliberate, but it can be manipulative if it breeds confusion.

The problem of manipulation arises when choosers can justly complain that because of the intentional actions of a manipulator, they have not, in a sense, *had a fair chance to make a decision on their own*.[19] Often the distinguishing mark of manipulation is a justified sense of *betrayal*: Having found out what happened, or having reflected on it a bit, people think that they have not been treated properly.

Of course there are degrees of manipulation, as some forms of influence attempt to bypass deliberation altogether (such as subliminal advertising), and other forms merely try to influence it by triggering certain forms of automatic processing (e.g., through framing a problem so as to provoke the desired response). Some forms of manipulation can claim explicit or implicit consent. Romantic partners sometimes manipulate one another, and it can be fine, even fun (though sometimes of course not so much). Some forms of manipulation are modest and relatively benign. In the Kodak commercial, the goal is to connect the product with a set of evocative associations – childhood, a carousal, and a magical ability to recapture, and make permanent, a lost past. Is that kind of thing

---

[19] There is, however, a set of cases that complicate the definition I offer here, and that suggest that it does not exhaust the category of manipulation. Suppose that people's judgments are properly and legitimately automatic and not a product of deliberation. (Immediate attractions to certain foods or persons are plausible examples.) We can imagine efforts to alter those automatic judgments through rational arguments that cannot be characterized as manipulative. But we can also imagine efforts to alter those judgments that do not involve rational arguments at all. A friend, or an outsider, might attempt to use associations, or vivid pictures of some kind, to create a relevant change. The question is: Mightn't such cases involve manipulation, even if they do not involve judgments that ought to involve reflection and deliberation? That question raises the possibility that nondeliberative efforts to alter properly nondeliberative judgments might also be counted as manipulative. But discussion of this possibility would take me beyond my focus here. I am grateful to Anne Barnhill for raising this point, and see her discussion in *What Is Manipulation?* (2014).

objectionable? Maybe so, but it's part of daily life, and it would be pretty fussy to wish it away.

Manipulation often occurs through such associations, which are a pervasive feature of political campaigns. Those who run for office are skilled in the art of manipulation, so understood, and increasingly the science too. Perhaps the most famous, or infamous, example of associative political advertising is Lyndon Johnson's genuinely terrifying "mushroom cloud" advertisement in his 1964 campaign against Barry Goldwater, ending, "The stakes are too high for you to stay home." If you look at any campaign, in any democratic nation, you will find politicians attempting to associate their opponents with something scary, ridiculous, foolish, or ugly, perhaps with effective music and graphics. Often they will be engaging in a form of manipulation – though we might question whether voters, once informed of the strategy, would feel betrayed, or would instead think something like "that's politics" or "all's fair in love and war, and in electoral campaigns."

Of course, the concept of manipulation extends far beyond the use of associations. Manipulators, inside and outside governments, often describe choices so as to make certain outcomes vivid and appealing (such as purchases of lottery tickets, which can lead to a life of ease and leisure), or vivid and unappealing (such as failures to buy life insurance, which can lead to a life of poverty and distress for survivors) – even though a more neutral frame would present the whole problem in a less tendentious manner, leaving the chooser in a more objective position to weigh the relevant variables (and in that sense more free).

Autonomy, Dignity, and Welfare

A central problem with manipulation is that it can violate people's autonomy (by making them instruments of another's will) and offend their dignity (by failing to treat them with respect). The manipulator is leading the chooser *to make a choice without sufficiently assessing, on the chooser's own terms, its costs and its benefits*. For this reason, the most strongly felt moral objections to manipulation involve dignity. The objections reflect a sense that people are not being treated respectfully. Their own capacities and their agency – to assess, to weigh, to judge – are not being given appropriate deference. For those who mount these objections, a central question is whether choosers have given appropriate consent to the act of manipulation, or whether the manipulator has properly inferred consent under the circumstances.

From the point of view of welfare, the objection to manipulation is much less straightforward. Some people can benefit (a great deal) from being manipulated. Consider a smoker or an alcoholic who desperately wants to quit, or someone on a terrific date who really wants to stay out late (but needs some cajoling). Within limits, being manipulated can be a lot of fun. In some forms, manipulation is a form of play, undertaken with a smile and a wink. (A speculation: Those who are intensely opposed to manipulation, in all its shades and forms, lack a sense of humor.) But in other forms, it is not fun at all, even deadly serious (consider efforts to manipulate kidnappers or terrorists). On welfarist grounds, there is no simple evaluation of manipulation, at least if we embrace the foregoing definition.

The foundation of the welfarist concern, I suggest, is the view, associated with Mill and Friedrich Hayek,[20] that the chooser, and not the manipulator, knows what is in his best interest. Of course Mill's principal concern, and Hayek's too, is with coercion, but the welfarist objection to manipulation stems from the same source: a belief that choosers know best. It follows that the anti-manipulation principle is strongly derivative of Mill's Harm Principle; it suggests that choosers ought to be able to make their own decisions, and that the role of others should be restricted to informing them or attempting to persuade them (without manipulation).

If choosers know best, then the welfare-increasing approach is to avoid manipulation and to engage (or boost) the chooser's deliberative capacities. But the manipulator refuses to do that. The skeptic wonders: *Why not?* A tempting answer is that the manipulator is promoting his own interests, and not those of the chooser. The use of manipulation, rather than (say) information or persuasion, creates a risk that the manipulator does not have the chooser's interests in mind. For that reason, manipulation undermines the welfare of the chooser. The welfarist analysis of manipulation closely parallels the welfarist analysis of fraud and deceit. In a sense, the manipulator can even be seen as a kind of thief, taking something from the chooser without real consent. In some cases, that is indeed the right way to assess an act of manipulation; it helps to illuminate recent initiatives in the area of consumer financial protection.

From the standpoint of the legal system, the problem is that as defined here, manipulation can plausibly be said to be pervasive. In a free society, it is inevitable. It can be found on television, on the Internet, in every

---

[20] Friedrich Hayek, *The Market and Other Orders*, in THE COLLECTED WORKS OF F. A. HAYEK 384 (Bruce Caldwell ed., 2013).

political campaign, in countless markets, in friendships, and in family life. Even if we insist (as we should) that manipulation cannot occur without intentional manipulators,[21] the scope of the practice is very wide. It would be odd and perhaps pointless to condemn practices that people encounter daily, and with which they live while mounting little or no objection. Indeed, it would be fussy and stern – even a bit inhuman – to try to excise it.

Because of the pervasiveness of manipulation, and because it often does little or no harm, the legal system usually does not attempt to prevent it. In this respect, the prohibition on manipulation is best seen as akin to a family of values that prominently includes civility and considerateness[22] – approved or mandated by social norms that lack legal sanctions. At least in general, the costs of regulating manipulation would far exceed the benefits. But as we shall see, the proper evaluation of acts of manipulation depends a great deal on context, including the expectations associated with particular roles. In some contexts, regulators do aim at manipulation, at least implicitly.[23]

Everyone knows that a car company wants to sell cars, and under existing conventions, it is acceptable to produce advertisements that do not exactly target people's deliberative capacities (at least if falsehoods are not involved). Something similar can be said about political campaigns. To be sure, there remains a question whether deliberative capacities are "sufficiently" engaged; in the political context, they are not usually on hold. But we can easily find cases in which the sufficiency requirement is not met. The ethical objection gains strength under two conditions: (1) when the manipulator's goals are self-interested or venal and (2) when the act of manipulation is successful in subverting or bypassing the chooser's deliberative capacities.

When both conditions are met, there is good reason for an ethical taboo on manipulation and perhaps even legal constraints. Some commercial

---

[21] Nature can, in a sense, manipulate people; cold weather and snow, for example, can affect people without sufficiently triggering deliberation. But it seems useful to limit the category to intentional efforts; in ordinary language, intentionality appears to be a defining characteristic of the concept of manipulation.

[22] See Edna Ullmann-Margalit, *Considerateness* (2011), *available at* http://ratio.huji.ac.il/sites/default/files/publications/dp584.pdf.

[23] An example involves a 2014 rule requiring integrated mortgage disclosures, 12 C.F.R. § 1024, 1026 (2015), *available at* http://files.consumerfinance.gov/f/201311_cfpb_final-rule_integrated-mortgage-disclosures.pdf. A useful but skeptical catalog of CFPB actions, some aimed at manipulative behavior, can be found in Adam Smith and Todd Graziano, *Behavior, Paternalism, and Policy: Evaluating Consumer Financial Protection* (2014), *available at* http://papers.ssrn.com/sol3/papers.cfm?abstract_id=2408083.

advertisements, and some financial products, are so plainly manipulative that legal responses are required. Of course governments generally should not interfere with political campaigns, because their own interests are at stake, but some campaigns are so manipulative that they deserve ethical condemnation for that reason. As we shall see, there is also reason for heightened concern, from the standpoint of the free speech principle, when the government compels speech in order to manipulate those who encounter it (such as smokers); in cases of this kind, the government should face an elevated burden of justification.

Insulting Deliberation

A great deal of effort has been devoted to the definition of manipulation, almost exclusively within the philosophical literature.[24] Many of the efforts focus on the effects of manipulation in counteracting or undermining people's ability to engage in rational deliberation. On one account, for example, manipulation "is a kind of influence that bypasses or subverts the target's rational capacities."[25] Wilkinson urges that manipulation "subverts and insults a person's autonomous decision making," in a way that treats its objects as "tools and fools."[26] He thinks that "manipulation is intentionally and successfully influencing someone using methods that pervert choice."[27]

Recall, for example, efforts to enlist attractive people to sell cars, or to use frightening music and ugly photos to attack a political opponent. We might think that in such cases, customers and voters are being insulted in the sense that the relevant speaker is not giving them anything like a straightforward account of the virtues of the car or the vices of the opponent, but is instead using associations of various kinds to press the chooser in the manipulator's preferred direction. On a plausible view, manipulation is involved to the extent that deliberation is insufficient. Here again, it is important to notice that we should speak of degrees of manipulation, rather than a simple on-off switch.

In a related account, Ruth Faden and Tom Beauchamp define psychological manipulation as "any intentional act that successfully influences a person to belief or behavior by causing changes in mental processes *other than those involved in understanding.*"[28] Joseph Raz suggests that

---

[24] An excellent overview is MANIPULATION (Christian Coons and Michael Weber eds., 2014).
[25] Coons and Weber, *Introduction*, in *id.* at 11.
[26] Wilkinson, *Nudging and Manipulation* (2013), at 345.　　[27] *Id.* at 347.
[28] RUTH FADEN AND TOM BEAUCHAMP, A HISTORY AND THEORY OF INFORMED CONSENT 354–368 (1986).

"Manipulation, unlike coercion, does not interfere with a person's options. Instead it perverts the way that person reaches decisions, forms preferences or adopts goals."[29]

Of course the idea of "perverting" choice, or people's way of reaching decisions or forming preferences, is not self-defining; it can be understood to refer to methods that do not appeal to, or produce, the right degree or kind of reflective deliberation. If so, an objection to manipulation is that it "infringes upon the autonomy of the victim by subverting and insulting their decision-making powers."[30] The objection also offers one account of what is wrong with lies, which attempt to alter behavior not by engaging people on the merits and asking them to decide accordingly, but by enlisting falsehoods, usually in the service of the liar's goals (an idea that also points the way to a welfarist account of what usually makes lies wrong[31]). A lie is disrespectful to its victims, not least if it attempts to exert influence without asking people to make a deliberative choice in light of relevant facts. But when lies are not involved, and when the underlying actions appear to be manipulative, the challenge is to concretize the ideas of "subverting" and "insulting."

It is tempting to adopt a simple definition, to this effect: *A statement or action is manipulative to the extent that it does not engage or appeal to people's capacity for reflective and deliberative choice.* The problem with this definition is that it is far too broad, sweeping up much action that is a standard part of daily life, and that is rarely taken as manipulative. Suppose, for example, that a good friend frames an option in the most attractive light, with a cheerful voice, and a seductive smile; or that the Department of Transportation embarks on a vivid, even graphic public education campaign to reduce texting while driving; or that a politician argues in favor of same-sex marriage in a way that points, in an emotionally evocative way, to the lived experience of specific same-sex couples. In all of these cases, we might have long debates about whether the relevant statements are appealing to people's capacity for reflective and deliberative choice. And even if we conclude that they are not, we should not therefore be committed to the view that manipulation is involved.

To warrant that conclusion, the word "sufficiently" is required, to add the suggestion that people have been in some sense tricked or fooled, or at

---

[29] Joseph Raz, The Morality of Freedom 377–379 (1986).
[30] See Wilkinson, *Nudging and Manipulation* (2013).
[31] Of course some lies are justified; the intentions of the liar might matter (e.g., to spare someone's feelings), and the consequences might be exculpatory (to prevent serious harm). See Bok, Lying (2011).

least that their deliberative capacities have not been adequately engaged. In this sense, there is a connection between the idea of manipulation and the idea of deceit; we can even see the former as a lighter or softer version of the latter. With an act of deceit, people almost inevitably feel betrayed and outraged once they are informed of the truth. (I bracket cases in which the deception turns out to be necessary to prevent harm or to provide benefits; consider surprise parties.) The same is true of manipulation. Once the full context is revealed, those who have been manipulated tend to feel used. They ask: *Why wasn't I allowed to decide for myself?*

In an illuminating discussion, with strong implications for policy and law and the legitimacy of nudging, the philosopher Anne Barnhill defines manipulation as "directly influencing someone's beliefs, desires, or emotions, such that she falls short of ideals for belief, desire, or emotion in ways typically not in her self-interest or likely not in her self-interest in the present context."[32] Notwithstanding its ambiguity and need for specification, the idea of "falling short of ideals" is helpful, and it should be seen as an effort to capture the same idea as the word "sufficiently."

Note that the standard here is best taken as objective, not subjective. The question is whether someone has, in fact, sufficiently engaged a chooser's deliberative capacities – not whether the chooser so believes. But there is a possible problem with Barnhill's definition, which is that it might be taken to exclude, from the category of manipulation, influences that are in the interest of the chooser. Some acts of manipulation count as such even if they leave the chooser better off. You might be manipulated to purchase a car that you end up loving, or to go on a vacation that turns out to be a lot of fun, or to start a diet that really is in your interest. We might say that such acts are justified – but they are manipulative all the same.

To understand manipulation in my general way, it should not be necessary to make controversial claims about the nature of choice or the role of emotions. We should agree that many of our decisions are based on unconscious processing, or System 1, and that we often lack a full sense of the wellsprings of our own choices. That might not be a problem in general – but it might make a big difference whether actions are determined by our own impulses or drives, or instead by factors intentionally designed by other people to influence us. It might well be a problem if a manipulator imposes some kind of influence that unduly undermines or bypasses our powers of reflection and deliberation. It is also possible to

---

[32] Barnhill, *What Is Manipulation?* (2014), at 50, 72. Barnhill builds on Robert Noggle, *Manipulative Actions: A Conceptual and Moral Analysis*, 34 Am. Phil. Q. 57 (1995).

acknowledge that emotions might themselves be judgments of value[33] while also emphasizing that manipulators attempt to influence people's choices without promoting much in the way of reflective thinking about the values at stake. In ordinary language, the idea of manipulation is invoked by people who are not committed to controversial views about psychological or philosophical questions. It is probably best to understand that idea in a way that brackets the most serious controversies.

Manipulating System 1

Recall that in the social science literature, System 1 is the automatic, intuitive system, prone to biases and to the use of heuristics, while System 2 is more deliberative, calculative, and reflective. Manipulators often target System 1, and they attempt to bypass or undermine System 2. We need not venture contested claims about the nature of the two systems in order to find it helpful to suggest that many actions count as manipulative because they appeal to System 1, and because System 2 is being subverted, tricked, undermined, or insufficiently involved or informed. Consider the case of subliminal advertising, which should be deemed manipulative because it operates "behind the back" of the person involved, without appealing to his conscious awareness. People's decisions are affected in a way that entirely bypasses their own deliberative capacities.

If this is the defining problem with subliminal advertising, we can understand why involuntary hypnosis would also count as manipulative. But most people do not favor subliminal advertising (for evidence, see Chapter 6), and to say the least, the idea of involuntary hypnosis lacks much appeal. The question is whether admittedly taboo practices can shed light on actions that are more familiar or that might be able to command broader support. It is also true that some forms of manipulation involve overloading System 2 and do not implicate System 1 at all.

Testing Cases

Consider some cases that test the boundaries of the concept of manipulation.

1. Public officials try to persuade people to engage in certain behavior with the help of relative risk information: "If you do not do X, your chances of death from heart disease will triple!"[34] Their goal is unquestionably to

---

[33] See Martha Nussbaum, Upheavals of Thought (2003).
[34] Wilkinson, *Nudging and Manipulation* (2013) at 347, uses this example.

nudge, and they use relative risk information for that purpose. The information is accurate, but it can be misleading. Suppose that for the relevant population, the chance of death from heart disease is very small – say, one in 100,000 – and people are far more influenced by the idea of "tripling the risk" than they would be if they learned what is also true, which is that if they do not do X, they could increase a 1/100,000 risk to a 3/100,000 risk (to say the least, a modest increase). If the goal is to change behavior, the relative risk frame is far more attention-grabbing, and probably far more effective, than the absolute risk frame. A tripling of a risk sounds alarming, but if people learn that the increase is by merely 2/100,000, they might not be much concerned. It is certainly reasonable to take the choice of the relative risk frame (which suggests a large impact on health) as an effort to frighten people and to activate System 1 – and thus to manipulate them (at least in a mild sense).

It is true that any description of a risk requires some choices. People who describe risks cannot avoid some kind of framing, and framing is a nudge. But framing, as such, need not entail manipulation. There is a good argument that the use of the relative risk frame does not sufficiently engage, or show a great deal of respect for, people's deliberative capacities; it might even be an effort to aim specifically at System 1. As we shall see, that conclusion does not mean that the use of the relative risk frame is necessarily out of bounds. This is hardly the most egregious case of manipulation, and if it saves a number of lives across a large population, it might be justified. But it can be counted as manipulative.

2. Public officials are alert to the power of loss aversion, and hence they use the "loss frame," so as to trigger people's concern about the risks associated with obesity and excessive energy consumption. They might deliberately choose to emphasize, in some kind of information campaign, how much people would *lose from not using* energy conservation techniques, rather than how much people would *gain from using* such techniques.[35] That choice embodies a kind of nudge. Is the use of loss aversion, with its predictably large effects, a form of manipulation?

The answer is not obvious, but there is a good argument that it is not, because deliberative capacities remain sufficiently involved. Even with a loss frame, people remain fully capable of assessing overall effects. But it must be acknowledged that the deliberate use of loss aversion might be an effort to trigger the negative *feelings* that are distinctly associated with losses. Loss aversion might well trigger System 1. To that extent, reasonable

---

[35] See Elliott Aronson, The Social Animal 124–125 (6th ed. 1996).

people could deem it to be manipulative – and could argue that any frame should aspire to neutrality. One way to move toward that aspiration would be to use both loss and gain frames in the same communication. Consider here the fact that while the U.S. government allows companies to say that their products are "90 percent fat-free," it also requires them to disclose that if so, they are "10 percent fat." An evident goal of the requirement is to prevent a form of manipulation that might come from a selective frame.

Here too, it is a separate question whether the use of loss aversion raises serious ethical objections. Within the universe of arguably manipulative statements, those that enlist loss aversion hardly count as the most troublesome, and in the case under discussion, the government's objectives are entirely laudable. If the use of loss aversion produces large gains (in terms of health or economic benefits), we would not have grounds for strong objections.

But it is easy to identify cases in which the use of loss aversion is venal or self-interested, and in which the surrounding context makes it an unambiguous example of manipulation.[36] Consider the efforts of banks, in the aftermath of a new regulation from the Federal Reserve Board (discussed in the Introduction), to enlist loss aversion to encourage customers to opt in to costly overdraft protection programs by saying, "Don't lose your ATM and Debit Card Overdraft Protection" and "STAY PROTECTED with [ ] ATM and Debit Card Overdraft Coverage."[37] In such cases, banks are making a clear effort to trigger a degree of alarm, and hence it is reasonable to claim that customers were being manipulated, and to their detriment. The example suggests that the ethical evaluation of arguable acts of manipulation turns into partly on the *extent* of the manipulation and partly on its purposes and its effects – a point to which I will return.

3. Alert to the behavioral science on social influences, a planner might consider the following approaches:

a. Inform people that most people in their community *are engaging in undesirable behavior* (drug use, alcohol abuse, delinquent payment of taxes, and environmentally harmful acts)
b. Inform people that most/many people in their community *are engaging in desirable behavior*
c. Inform people that most/many people in their community *believe that people should engage in certain behavior*

---

[36] *See generally* Lauren E. Willis, *When Defaults Fail: Slippery Defaults*, 80 U. Chi. L. Rev. 1155 (2012).
[37] *Id.* at 1192.

All of these approaches are nudges, and they can have substantial effects. The first two rely on "descriptive norms," that is, norms about what people actually do.[38] The third approach relies on "injunctive norms," that is, norms about what people think that people should do. As an empirical matter, it turns out that descriptive norms are ordinarily more powerful.[39] If choice architects want to change people's behavior, then they should emphasize that most or many people actually do the right thing. But if most/many people do the wrong thing, so that any descriptive norm would be harmful (or a lie), it can be helpful to invoke injunctive norms.[40]

Suppose that public officials are keenly aware of these findings and use them to nudge people in the preferred direction. Are they engaged in manipulation? The word "sufficiently" becomes relevant here as well. Without doing much violence to ordinary language, some people might think it that it is manipulative for public officials to choose the formulation that will have the largest impact. At least this is so if social influences work as they do because of their impact on the automatic system, and if they bypass deliberative processing.[41] But as an empirical matter, this is far from clear; information about what other people do, or what other people think, can be part of reflective deliberation, and hardly opposed to it. So long as officials are being truthful, it would strain the boundaries of the concept to accuse them of manipulation: When they are informed about what most people do, people's powers of deliberation are sufficiently engaged.

4. We have seen that default rules often stick, in part because of the force of inertia, in part because of the power of suggestion. Suppose that a public official is aware of that fact and decides to reconsider a series of default rules in order to exploit the stickiness of defaults. Seeking to save money, she might decide in favor of a double-sided default for printers. Seeking to reduce pollution, she might promote, or even require, a default rule in favor of green energy. Seeking to increase savings, she might promote, or even require, automatic enrollment in retirement plans.

Are these initiatives manipulative? One reason that default rules are effective is that they carry an element of suggestion, a kind of informational

---

[38] *See generally* Robert Cialdini, *Crafting Normative Messages to Protect the Environment*, 12 CURRENT DIRECTIONS IN PSYCHOLOGICAL SCIENCE 105 (2003).

[39] *Id.*

[40] *Id.;* Wesley Schultz et al., *The Constructive, Destructive, and Reconstructive Power of Social Norms*, 18 PSYCH. SCI. 429 (2007).

[41] For relevant (but not decisive) findings, *see generally* Caroline J. Charpentier et al., *The Brain's Temporal Dynamics from a Collective Decision to Individual Action*, 34 J. NEUROSCIENCE 5816 (2014).

signal, suggesting what it makes best sense for people to do. To the extent that people are affected by that signal, there is nothing manipulative about default rules. Such rules appeal to deliberative capacities insofar as they convey information about what planners think people ought to be doing. But insofar as default rules stick because of inertia, the analysis is more complicated: Without making a conscious choice, people end up enrolled in some kind of program or plan. In a sense, the official might be thought to be exploiting System 1, which is prone to inertia and procrastination. The question is whether automatic enrollment fails "sufficiently" to engage reflection and deliberation.

In answering that question, it is surely relevant that an opt-in default is likely to stick as well, and for the same reasons – which means that the question is whether *any* default rule counts as a form of manipulation. The answer to that question is plain: Life cannot be navigated without default rules, and so long as the official is not hiding or suppressing anything (and is thus respecting transparency), the choice of one or another should not be characterized as manipulative. Note that people do reject default rules that they genuinely dislike, so long as opt-out is easy – an empirical point in favor of the conclusion that such rules should not be counted as manipulative.

But some objectives do think that if default rules stick because of inertia, it is legitimate to ask whether people are, in a sense, being manipulated. The problem is deepened if we think that the particular default rule serves the interests of the choice architect rather than the chooser. To the extent that the risk of manipulation is real, it is particularly important to make it clear to people, in a way that is salient and timely, that they are permitted to opt out if they like. It may also be important to consider the use of active choosing as an approach that ensures the actual expression of agency, rather than to mere opportunity to choose (see Chapter 6).

A potpourri. There is no question that much of modern advertising is directed at System 1, with attractive people, bold colors, and distinctive aesthetics. (Consider advertisements for Viagra.) Often the goal is to trigger a distinctive affect and more specifically to enlist the "affect heuristic," in accordance with which people use their emotional reactions to good, services, or activities as a kind of heuristic for a full consideration of the variables at stake.[42] Instead of considering those variables, which might be hard, people ask a much easier question: *How do I feel about that?*

---

[42] *See* Paul Slovic THE FEELING OF RISK: NEW PERSPECTIVES ON RISK PERCEPTION 3–20 (2010).

Insofar as choice architects are enlisting the affect heuristic, they are putting the question of manipulation in stark relief.

Much of website design is an effort to trigger attention and to put it in exactly the right places.[43] Cell phone companies, restaurants, and clothing stores use music and colors in a way that is designed to "frame" products in a distinctive manner. Doctors, friends, and family members (including spouses) sometimes do something quite similar. Is romance an exercise in manipulation? Some of the time, the answer is surely yes, though the question of "sufficiently" raises special challenges in that context.

Acting as advocates, lawyers may be engaged in manipulation; that is part of their job, certainly in front of a jury, and even during processes of negotiation. (Good negotiators know how to use loss aversion, and also anchoring, and they really work.) The same can be said about those who run for public office, who standardly enlist the affect heuristic. Politicians know that many voters will not carefully scrutinize a wide range of a candidate's policy positions. They don't have time to do that, and they might not enjoy the effort. They will ask instead: *Do we like him?* Something similar is true for some aspects of the provision of medical care, when doctors want patients to choose particular options and enlist behaviorally informed techniques to influence, nudge, or perhaps manipulate them to do so. Doctors might use a smile or a frown, whether or not consciously, to influence patients to feel upbeat about some treatments and negative about others.

Or consider certain uses of social media, which unquestionably involve nudging, and which can cross the line into manipulation. A vivid example is Facebook's successful attempt to affect (manipulate) the emotions of 689,003 people though the display of positive or negative stories, to see how those stories affected people's moods. As it happens, emotions are quite contagious; sadness breeds sadness, anger foments anger, and joy produces more joy. (Living with a happy person can make you happy.) For that reason, Facebook's efforts to filter stories did, in fact, influence the emotions of users, as measured by the affect associated with their own subsequent posts.[44] A great deal of conduct, however familiar, can be counted as manipulative in the relevant sense.

---

[43] Steve Krug, Don't Make Me Think Revisited: A Common Sense Approach to Web and Mobile Usability 10–19 (2014).

[44] *See* Adam Kramer et al., *Experimental Evidence of Massive-Scale Emotional Contagion through Social Networks*, 111 Proc. of the Nat'l Acad. of Sci. 8788 (2014).

What's Wrong with Manipulation?

Autonomy and Dignity

Respect. The most obvious problem with manipulation is that it can insult both autonomy and dignity. From the standpoint of autonomy, the objection is that manipulation can deprive people of agency; it rests on a continuum for which coercion is the endpoint. (If people are manipulated into buying a product, they might even feel coerced.) From the standpoint of dignity, the problem is that manipulation can be humiliating. Healthy adults, not suffering from a lack of capacity, should not be tricked or fooled; they should be treated as capable of making their own decisions. Their authority over their own lives should not be undermined by approaches that treat them as children or as puppets. An act of manipulation does not treat people with respect.[45]

Suppose, for example, that someone thinks, "I want all my friends to do certain things, and I know a number of strategies to get them to do those things. I have read a great deal of psychology and behavioral science, including the best work on social influence, and I aim to use what I know to manipulate my friends." Such a person would not be respecting her friends' autonomy. She would be using them as her instruments. Indeed, her actions would be inconsistent with the nature of friendship itself, which entails a relationship that is not strictly or mostly instrumental. (Compare a husband who treated his wife in this way.)

Now turn to the case of government. Suppose that public officials – say, in a governor's office – similarly learn a great deal about how to influence people, and suppose that they decide to use what they learn to achieve certain policy goals. Suppose that some of the relevant instruments attempt to subvert or bypass deliberation. To evaluate the resulting actions, we need to know the details: What, exactly, are public officials doing? If they are making it easier for people to qualify for benefits, or more attractive for them to do so, we do not have a case of manipulation. But if the

---

[45] *See* Marcia Baron, *Manipulativeness*, 77 PROC. AND ADDRESSES OF THE AM. PHIL. ASS'N 37 (2003), and in particular this suggestion: "By contrast, the person who has the virtue corresponding to manipulativeness – a virtue for which we do not, I believe, have a name – knows when it is appropriate to try to bring about a change in another's conduct and does this for the right reasons, for the right ends, and only where it is warranted (and worth the risks) and only using acceptable means. The virtuous person tries to reason with the other, not cajole or trick him into acting differently. . . . [B]eing manipulative is a vice because of its arrogance and presumption, and because the manipulative person is too quick to resort to ruses." *Id.* at 48, 50.

communications take an extreme form – designed, for example, to frighten people into doing something – it might be fair to say that manipulation is involved and that public officials are not sufficiently respecting their citizens' autonomy. Imagine that they are attempting to influence people to engage in certain behavior not through substantive arguments, but through psychologically astute efforts to appeal to emotions or to System 1. Perhaps they seek to promote concern with some risk – earthquakes, climate change – in this way.

Again we need to know the details, but it could also be fair to say that such officials are not treating citizens with respect; they might be using them as instruments or as puppets for their own ends (or perhaps for the public-spirited ends that they favor). It would be extreme to insist that in the political domain, all arguments must be statistical, but in a democracy that aspires to be deliberative, System 2 should not be bypassed altogether.

Role. We should be able to see, in this light, that *role* greatly matters to the assessment of manipulation. Suppose that Jones is trying to obtain a job. It is hardly unacceptable for Jones to attempt to get prospective employers to like him, and if Jones learns about social influence and the operations of System 1, it would hardly be illegitimate for him to take advantage of what he learns. To be sure, there are ethical limits on what Jones can do, and even for someone seeking a job, lies, deception, and the most egregious forms of manipulation (consider heavy flirting) would cross the line. But in interactions or relationships that are instrumental, and that are so understood, the constraints on manipulation are weakened or at least different.

In an advertising campaign, everyone knows the nature of the interaction. Manipulation is the coin of the realm. The purpose of advertisements is to sell products, and while we can find purely factual presentations, many advertisements do not appeal to reflection or deliberation at all. They try to create certain moods and associations; the affect heuristic looms large. On one view, that is the free market in action, and we should rely on competition to protect consumer welfare. On another view, it is a serious problem, and competition cannot cure it; it might make things worse. In an impressive book, Nobel Prize winners George Akerlof and Robert Shiller argue that in free markets, "phishermen" prey on the ignorance or the biases of "phools" (ordinary people).[46] Akerlof and Shiller contend that the invisible hand ensures that phishermen will be

---

[46] *See* GEORGE AKERLOF AND ROBERT SHILLER, PHISHING FOR PHOOLS (2015).

plentiful, and succeed, because companies that do not prey on ignorance or biases will be at a competitive disadvantage. The invisible hand promotes certain kinds of manipulation. The world of advertising is certainly a point in favor of Akerlof and Shiller's argument. If they are right, we have grounds for stronger regulatory controls on manipulation by commercial actors; the invisible hand is not promoting people's welfare.

As we have seen, the relationship between a campaign and voters has an instrumental character: Campaigns want votes, and everyone understands that. In the process, both advertisements and speeches will have manipulative features. It would be extravagant to say that in such cases, people have consented to manipulation in all imaginable forms. Here too, lines can be crossed, and ethical objections can have force. But it is important that people are aware of the distinctive nature of the relevant enterprises.

Other roles are accompanied by radically different norms, and manipulation might not fit with, or might violate, those norms. If employers treated their employees the same way that advertisers treat consumers, they would be acting unethically. When governments deal with their citizens, they face radically different norms from those that apply in campaigns. At least this is so in free and democratic societies, in which it is understand that the public is ultimately sovereign. To be sure, public officials are hardly forbidden from framing options and characterizing approaches in a way that casts those they prefer in the most favorable light. That is a perfectly legitimate part of governance. But as the manipulative characteristics of their actions become more extreme, the scope for objections becomes greater.

Welfare

Suppose that we are welfarists and that we believe that what matters is how people's lives are going.[47] Suppose too that we care about violations of autonomy and dignity only insofar as such violations affect people's subjective experiences (e.g., by making them feel confined or humiliated). If, how should we think about manipulation?

It should be clear that there is no taboo on the practice. As we shall see, manipulation might promote people's welfare. Everything depends on

---

[47] I am bracketing here various questions about how welfarism is best understood. It is possible to have a conception of welfare that includes consideration of autonomy and dignity. See AMARTYA SEN, DEVELOPMENT AS FREEDOM (2000); MARTHA NUSSBAUM, CREATING CAPABILITIES (2011); *Utilitarianism and Welfarism*, 76 J. PHIL. 463 (1979). For instructive discussion, see MATTHEW ADLER, WELL-BEING AND FAIR DISTRIBUTION (2011).

whether it does, and so welfarists do not oppose manipulation as such. But there is a distinctive welfarist objection to manipulation, which takes the following form. As a general rule, it might be thought that choosers know what is in their best interest (at least if they are adults, and if they do not suffer from a problem of capacity, such as mental illness[48]). They have unique access to their situations, their constraints, their values, and their tastes. If they are manipulated, they are deprived of the (full) ability to make choices on their own, simply because they are not give a fair or adequate chance to weigh all variables. If someone wants to help people to make better choices, his obligation is to inform them, so that they can themselves engage in such weighing.

The problem with the manipulator is that he lacks relevant knowledge – about the chooser's situation, tastes, and values. Lacking that knowledge, he nonetheless subverts the process by which choosers make their own decisions about what is best for them. Things are even worse if the manipulator is focused on his own interests rather than on those of choosers. It is in this sense that a self-interested manipulator can be said to be stealing from people – both limiting their agency and moving their resources in the preferred direction.

For these reasons, the welfarist objection to paternalism is rooted in the same concerns that underlie Mill's Harm Principle. We have seen that in Mill's view, the problem with outsiders, including government officials, is that they lack the necessary information. Recall Mill's claim that the "ordinary man or woman has means of knowledge immeasurably surpassing those that can be possessed by any one else." When society seeks to overrule the individual's judgment, it does so on the basis of "general presumptions," and these "may be altogether wrong, and even if right, are as likely as not to be misapplied to individual cases." These points apply to those engaged in manipulation no less than to those engaged in coercion.

Notwithstanding Mill's points, we should reiterate that from the welfarist standpoint, the ban on manipulation cannot be defended in the abstract; it needs an empirical justification.[49] Behavioral science raises

---

[48] A child, or a person suffering from some form of dementia, has a weaker objection to manipulation. Parents manipulate young children all the time, partly to promote their welfare. Caretakers manipulate people who are suffering from dementia. These practices are largely taken for granted, but we could imagine situations in which they would raise serious ethical questions. Even if the relevant manipulation is in the interest of those who are being manipulated, the interests in autonomy and dignity impose constraints here as well.

[49] Note that the question here is whether manipulation increases or decreases welfare; it is not whether the law, or some regulator, should ban manipulation. The latter question raises issues about institutional competence and decision costs. It also requires attention to the effect of manipulation

serious questions about whether such a justification is available, and in any case, everything depends on whether manipulation improves people's welfare. To see the point, imagine a benign, all-knowing, welfare-promoting manipulator – a kind of idealized friend or parent – who is concerned only with the welfare of those who are being manipulated, who has all the knowledge he needs, and who simply does not make mistakes. By hypothesis, the welfare-promoting manipulator should be celebrated rather than challenged on welfarist grounds – at least if the best way to promote welfare is through manipulation rather than otherwise.

The major qualification is that if people know that they are being manipulated, and do not like it, there will be a welfare loss, and that loss will have to be counted in the overall assessment. If people hate manipulators, manipulation is less likely to be supportable on welfare grounds (unless it is hidden, which raises problems of its own; hidden manipulation is risky, because it might be disclosed, and people will not be happy to learn that it has been hidden). But if manipulation really does increase welfare, then it would seem to be justified and even mandatory on ethical grounds.

The main problem with the thought experiment is its extreme lack of realism. Manipulators are unlikely to be either benign or all-knowing. Often they have their own agendas, and the fact that they engage in manipulation attests to that fact. If they are genuinely concerned about the welfare of the chooser, why not try to persuade them? Why cross the line into manipulation? We have seen that people err in various ways and that Mill was wrong to be so confident in thinking that people's choices will promote their welfare. Behavioral scientists have specified exactly why he was wrong, and sometimes, at least, outsiders can provide a lot of help, not least through nudges. But if the outsider can help, why not inform, remind, or warn? Why not rely on a default rule? Why manipulate?

To be sure, the manipulator might be able to answer these questions if, for example, time is of the essence, or if the chooser lacks capacity (because, e.g., he is a child or very ill). Or suppose that graphic health warnings, aimed directly at System 1, save numerous lives; suppose too that numerous lives cannot be saved with a merely factual presentation

---

on large populations with heterogeneous understandings. In response to an advertising campaign, for example, some people might be manipulated (in the sense that System 1 is essentially all that is affected) while others are not (because the campaign triggers a significant amount of deliberation).

unaccompanied by graphic health warnings. On welfarist grounds, a great deal might be said on behalf of graphic health warnings.[50]

The example shows that from the standpoint of welfare, everything depends on the context; the fact that manipulation is involved does not *necessarily* impeach the manipulator's welfare calculus. But in many situations, suspicion about manipulators' goals is perfectly justified. To this point it must be added that even when those goals are admirable, manipulators may not know enough to justify their actions. Recall here Hayek's claim that "the awareness of our irremediable ignorance of most of what is known to somebody [who is a planner] is *the chief basis of the argument for liberty*."[51]

Manipulation with Consent: "I Welcome It!"

Suppose that people consent to manipulation.[52] An alcoholic might tell his wife: "I am trying so hard to quit. Please use whatever techniques you can think of to help me. Manipulation is very much on the table. I welcome it!" A gambler might tell his friends and family: "I have a terrible problem, and it is ruining my life. Feel free to manipulate me!" Or suppose that the overwhelming majority of smokers tell their government: "I want to stop! If you can find a way to help me to overcome my addiction, I would be most grateful." T. M. Wilkinson notes that it is too crude to say that manipulation infringes upon autonomy, because "manipulation could be consented to. If it were consented to, in the right kind of way, then the manipulation would at least be consistent with autonomy and might count as enhancing it."[53]

The conclusion has a great deal of force. We can understand consent as suggesting support from System 2, which might welcome a little manipulation (or possibly a lot) as a way of cabining the adverse effects of System 1. (Recall the discussion in Chapter 2 of self-control problems and preferences about preferences.) The tale of Ulysses and the Sirens is instructive here, whether Ulysses was requesting manipulation or something else.[54]

---

[50] Christine Jolls, *Product Warnings, Debiasing, and Free Speech: The Case of Tobacco Regulation*, 169 J. INSTITUTIONAL AND THEORETICAL ECONOMICS 53 (2013).

[51] *See* FRIEDRICH HAYEK, THE MARKET AND OTHER ORDERS 384 (Bruce Caldwell ed., 2013) (emphasis added).

[52] On one view, the concept of manipulation presupposes a lack of consent. *See* Robert Goodin, *Manipulatory Politics* 9 (1980) (discussing the idea of "unknown interference"). But the examples given in text suggest that manipulation can be a product of consent and even invitation.

[53] Wilkinson, *Nudging and Manipulation* (2013), at 345.

[54] *See* JON ELSTER, ULYSSES AND THE SIRENS (1983).

Nor is there an obvious objection, in the case of consent, from the standpoint of welfare. The chooser has decided that he will be better off if he is manipulated. If we see his choice as presumptively promoting his welfare, we should respect it, even if what he chose is manipulation.

In the easiest cases, consent is explicit. In harder cases, it is only implicit, in the sense that the manipulator infers it from the circumstances or believes, with good reason, that the chooser would consent if asked. If the inference is less than reliable, the consent justification is correspondingly weakened. If the belief is reasonable but potentially wrong, it might make sense to insist on obtaining explicit consent in order to avoid the risk of error. It is important to see that consensual manipulation is an unusual case; those who need help do not ordinarily ask, "Please manipulate me." But such cases certainly do exist, at least when people face serious problems of self-control.

Transparency and Manipulation

The idea of manipulation is sometimes taken to imply a lack of transparency, as if something important is being hidden or not being disclosed, and often it is crucial that manipulators are hiding something.[55] If a manipulator is acting as a puppeteer, he might be failing to reveal his own role; that can be an important feature of manipulation. With respect to manipulation, however, it is not entirely clear what transparency even means. Transparency about what, exactly? About the manipulator's own actions? About some aspect of the situation? About the reason that an influence turns out to work? About something else?

Hiding something

Typically manipulation does consist in a lack of transparency about a key feature of a situation; that is itself the manipulation involved. A father tells a small child: *If you are very good, Santa Claus will bring you a toy giraffe.* The father is not transparent about the fact that he is actually Santa Claus. (True, that is a lie as well as a form of manipulation.) Or – to return to a defining case of manipulation – a company uses subliminal advertising to get people to buy its products. Once the relevant feature is brought

---

[55] *See* GOODIN, MANIPULATORY POLITICS (1980), at 7–12.

out into the open, the objects of the manipulation feel betrayed, asking, "What didn't you tell me that?" With transparency, the attempted manipulation cannot be effective.

In the pivotal scene in *The Wizard of Oz*, the Wizard says, "Pay no attention to the man behind the curtain." The man behind the curtail is of course a mere human being, masquerading as the great Wizard – and he is claiming far more authority than he has or deserves, and also designing social situations in a way that hides features that, if revealed, would greatly alter people's judgments and choices. The Wizard is a terrific manipulator of people's beliefs and emotions – perhaps even at the end, when, unmasked, he offers symbolic gifts to the Scarecrow, the Tin Man, and the Cowardly Lion, in order to convince them that they have a brain, a heart, and courage. The Wizard manipulates precisely through a lack of transparency. (But didn't he increase their welfare?)

Or consider a less celebrated movie, *The Truman Show*, in which the life course of Truman, the movie's hero-protagonist, is affected by multiple decisions from a master manipulator, who conceals two facts: (1) Truman is the unwitting star of a television show and (2) his friends and acquaintances are mere actors. Covertness and hiding are common features of manipulation. Whenever people who are imposing influence conceal their own role, it seems reasonable to object. (That certainly happens in politics.) As we have seen, a lack of transparency offends both autonomy and dignity. Although Truman did not suffer from a lack of welfare, most people do not want to live as he did, with authorities designing a choice architecture to give us a bright, sunny life. Here as well, manipulation consists in a lack of transparency.

From the standpoint of welfare, an absence of transparency creates a different problem. We might ask why, exactly, someone has failed to be upfront with the chooser, who ought to be able to make his own decisions, armed with relevant information. As before, however, the analysis of welfare is more complex, for we could imagine cases in which transparency is not necessary and may in fact be a problem. Suppose that someone suffers from a serious self-control problem and that his life is in danger (from, say, alcohol or drug addiction). Suppose too that a manipulator has come across a life-saving strategy and that transparency would render the manipulation less effective. By hypothesis, welfarist considerations argue against transparency. Points of this kind have the strongest intuitive force when applied to people who lack capacity (young children, the mentally ill), but we can imagine contexts in which adults with full capacity would benefit from being manipulated and would be harmed by transparency.

From the standpoint of welfare, there might also be a justification for hidden manipulation in other extreme circumstances – as, for example, when people are trying to stop a kidnapping or to save a kidnapping victim. A kidnapper has forfeited his right to be free from manipulation. If the goal is to stop a wrongdoer, or someone who threatens to do real harm, it might be perfectly acceptable or even obligatory to manipulate them and to hide that fact. They have lost their right to be treated with respect, and their welfare, as choosers, is not a matter of much concern.

Transparency does not justify manipulation

In standard cases, however, this argument will be unavailable. It follows that most of the time, an actually or arguably manipulative action should not be hidden or covert, even when it is justified; return to the case of graphic health warnings. Transparency is a necessary condition. Note, however, that it is not sufficient to justify manipulation. One person might flirt with another, not because of a romantic attraction but to get the latter to do something, and the flirtation might count as manipulation – but it is not exactly hidden and it is not exactly justified. (What is hidden is the reason for the flirtation; disclosure of that reason would usually be self-defeating.) Some acts can be both manipulative and fully revealed to those who are being manipulated. Recall the use of relative risk information, where the nature of the disclosure is hardly hidden. A graphic health warning is perfectly transparent – and if it is required by regulation, it is even likely to be preceded by a period for public comment.[56]

Subliminal advertising could itself be preceded by an explicit warning: "This movie contains subliminal advertising." Subliminal advertising would not become acceptable merely because people were informed about it. If a movie chain announced that its previews would be filled with subliminal advertisements, people could fairly object – certainly on grounds of autonomy, and on plausible assumptions on grounds of welfare as well.

---

[56] As was the case for the FDA regulation invalidated by the court of appeals. R. J. Reynolds Tobacco Co. v. U.S. Food & Drug Admin., 823 F. Supp. 2d 36 (D.D.C. 2011), aff'd, 696 F.3d 1205 (D.C. Cir. 2012).

Transparency about psychology?

I have said that the idea of transparency contains ambiguity, and we can now see why. Use of relative risk information is open and public, but it does not *disclose the psychological mechanism that makes it effective.* No one says, "We are using relative risk information because we want you to change, and we know that if we say that your mortality risk will be tripled, you are more likely to change. Of course it is also true that even if you do not change, your mortality risk will remain very low." A default rule is not hidden, but it does not disclose this: "Default rules have an effect in part because people tend to procrastinate and suffer from inertia, and we are counting on your procrastination, and your tendency to inertia, to help us to achieve our policy goals for you."

Is it manipulative not to be transparent about the psychological mechanisms that make influences work? Without straining the ordinary meaning of the word, we could conclude that it is, but my own definition does not require or even support that conclusion. If the act is itself transparent, and if deliberative capacities are sufficiently involved, then a failure to tell people about the underlying psychological mechanisms does not mean that manipulation is necessarily involved. For government action, however, reason-giving is ordinarily required, and reason-giving should include an explanation of why a particular form of influence has been chosen – which includes an account of psychological mechanisms. I will return to this issue in the next chapter.

Democratically Authorized Manipulation

What if manipulation is democratically authorized? Suppose that a national legislature expressly votes for it, perhaps in order to improve public health (as, e.g., by discouraging smoking, or drug use, or unhealthy eating), or perhaps to promote other goals (such as enlistment in the military or adoption of the currently preferred ideology). In relatively benign cases, involving little or no manipulation, a legislature might support an educational campaign that is designed to reduce illnesses and deaths and that enlists a series of behaviorally informed strategies, targeting System 1, to accomplish its goals.

It should be clear that democratic authorization ought not by itself to dissolve otherwise reasonable objections to manipulation. The most obvious problems arise if the national legislature has illegitimate ends (say, the incul-cation of racial prejudice or self-entrenchment of some kind). If a political majority supports efforts to manipulate people in order to entrench itself, or to promote second-class citizenship for certain social groups, the fact of majority support is hardly a justification. It might even make things worse. But the familiar objections to manipulation – involving autonomy, dignity, and welfare – apply even if the ends are perfectly legitimate. If a national legislature authorizes subliminal advertising, it remains fully possible to complain on grounds of offense to both autonomy and dignity. An objection from the standpoint of welfare is also possible: Why did the democratic process authorize manipulation, rather than some other kind of communication, which promotes reflective judgments by people themselves?

To be sure, we could understand democratic authorization as a form of majority or collective consent, suggesting support from System 2, which might welcome a little manipulation (or possibly a lot) as a way of cabining the adverse effects of System 1. Suppose a strong majority really wants to government to help to combat a public health problem, and that it agrees that the best and most effective way to do so is to target System 1. We might be inclined to speak of consent in cases of this kind. Society as a whole might be trying to vindicate its reflective judgments, or its preferences about preferences, in the face of individual myopia or reck-lessness. Society might be like Ulysses, protecting itself from the Sirens, or vindicating its own highest aspirations (say, to equality on the basis of race or sex).

It is possible, and it happens, but in general, there are evident risks in authorizing public officials to pursue this line of argument. The objection to manipulation comes from *individuals*, who do not want to be manipu-lated; the fact that a majority wants to manipulate them is no defense. The idea of majority or collective consent is a mystification, at least when the rights of individuals are involved. If a majority wants to convince a minority to believe something, or to do something, it should not resort to manipulation.

But in certain contexts, the argument on behalf of at least a modest degree of manipulation might not be implausible, certainly on welfare grounds,[57] and it is strengthened if the democratic process has supported

---

[57] *See* Jonathan Baron, *A Welfarist Approach to Manipulation*, J. Behavioral Marketing (forthcoming).

it. Imagine, for example, a public education campaign that is designed to reduce the risks associated with texting while driving, or an effort to combat the use of dangerous drugs or to convince people to stay in school. Many such campaigns are vivid and have an emotional component; they can be understood as efforts to combat self-control problems and to focus people on the long term.

If government is targeting System 1 – perhaps through framing, perhaps through emotionally evocative appeals – it might be responding to the fact that System 1 has already been targeted, and to people's detriment. In the context of cigarettes, for example, it is plausible to say that previous manipulations – including advertising and social norms – have influenced people to become smokers. If this is so, perhaps we can say that public officials are permitted to meet fire with fire. But some people might insist that two wrongs do not make a right – and that if the government seeks to lead people to quit, it must treat them fully as adults and appeal only or mostly to their deliberative capacities. In my view, that position is reasonable but too strict, at least in the context of behavior that is at once addictive and life-threatening. If graphic warnings can save significant numbers of lives, they should not be ruled out of bounds.[58]

Recall that there are degrees of manipulation, and there is a large difference between a lie and an effort to frame an alternative in an appealing, unappealing, or ugly light. In ordinary life, we would not be likely to accuse our friends or loved ones of manipulation if they characterized one approach as favored by most members of our peer group, or if they emphasized the losses that might accompany an alternative that they abhor, or if they accompanied a description of one option with a grave look and a frown. These are at most mild forms of manipulation, to be sure, and it is important to see that mild forms might well be acceptable and benign (and a bit fun) if they promote the interests of those people at whom they are aimed. No legal system makes it unlawful for people to exploit one another's cognitive biases.[59]

---

[58] *Id.* and in particular this suggestion: "The two dimensions of outcome valence and deceit may be correlated in the real world, or people may think they are. When two dimensions are correlated, people sometimes use one of them to make inferences about the other. This attribute-substitution effect may lead people to be suspicious of beneficial manipulation, such as those involved in nudges. For example, people may think of beneficial nudges as violations of autonomy to the extent to which they actually work. This confusion could hold back the adoption of beneficial nudges."

[59] *But see* AKERLOF AND SHILLER, PHISHING FOR PHOOLS (2015), for an assortment of concerns, suggesting the possible value of a larger regulatory role.

Unifying Strands

If the various arguments are put together, we might be able to evaluate acts of manipulation with the help of the following matrix:

	Benign and informed	Malign or uninformed
Not highly manipulative	Acceptable on welfare grounds; might be acceptable by reference to autonomy or dignity	Unacceptable
Highly manipulative	Acceptable on welfare grounds; objectionable on grounds of autonomy and dignity	Highly unacceptable

The matrix helps to orient the appropriate response to manipulation from the standpoint of ethics, politics, and law, and indeed it captures widespread intuitions. In the bottom right cell, we can find actions by self-interested or venal public officials in both undemocratic and democratic systems. In the top right, we can find foolish or venal statements or actions by choice architects that do not entirely bypass people's deliberative capacities, but that hardly do justice to them. Many government agencies, and many ordinary companies, act in accordance with the top left cell; they depict their behavior in an appealing light, and they try to attract favorable attention, but the particular form of manipulation is hardly egregious. Many governments act in a way that fits in the bottom left cell; some graphic campaigns are examples.

The matrix also provides a start toward an analysis of how the legal system should respond to manipulation. From the standpoint of welfare, the central question is whether the benefits of restricting the manipulative action or statement justify the costs. To answer that question, we need to know what would happen if the action or statement were not made (or were transformed into a nonmanipulative version). In this respect, the analysis of manipulation closely parallels the analysis of deception. The costs of manipulation depend, in large part, on whether the manipulator is malign or uninformed. To the extent that it is, there is a risk of serious welfare losses. But suppose that an advertiser is part of a well-functioning competitive process, and that its advertisement includes a degree of manipulation in order to sell a product. If the competitive process is genuinely well-functioning, consumers are not likely to lose much, and market pressures might discipline the use and the effectiveness of manipulation.[60] But if people lack information and suffer from behavioral biases, the invisible hand might even promote manipulation and punish competitors who do not resort to it, potentially leading to serious welfare losses.[61]

The question, then, is whether some kind of market failure exists, so that manipulative behavior can persist or be rewarded. In light of information problems and behavioral biases, the answer is likely to be affirmative, at least in many markets.[62] Of course consumers will have diverse understandings of, and reactions to, statements and actions that plausibly fall within the category of manipulation. Some consumers will see right through it; others will be completely fooled. Empirical testing of representative populations could provide highly informative here. The fact of heterogeneous understandings will create serious challenges for regulators seeking to prevent arguably harmful forms of manipulation. As we shall see, however, some manipulative acts are so plainly welfare-reducing that it makes sense to restrict them.[63]

Compelled Speech

Under established constitutional principles in American law, government can regulate threats ("your money or your life!").[64] It can also regulate false or misleading commercial speech ("if you use this product, you will never get cancer!")[65] and certain forms of coercive speech ("if you vote for a union, I will fire you").[66] May government also regulate manipulation? It is also clear that government can compel certain kinds of speech, at least if it is trying to ensure that consumers know what they are buying.[67] May it compel speech that is arguably manipulative?

As a testing case, consider the efforts of the Food and Drug Administration (FDA) to require cigarette packages to contain graphic health warnings. Many countries impose such warnings, and their actions are

---

[60] See Edward L. Glaeser, *Paternalism and Psychology*, 73 U. Chi. L. Rev. 133 (2006).

[61] See AKERLOF AND SHILLER, PHISHING FOR PHOOLS (2015).

[62] See BAR-GILL, SEDUCTION BY CONTRACT (2011).

[63] See Eric Posner, *The Law, Economics, and Psychology of Manipulation* (2015), *available at* http://papers.ssrn.com/sol3/papers.cfm?abstract_id=2617481.

[64] Watts v. United States, 394 U.S. 705 (1969).

[65] Va. State Pharmacy Bd. v. Va. Citizens Consumer Council, 425 U.S. 748 (1976).

[66] NLRB v. Gissel Packing Co., 395 U.S. 575 (1969).

[67] See Note, *The Future of Government-Mandated Health Warnings*, 163 U. Pa. L. Rev. 177 (2014).

usually not thought to create any kind of constitutional problem. In my view, that is exactly the right approach. Free speech is centrally about protection of self-government, not commercial advertisers, and graphic health warnings might well save a lot of lives – which is a sufficient justification for them. But under American constitutional law as it has developed over time, the constitutional question is real. In 2012, a federal court of appeals invalidated the FDA's requirement on free speech grounds, concluding that the FDA lacked sufficient evidence to justify the compelled speech.[68] In so ruling, the court did not emphasize the arguably manipulative nature of the graphic warnings. But the lower court opinion did exactly that.[69]

That court found it highly relevant that "the Rule's graphic-image requirements are *not* the type of purely factual and uncontroversial dis-closures that are reviewable under this less stringent standard." It added, plausibly, that "it is abundantly clear from viewing these images that the emotional response they were crafted to induce is calculated to provoke the viewer to quit, or never to start, smoking: an objective wholly apart from disseminating purely factual and uncontroversial information." The court concluded that when the government compels speech that does not involve the "purely factual and uncontroversial," it has to meet a higher burden of justification.

The central idea here lacks support in Supreme Court decisions, but it has some appeal: *The free speech principle imposes special barriers against government efforts to require speech that does not merely appeal to deliberative or reflective capacities, but that engages and attempts to activate System 1.* On this view, there is no firm rule against compelling manipulative speech of that kind (so long as it is not false or deceptive), but if government is engaging in such compulsion, it must have a strong justification for doing so.

This analysis raises an assortment of issues. Do the graphic warnings really count as manipulative? They are certainly designed to create a visceral response (and they do exactly that). But the question is whether they do not sufficiently engage or appeal to people's capacity for reflective and deliberative choice. Here the answer has to come from specifying the idea of "sufficiently." There is an empirical component to the specification: What, exactly, do people understand after they see the warnings? Suppose

---

[68] *See* R. J. Reynolds Tobacco Co. v. U.S. Food & Drug Admin.,), *aff'd*, 696 F.3d 1205 (D.C. Cir. 2012), 823 F. Supp. 2d 36 (D.D.C. 2011).
[69] *Id.*

that for a large part of the population, understanding is actually improved; people have a better sense of the risks.[70] If so, there is a good argument that manipulation is not involved. But suppose that understanding is not improved. Can the warnings nonetheless be justified?

We could imagine two such justifications. The first involves welfare: Graphic health warnings will save a significant number of lives, and purely factual information will have a far weaker effect. If this is so, then the graphic health warnings do have a sufficient justification.[71] The second is rooted in autonomy: Smokers, and prospective smokers, do not sufficiently appreciate the health risks of smoking, and graphic warnings can promote a kind of "debiasing" that purely statistical information fails to provide.[72] To this point, it might be added that government regulation is hardly being imposed on a blank slate. Recall that efforts to promote smoking involve a high degree of manipulation, with the help of the affect heuristic – portraying happy, healthy, attractive smokers – and in my view, the government can legitimately respond. In light of the number of lives at risk and the underlying evidence, these kinds of justifications do seem sufficient in the particular context of smoking.

Regulating Manipulation

Should government regulate manipulation? In the context of political speech? Commercial advertising? We could imagine, or find, egregious cases in which it is tempting to say that it should. But the free speech barriers are severe.

Political speech and public figures. In the context of political speech, the leading case in American constitutional law is Hustler Magazine v. Falwell,[73] where the Court said that the free speech principle protects a cruel and offensive parody, depicting Protestant minister Jerry Falwell as engaged in an incestuous act with his mother at an outhouse. The parody was satirical, but it should also be seen as a form of manipulation, designed to lead readers to see Falwell as a ridiculous figure and also a hypocrite. In

---

[70] *See* Christine Jolls, *Debiasing through Law and the First Amendment*, 67 STAN. L. REV. 1411 (2015).

[71] *See* Baron, *A Welfarist Approach to Manipulation* (forthcoming).

[72] This is a possibility, and it might be questioned. By themselves, graphic warnings do not provide statistical information; they might be taken as a kind of red light, or a general statement of alarm. As noted, whether they increase knowledge is an empirical question. *See* Jolls, *Debiasing through Law and the First Amendment* (2015).

[73] 485 U.S. 46 (1988).

the terms used here, the parody was an effort to appeal directly to System I, so that people would not be able to regard Falwell in the same light in the future. Whenever they saw him, or heard him, the parody might echo in their minds, even if they were not consciously aware of it.

The Court unanimously ruled that the Constitution protected the parody. The Court acknowledged that to prevent genuine harm, states could regulate false statements of fact, which "are particularly valueless; they interfere with the truth-seeking function of the marketplace of ideas, and they cause damage to an individual's reputation that cannot easily be repaired by counterspeech, however persuasive or effective."[74] But satire must be treated differently. "Were we to hold otherwise, there can be little doubt that political cartoonists and satirists would be subjected to damages awards without any showing that their work falsely defamed its subject." Even the most outrageous forms of satire are protected, because the idea of outrageousness has "an inherent subjectiveness about it which would allow a jury to impose liability on the basis of the jurors' tastes or views, or perhaps on the basis of their dislike of a particular expression."[75]

To be sure, the Court's reasoning was not unbounded. It acknowledged that the established "actual malice" standard – allowing people to recover damages for statements known to be false or made with reckless indifference to the question of truth or falsity[76] – would apply if readers had taken the parody as depicting actual facts. But readers could not so take the parody here. This point leaves open the possibility that even in the political domain, certain forms of manipulation could be regulated if readers or viewers were affirmatively misled. But in view of the fact that the Court has pointedly declined to create a *general* exception to the First Amendment even for false statements of fact, any effort to regulate manipulative speech in the political context would run into severe constitutional trouble.[77]

With the design of any restrictions on such speech, there are independent questions of vagueness and overbreadth. If a government wants to prohibit the most egregious forms of manipulation in the political context, what, exactly, would it say? I have ventured a definition of manipulation here, but it is not exactly easy to adapt that definition to fit a provision of

---

[74] *Id.* at 52.   [75] *Id.* at 47.   [76] New York Times v. Sullivan, 376 U.S. 254 (1964).

[77] At a minimum, it would be necessary to show that the manipulative statement created serious harm, and in the political context, such a showing would be highly unlikely to be enough, given the general commitment to the principle that the best correction, for arguably harmful speech, is more speech rather than enforced silence. *See* Whitney v. California, 274 U.S. 357, 374 (1927) (Brandeis, J., dissenting).

civil or criminal law. As we have seen, manipulation has at least fifty shades – which means that any effort to restrict it would likely be too vague and too broad.

Commercial speech. The context of commercial advertising is different, because the burden on regulators is lighter.[78] But here as well, the free speech obstacles are formidable. So long as the relevant speech is neither false nor deceptive, the government would need a powerful justification for imposing regulation.[79] The definitional issues remain challenging, and even if they could be resolved, it would be plausible to say, in the general spirit of *Hustler Magazine*, that the marketplace of ideas is full of efforts to appeal to System 1, and to downplay or bypass deliberation and reflection.

Even if the commercial sphere is less immune from speech regulation, it is emphatically a place where manipulation is pervasive.[80] The hope is that consumers will understand that advertisements are generally self-serving and that the process of competition will provide a sufficient corrective. We have seen that behavioral economics has raised quite serious questions about the realism of that hope.[81] But it is highly doubtful that those questions provide a sufficient basis for a general "manipulation exception" to the existing protection accorded to commercial speech.

Consumer Protection

None of these conclusions mean that narrower forms of regulation could not be imagined. The law of contract has long recognized the problem of manipulation and taken steps to address it, largely by forbidding manipulators to take advantage of contract terms that they have been able to obtain only through manipulation.[82] In the context of consumer financial products, various forms of manipulation are a widespread problem. Indeed, manipulation can be seen as a defining motivation for regulatory initiatives that followed the financial crisis of 2007 and 2008.[83] The Dodd-Frank Wall Street Reform and Consumer Protection Act states that the CFPB should ensure that "markets for consumer financial products and services are fair,

---

[78] *See* Va. State Pharmacy Bd. v. Va. Citizens Consumer Council, 425 U.S. 748 (1976).For a valuable discussion from an economic perspective, see Richard Craswell, *Regulating Deceptive Advertising: The Role of Cost-Benefit Analysis*, 64 SOUTHERN CAL. L. REV. 549 (1991).

[79] Cent. Hudson Gas & Elec. Corp. v. Pub. Serv. Comm'n, 447 US 557 (1980).

[80] *See* AKERLOF AND SHILLER, PHISHING FOR PHOOLS (2015).

[81] *See* OREN BAR-GILL, SEDUCTION BY CONTRACT (2011).

[82] Posner, *The Law, Economics, and Psychology of Manipulation* (2015).

[83] *See* BAR-GILL, SEDUCTION BY CONTRACT (2011); Ryan Bubb and Richard H. Pildes, *How Behavioral Economics Trims Its Sails and Why*, 127 HARV. L. REV. 1593–1678.

transparent, and competitive."[84] It calls for attention not only to "unfair and deceptive" acts and practices but also to "abusive" ones, which can be taken as a reference to the worst forms of manipulation. In monitoring finanical markets, the CFPB must consider the "understanding by consumers of the risks of a type of consumer financial product or service"[85] – a phrase that can easily be read to reflect a concern about manipulation.

Implementing these requirements, the CFPB has adopted as its slogan "Know before you owe," and its various efforts to ensure informed choices can be understood as an attack on manipulation as I have understood it here.[86] In consumer markets, of course, one problem is complexity, which can defeat understanding. But another problem falls in the general category of manipulation, as in the form of "teaser rates" and various inducements that fall short of deceit, but that emphatically prey on System 1.

A short, simple credit card agreement, of the sort provided by the CFPB, can be seen as a direct response to the risk of manipulation[87] – and as an effort to ensure that System 2 is firmly in charge. Proposals to ban or restrict teaser rates can be understood in similar terms.[88] In cases of this kind, there is ample room for considering the problem of manipulation in deciding how best to regulate financial products. It is important to see that in such cases, government is regulating commercial practices, not advertising, and that its real concern is with practices that do not sufficiently trigger reflective deliberation on the part of consumers. We have seen that this is far from a self-defining category, but the CFPB's initiatives can be taken as initial efforts to specify it. We can hope that the United States and other nations will go further.[89]

Manipulation: Final Words

A statement or action can be counted as manipulative to the extent that it does not sufficiently engage or appeal to people's capacity for reflective and deliberative choice. Most nudges do not fall within this definition, but some certainly do, and others are at the borderline.

---

[84] 12 U.S.C. § 5511 (2010).   [85] 12 U.S.C. § 5512 (2010).

[86] *See* Consumer Financial Protection Bureau, Credit Cards: Know before You Owe, *available at* www.consumerfinance.gov/credit-cards/knowbeforeyouowe/.

[87] *Id.*

[88] Oren Bar-Gill and Ryan Bubb, *Credit Card Pricing: The Card Act and Beyond*, 97 Cornell L. Rev. 967 (2012).

[89] For theoretical foundations, *see* Akerlof and Shiller, Phishing for Phools (2015).

Some forms of manipulation are pretty egregious, as where a vivid, graphic description of a terrible outcome (losing a child, losing a war) is offered to convince people to engage in certain conduct (to buy extra life insurance, to vote for a political candidate). Some arguable forms of manipulation are mild, as when a politician, an employer, or a waiter uses loss aversion, tone of voice, and facial expressions to encourage certain decisions. Thus defined, manipulation is a pervasive feature of human life. It is for this reason that while the legal system is generally able to handle lies and deception, it has a much harder time in targeting manipulation.

In their most troublesome forms, manipulative acts fail to respect choosers; they undermine people's autonomy and do not respect their dignity. The welfarist objection, rooted in the idea that choosers know what is in their best interest, is that when people's choices are products of manipulation, those choices may not promote their own welfare, precisely because choosers have not been put in a position to deliberate about relevant variables and values. This is likely to be true if the manipulator is ill-motivated, but it might also be true because the manipulator lacks relevant information.

From the welfarist point of view, manipulation is only presumptively disfavored. A benign, knowledgeable manipulator could make people's lives go better and possibly much better. But under realistic assumptions, the presumption against manipulation is justifiably strong, because manipulators are unlikely to be either benign or knowledgeable.

CHAPTER 6

Do People Like Nudges? Empirical Findings

What do people actually think about nudging and choice architecture? Do they have serious ethical objections? Or do they believe that nudges are acceptable or desirable, or even morally obligatory? Do they distinguish among nudges, and if so, exactly how?

The answers cannot, of course, dispose of the ethical questions. The issue is how to resolve those questions in principle, and empirical findings about people's answers are not decisive. Perhaps those answers are confused, insufficiently considered, or wrong. There is a risk that if people are responding to survey questions, they will not have time or opportunity to reflect, especially if those questions do not offer relevant facts (e.g., about the costs and the benefits of the policies in question).[1] Even if their answers are reflective, perhaps people do not value autonomy or dignity highly enough, or perhaps they do not quite know what those concepts means. Perhaps people pay too little attention to social welfare,[2] or perhaps their judgments about social welfare are off the mark, at least if they are not provided with a great deal of information.

Perhaps different nations, and different groups within the same nation, offer different answers, suggesting an absence of consensus. Behavioral scientists would emphasize a related point: People's answers to ethical questions, or questions about moral approval or disapproval, might well depend on how such questions are framed; slight differences in framing can yield dramatically different answers. Those differences are themselves a nudge; they can have major effects, and they are not easy to avoid.[3]

---

[1] This is a reasonable concern about people's general approval of compulsory labeling of genetically modified organisms, see infra note 35, and also about their favorable attitude toward mandatory automatic enrollment in "green" energy (in a question that does not specify the costs or benefits of such energy).

[2] See generally LOUIS KAPLOW AND STEVEN SHAVELL, FAIRNESS VERSUS WELFARE (2006).

[3] See generally PERSPECTIVES ON FRAMING (Gideon Keren ed., 2010).

Here is a small example of how ethical judgments can depend on framing.[4] If people are asked whether they think that young people should be valued more than old people, they will usually say, "certainly not." They will strenuously resist the idea that government should give a higher value to young lives than to old ones. But suppose that people are asked whether they want either (1) to save 70 people under age of 5 or (2) to save 75 people over the age of 80. It is reasonable to speculate (and evidence confirms) that most people will choose (1), thus demonstrating that they are willing to value a young person more than an old one.[5] It would be child's play to frame nudges so as to elicit one's preferred answer to ethical questions.

Notwithstanding these points, people's answers to carefully designed questions are interesting in themselves, because they show patterns of thinking among those who are not required to spend a great deal of time on them. They can also help to illuminate political, legal, and ethical problems, and for three different reasons. The first and most important is that in a democratic society, it is inevitable that public officials will attend to what citizens actually think. If citizens have strong ethical objections, democratic governments will hesitate before proceeding (if only because of electoral self-interest). Such objections can operate as a kind of presumptive or de facto veto. No public official will entirely disregard a strongly felt moral concern on the part of significant segments of the public. And if people do not have moral objections, and if they welcome nudges as helpful and desirable, public officials will be attentive to their views. Widespread public approval can operate as a license or a permission slip, or perhaps as a spur or a prod.[6]

The second reason is epistemic: People's judgments provide relevant information about to think about the ethical issues even if that information is not conclusive. It is not necessary to make strong claims about the wisdom of crowds, especially on contested ethical issues, in order to believe that an ethical judgment, on the part of those who might be subject

---

[4] *See* Shane Frederick, *Measuring Intergenerational Time Preference: Are Future Lives Valued Less?*, 26 J. Risk and Uncertainty 39, 40 (2003) (showing that people's preferences for life-saving programs depend on framing).

[5] *See id,* See also Maureen L. Cropper, Sema K. Aydede, and Paul R. Portney, *Preference for Life Saving Programs: How the Public Discounts Time and Age,* 8 J. Risk and Uncertainty 243, 258–259.

[6] I am bracketing here questions about interest-group dynamics and coalition formation, which can of course complicate official judgments. Politicians are interested in many things that bear on reelection, not merely the views of the median voter. And of course there are important differences between the legislative and executive branches on this count, with the latter frequently having more "space" for technocratic judgment. *See* Cass R. Sunstein, *The Most Knowledgeable Branch*, U. Pa. L. Rev. (forthcoming).

to nudges, deserves respectful attention. Public officials should be humble and attentive to the views of others, and if strong majorities favor or oppose nudges, then their views are entitled to consideration.

The third reason involves the commitment to democratic self-government. If that commitment matters, officials should pay attention to what people think, even if they disagree.[7] It is true that people's considered judgments might diverge from what emerges from brief surveys. And if public officials have a clear sense that an approach would reduce social welfare, there is a strong argument that they should not adopt that approach even if people would like them to do so – just as there is a strong argument that they should adopt an approach that increases social welfare even if people oppose it.[8] But whenever public officials are uncertain about whether an approach is desirable, it would be reasonable, in the name of self-government, for them to give consideration to the views of members of the public.

As we shall see, current research, including a nationally representative survey outlined here, supports a single conclusion. Most people have no views, either positive or negative, about nudging in general; their assessment turns on whether they approve of the purposes and effects of particular nudges. Strong majorities tend to be supportive of nudges of the kind that have been seriously proposed, or acted on, by actual institutions in recent years. Within the United States, this enthusiasm extends across standard partisan lines; perhaps surprisingly, it unifies Democrats, Republicans, and independents. So long as people believe that the end is both legitimate and important, they are likely to favor nudges in its direction. This is an important finding, because it suggests that most people do not share the concern that nudges, as such, should be taken as unacceptably manipulative or as an objectionable interference with autonomy. Revealingly, they are far more negative about mandates and bans, even when these are taken to have perfectly legitimate ends; many people do care about freedom of choice as such, and they will reject many well-motivated policies that do not allow for it.[9]

---

[7] This statement is not meant to take a stand on contested issues about the precise role of the representative. The classic study is HANNA PITKIN, THE CONCEPT OF REPRESENTATION (1972).

[8] Public approval or disapproval might also be counted as an ingredient in social welfare, but at least in general, it is likely to be a modest one. Outside of highly unusual circumstances, the welfare effect of a requirement of calorie labels, or of automatic enrollment in a savings plan, will depend on its consequences for behavior and outcomes, not on whether people like those policies in the abstract.

[9] Within Denmark, a similar finding is discussed in Sofie Kragh Pederson et al., *Who Wants Paternalism*, 66 BULLETIN OF ECONOMIC RESEARCH S147 (2014).

People are most likely to oppose those nudges that (a) promote what they see as illicit goals or (b) are perceived as inconsistent with either the interests or values of most choosers. This proposition dominates the survey findings, and it accounts for the bulk of cases in which people disapprove of nudges. A more particular finding, one that counts against some default rules, is that people *do not want choice architects to produce economic or other losses by using people's inertia or inattention against them.* They believe that if people are to lose money, it must be a result of their explicit consent.

In addition, people tend to prefer nudges that target deliberative processes to those that target unconscious or subconscious processes, and they may react against the latter – though they do not by any means rule the latter out of bounds and will often approve of them as well. In other words, people tend to prefer System 2 nudges to System 1 nudges, though when they learn that System 1 nudges are more effective, many people shift in their direction. When nudging is associated with one or another political viewpoint, people's evaluation of nudges is much affected by which political viewpoint it is associated with – which reinforces the general view that in most cases, it is people's assessment of the ends of particular nudges, rather than of nudging as such, that settles their judgments.

If people focus on particular nudges that they think to be ill-motivated, intrusive, threatening, or otherwise objectionable, they become likely to oppose nudges as such, and if they focus on particular nudges of which they approve, their overall evaluation tends to be positive. Moreover, there is evidence that transparency about the fact of nudging does not reduce the effectiveness of nudges, because most nudges are already transparent, and because people will not, in general, rebel against nudges.

At the same time, this last conclusion must be taken with caution, not least in light of ambiguities in the very idea of transparency. Officials might be transparent about the nudge itself but might not disclose the intention behind it, or the psychological mechanism that makes the nudge effective. Is that a problem? Some people certainly think so. There is also preliminary but suggestive evidence of potential "reactance"[10] against certain nudges. Reactance refers to people's occasionally negative reactions to orders or commands, leading people to do the opposite of what is mandated. A nudge is not a mandate, but it could trigger reactance; people might think, "I do not want to be nudged," and therefore rebel. Some people just don't like being nudged, or even the idea of being nudged, and

---

[10] *See generally* SHARON BREHM AND JACK BREHM, PSYCHOLOGICAL REACTANCE: A THEORY OF FREEDOM AND CONTROL (1981).

when a nudge is proposed, they will tend to dislike it. As we will see, those who show reactance tend to like some kinds of nudges better than others.

An important disclaimer before we begin: Most of the evidence discussed here comes from the United States, and it is natural to wonder whether the findings would be replicated in other nations. What kinds of divergences might be expected from people in other countries? We shall see that there is some preliminary evidence on exactly that question, with valuable data from Sweden, and evidence that people in Denmark, France, Germany, Hungary, Italy, and the United Kingdom have broadly similar reactions to those of Americans.[11] On the basis of that evidence, it is reasonable to think that people in diverse nations hold the same basic principles and that their divergences are relatively minor. Of course it is true that larger differences might be found in China, South Korea, South Africa, and Rwanda. That remains to be seen.

In some ways, moreover, the United States should be expected to be relatively unreceptive testing ground. With its distinctively pro-liberty culture and its general suspicion of government, the United States might well be more skeptical of nudges than most other nations (and on this count, the comparison with Sweden is especially illuminating). As we shall also see, the general principles that emerge from the existing evidence, even if it mostly involves the United States, should be expected to have cross-national appeal, even if there is some international variation, and even if citizens of different nations specify those general principles in different ways.

A Principled Public?

I devised a survey involving thirty-four nudges. The survey was administered by Survey Sampling International and included 563 Americans, invited via email, and paid a total of $2,073.75. The survey had a margin of error of plus or minus 4.1 percentage points. The group was nationally representative and hence diverse along all relevant lines (race, gender, age, geography, and wealth). From people's responses, two dominant findings emerge. *First*, Americans reject nudges that promote what they see as illicit ends (such as religious or political favoritism). *Second*, Americans reject nudges that they view as inconsistent with the interests or values of most choosers.

---

[11] *See* Lucia Reisch and Cass R. Sunstein, *Do Europeans Like Nudges?* (unpublished manuscript 2016).

By contrast, there is widespread support for nudges that are taken to have legitimate ends and to be consistent with the interests and the values of most choosers. It follows that numerous nudges – default rules, warnings, and public education campaigns – are likely to attract bipartisan support, so long as people approve of their ends and think that they are consistent with choosers' values and interests. Notably, most Americans are reluctant to reject nudges – even those that target System 1 – as unacceptably manipulative (though we shall also find evidence that they prefer System 2 nudges in pairwise comparisons). Several of the policies tested here can be counted as highly tendentious and as arguably manipulative. Nonetheless, they attracted majority support, with the single (and highly exotic) exception of subliminal advertising (which, surprisingly, receives substantial minority support in the context of efforts to combat smoking and overeating).

As we will see, political divisions sometimes affect the *level* of support, because Democrats are more favorably disposed toward health and safety nudges than Republicans. Certain people do reject nudges even if they think that they are well-motivated, and many people have qualms about nudges that target System 1. In cases that raise strong partisan differences, such divisions will map onto nudges as well. But across a wide range, clear majorities of Democrats and Republicans (and also independents) are in full agreement about what they support and what they reject.

Popular Nudges

In the United States, the federal government has adopted or promoted a large number of nudges. Three of the most prominent include (1) mandatory calorie labels at chain restaurants;[12] (2) mandatory graphic warnings on cigarette packages[13] (struck down by a federal court of appeals);[14] and (3) automatic enrollment in savings plans, subject to opt out.[15] The nationally representative sample found substantial majority support for all three policies, including support for (3) regardless of whether it consists of the current federal "encouragement" of such enrollment or a federal

---

[12] 79 Fed. Reg. 71156.   [13] 75 Fed. Reg. 69524.

[14] On the FDA's effort to require graphic warnings on packages, *see* R. J. Reynolds Tobacco Co. v. U.S. Food & Drug Admin., 823 F. Supp. 2d 36 (D.D.C. 2011), *aff'd on other grounds*, 696 F.3d 1205 (D.C. Cir. 2012).

[15] For discussion of relevant laws and policies, *see generally* AUTOMATIC: CHANGING THE WAY AMERICA SAVES (William Gale et al. eds., 2009).

Table 1: *American Attitudes toward Prominent Recent Nudges*

	Calorie labels	Graphic warnings (cigarettes)	Federal encouragement: auto-enrollment	Federal mandate: auto-enrollment
Total support (percentage)	87/13	74/26	80/20	71/29
Democrats	92/8	77/23	88/12	78/22
Independents	88/12	74/26	75/25	67/33
Republicans	77/23	68/32	73/27	62/38

mandate for automatic enrollment, imposed on large employers. (Such a mandate does not exist.)

About 87 percent of Americans favored calorie labels,[16] and 74 percent favored graphic warnings. Both policies had strong majority support from Democrats, Republicans, and independents. Overall, 80 and 71 percent respectively approved of encouraging and mandating automatic enrollment plans. Here as well, all three groups showed strong majority support.[17]

Three educational campaigns also attracted widespread approval. Respondents were overwhelmingly supportive of a public education campaign from the federal government to combat childhood obesity (82 percent approval, again with strong support from Democrats, Republicans, and independents). They were highly supportive of a public education campaign from the federal government designed to combat distracted driving, with graphic stories and images (85 percent approval). About 75 percent of people favored a federal education campaign to encourage people not to discriminate on the basis of sexual orientation, though here there was a noteworthy division across party lines (85 percent of Democrats, 57 percent of Republicans, and 75 percent of independents).

Three other educational campaigns attracted majority support, but at significantly lower levels, and with only minority approval from

---

[16] Note that there were statistically significant differences with respect to calorie labels between Republicans (77 percent approval) and both Democrats (92 percent approval) and independents (88 percent approval).

[17] Here as well, there were statistically significant differences between Democrats and Republicans for both policies and between Democrats and independents with respect to encouragement. (Encouraged: 88 percent of Democrats, 73 percent of Republicans, and 75 percent of independents. Mandated: 78 percent of Democrats, 62 percent of Republicans, and 67 percent of independents.)

Table 2: *American Attitudes Toward Five Educational Campaigns[18]*

	Childhood obesity	Distracted driving	Sexual orientation discrimination	Movie theaters	Animal Welfare Society	Obesity (arguably manipulative)
Total support (percentage)	82/18	85/15	75/25	53/47	52/48	57/43
Democrats	90/11	88/12	85/15	61/39	59/41	61/40
Independents	81/19	84/16	75/25	51/49	55/45	60/40
Republicans	70/30	80/20	57/43	41/59	34/66	47/53

Republicans. About 53 percent of Americans favored a federal requirement that movie theaters run public education messages to discourage people from smoking and overeating. Democrats showed higher approval ratings than Republicans (61 percent as opposed to 41 percent, with independents at 51 percent). By a very small majority (52 percent), Americans supported a public education campaign, by the federal government itself, to encourage people to give money to the Animal Welfare Society of America (a hypothetical organization) (59 percent of Democrats, 34 percent of Republicans, and 55 percent of independents; party was a statistically significant factor). This latter finding seems surprising; it could not easily be predicted that respondents would want their government to design a campaign to promote donations to an animal welfare society.

About 57 percent of people supported an aggressive public education campaign from the federal government to combat obesity, showing obese children struggling to exercise, and showing interviews with obese adults, who are saying such things as "My biggest regret in life is that I have not managed to control my weight" and "To me, obesity is like a terrible curse." This question was designed to test people's reactions to a tendentious and arguably offensive and manipulative campaign, which might have been expected to receive widespread disapproval, as it did not. Indeed, one of the goals of the question was to establish such disapproval – but it was not found here. Here there was a significant disparity between Democrats (61 percent approval) and independents (60 percent approval) on the one hand and Republicans on the other (47 percent approval); the difference between Democrats' and Republicans' views was statistically significant.

---

[18] Percentages may not total 100 due to rounding.

Most Americans were also supportive of multiple efforts to use choice architecture to promote public health and environmental protection. In recent years, there has been considerable discussion of "traffic light" systems for food, which would use the familiar red, yellow, and green to demarcate health rankings. Some evidence suggests that such systems can be highly effective.[19] In the United States, the national government has shown no official interest in these initiatives, but with respondents in the nationally representative survey, the idea attracted strong support (64 percent). There was also majority approval of automatic use of "green" energy providers, subject to opt out (see Chapter 7) – perhaps surprisingly, with support for automatic use of green energy whether it consisted of federal "encouragement" (72 percent) or instead a federal mandate on large electricity providers (67 percent). In these cases, there were significant differences across partisan lines, but majorities of Democrats, Republicans, and independents were all supportive.

Most respondents were in favor of requiring companies to disclose whether the food they sell contains genetically modified organisms (GMOs) (86 percent approval).[20] There was strong majority support (73 percent) for a mandatory warning label on products that have unusually high levels of salt, as in "This product has been found to contain unusually high levels of salt, which may be harmful to your health." Perhaps surprisingly, most respondents (but not most Republicans) approved of a state requirement that grocery stores put their most healthy foods in prominent, visible locations (56 percent approval; 63 percent from Democrats, 43 percent from Republicans, and 57 percent from independents). Respondents also supported a state requirement that people must say, when they obtain their drivers' license, whether they want to be organ donors (70 percent approval; 75 percent from Democrats, 62 percent from Republicans, and 69 percent from independents). For all of these policies, the differences between Democrats and Republicans were statistically significant.

Five other forms of choice architecture, which might be expected to be far more controversial, nonetheless obtained majority support. The first would list the name of the incumbent politician first on every ballot.

---

[19] See Anne Thorndike et al., *Traffic-Light Labels and Choice Architecture*, 46 AM J. PREVENTIVE MEDICINE 143, 143 (2014).
[20] In my view, this is not a good idea. *See id.* at 130; Cass R. Sunstein, *Don't Mandate Labeling for Gene-Altered Foods*, BLOOMBERG VIEW (May 12, 2013), *available at* www.bloomberg.com/news/articles/2013-05-12/don-t-mandate-labeling-for-gene-altered-foods.

It might be expected that this pro-incumbent nudge would be widely rejected, because respondents might not want the voting process to be skewed in favor of incumbents, and because any effort to enlist order effects might be seen as manipulative (as indeed it should be). But a bare majority (53 percent) approved of this approach, perhaps because most people believed that it would promote clarity, perhaps because they did not see the risk of bias from order effects.

There was also majority approval (53 percent) for the approach, recently adopted in both Oregon and California, of automatically registering eligible citizens as voters, subject to opt-out. Interestingly, most Republicans (61 percent) rejected this approach. One reason might be that they believe that people who do not take the time to register to vote ought not to be counted as voters. Another reason is that they might believe that Oregon's approach would favor Democrats. Yet another reason is that they might believe that such an approach would increase the risk of fraud.

By a modest majority, most people (58 percent) also approved of an approach by which women's last names would automatically be changed to that of their husband, subject to opt-out. This approach obtained majority support from Democrats, Republicans, and independents. This result is especially noteworthy in view of the fact that an approach of this kind would almost certainly be an unconstitutional form of sex discrimination, even if it tracked behavior and preferences.[21] We might expect a difference between men and women on this question, but notably, 58 percent of both groups approved of this approach.

Finally, there was majority support for a federal labeling requirement for products that come from companies that have repeatedly violated the nation's labor laws (such as laws requiring occupational safety or forbidding discrimination), as in "This product is made by a company that has repeatedly violated the nation's labor laws." About 60 percent of participants supported that policy, with a significant difference between Democrats (67 percent approval) and Republicans (50 percent approval). There was also majority support for federally required labels on products that come from countries that have recently harbored terrorists, as in "This product comes from a nation that was recently found to harbor terrorists."

[21] *See Craig v. Boren*, 429 U.S. 190, 200–204 (1978). For valuable discussion of the general topic, see Elizabeth F. Emens, *Changing Name Changing: Framing Rules and the Future of Marital Names*, 74 U. Chi. L. Rev. 761, 772–774 (2007).

Table 3: *American Attitudes Toward Environmental and Public Health Nudges*

	GMO labels	Salt labels	Healthy food placement	Traffic lights	Organ donor choice	Encouragement: Green energy	Mandate: Green energy
Total support (percentage)	86/14	73/27	56/44	64/36	70/30	72/28	67/33
Democrats	89/11	79/21	63/37	71/29	75/25	82/18	79/21
Independents	87/13	72/28	57/43	61/39	69/31	66/34	63/37
Republicans	80/20	61/39	43/57	57/43	62/38	61/39	51/49

Table 4: *American Attitudes toward Some Potentially Provocative Nudges*[22]

	Listing incumbent politician first	Automatic voter registration	Husband's last name	Mandatory manufacturing label: labor violations	Mandatory manufacturing label: aiding terrorists
Total support (percentage)	53/47	53/47	58/42	60/40	54/46
Democrats	58/42	63/37	61/40	67/33	56/44
Independents	51/49	50/50	56/44	57/43	49/51
Republicans	47/53	39/61	57/43	50/50	58/42

This approach attracted 54 percent approval – 56 percent from Democrats, 58 percent from Republicans, and 49 percent from independents.

Unpopular Nudges

By contrast, twelve nudges were widely disapproved. Of these, seven involved uses of default rules. Two of these defaults were designed so as to be not merely provocative but also highly offensive, and strong majorities took them exactly as they were designed.

Under the first, a state would assume that people want to register as Democrats, subject to opt out if people explicitly say that they want to register as Republicans or independent. Of course a default rule of this kind should be taken as an effort to skew the political process (and it would

---

[22] Percentages may not total 100 due to rounding.

certainly be unconstitutional for that reason).[23] The overwhelming majority of people rejected this approach (26 percent total approval; 32 percent of Democrats, 16 percent of Republicans, and 26 percent of independents, with statistically significant differences between Democrats and Republicans). The second was a state law assuming that people are Christian, for purposes of the census, unless they specifically state otherwise. Such a default rule could also be seen as an attempt to push religious affiliations in preferred directions (and it would similarly be unconstitutional).[24] Here too there was widespread disapproval (21 percent overall approval; 22 percent of Democrats, 27 percent of Republicans, and 17 percent of independents).

The third unpopular default rule (completing the set of unconstitutional nudges) involved a state law assuming that upon (heterosexual) marriage, husbands would automatically change their last names to that of their wives, subject to opt out (24 percent total approval; 28 percent of Democrats, 18 percent of Republicans, and 23 percent of independents). Interestingly, there was no gender disparity here (just as with the question that involved the opposite defaults); 24 percent of both men and women approved. With the fourth, the federal government would assume, on tax returns, that people want to donate $50 to the Red Cross, subject to opt out if people explicitly say that they do not want to make that donation (27 percent approval; 30 percent of Democrats, 20 percent of Republicans, and 28 percent of independents). The fifth was identical but substituted the Animal Welfare Society for the Red Cross. Not surprisingly, that question also produced widespread disapproval (26 percent approval; 30 percent of Democrats, 20 percent of Republicans, and 25 percent of independents).

With the sixth, state government assumed that state employees would give $20 per month to the United Way, subject to opt out. It might be

---

[23] In principle, the problem would be most interesting in an area in which the default rule tracked reality. If most people are, in fact, Democrats, is it clearly objectionable if a city or state assumes that they are, for purposes of registration? The answer is almost certainly yes; political affiliations should be actively chosen, not assumed by government. This principle almost certainly has constitutional foundations (though it has not been tested): If a voting district consisted of 80 percent Democratic voters, it would not be acceptable to assume that all voters intend to register as Democrats. But I am aware that this brief comment does not give anything like an adequate answer to some complex questions about the use of "mass" default rules that track majority preferences and values. For discussion, *see* CASS R. SUNSTEIN, CHOOSING NOT TO CHOOSE 77 (2015).

[24] Here as well we could imagine interesting questions if the default rule tracked reality. But with respect to religion, as with respect to politics, there is a strong constitutional norm in favor of official neutrality, which would be violated even if a particular default reflected majority preferences and values.

Table 5: *Unpopular Defaults*

	Democrat registration	Christian on census	Wife's last name	Red Cross	Animal Welfare Society	United Way	Carbon emissions charge
Total support (percentage)	26/74	21/79	24/76	27/73	26/74	24/76	36/64
Democrats	32/68	22/78	28/72	30/70	30/70	26/74	43/57
Independents	26/74	17/83	23/77	28/72	25/75	25/75	34/66
Republicans	16/84	27/73	18/82	20/80	20/80	17/83	25/75

expected that because state government and state employees were involved, approval rates might grow. But they did not (24 percent approval; 26 percent of Democrats, 17 percent of Republicans, and 25 percent of independents). With the seventh, a majority (64 percent) disapproved of a federal requirement that airlines charge people, with their airline tickets, a specific amount to offset their carbon emissions (about $10 per ticket), subject to opt out if passengers said that they did not want to pay.

The five other unpopular nudges involved information and education. With the first and most extreme, a newly elected president adopted a public education campaign designed to convince people that criticism of his decisions is unpatriotic and potentially damaging to national security. There was overwhelming disapproval of this campaign (23 percent approval; 24 percent of Democrats, 21 percent of Republicans, and 22 percent of independents). What is perhaps most noteworthy here is not majority disapproval, but the fact that over one-fifth of Americans, on an essentially nonpartisan basis, were in favor of this most unusual public campaign.

With the second, the federal government adopted a public education campaign designed to convince mothers to stay home to take care of their young children. Over two-thirds of respondents rejected this nudge (33 percent approval; 33 percent of Democrats, 31 percent of Republicans, and 34 percent of independents). The third involved a government requirement that movie theaters run subliminal advertisements to discourage smoking and overeating. Here too, there was majority disapproval (41 percent approval; 47 percent of Democrats, 42 percent of Republicans, and 35 percent of independents). It is noteworthy and surprising, however, that over two-fifths of people actually supported this requirement.

Table 6: *Unpopular Education Campaigns and Disclosure*[25]

	Unpatriotic criticism	Stay-at-home-mothers	Subliminal advertising	Mandatory manufacturing label: Communism	Transgender
Total support (percentage)	23/77	33/67	41/59	44/56	41/59
Democrats	24/76	33/67	47/53	47/53	49/51
Independents	22/78	34/67	35/65	42/58	38/62
Republicans	21/79	31/69	42/58	43/57	29/71

With the fourth, the federal government would require all products that come from a Communist country (such as China or Cuba) to be sold with the label "Made in whole or in part under Communism." Slightly over half of respondents disapproved of this requirement (44 percent approval; 47 percent of Democrats, 43 percent of Republicans, and 42 percent of independents). With the fifth, a majority (59 percent) also rejected a public education campaign from the federal government informing people that it is possible for people to change their gender from male to female or from female to male, and encouraging people to consider that possibility "if that is really what they want to do." There is yet another surprise here, which is that this somewhat adventurous campaign was endorsed by 41 percent of respondents; note that approval rates differed between Democrats (49 percent) and Republicans (29 percent; independents, 38 percent).

Why Are Some Nudges Unpopular?

Implicit Principles

What separates the approved nudges from the rejected ones? As noted, two principles seem to dominate the cases. First, people *reject nudges that are taken to have illegitimate goals.* In a self-governing society, it is illegitimate to attempt to convince people that criticism of a public official is unpatriotic. At least in the United States, nudges that favor a particular religion or political party will also meet with widespread disapproval, even among

---

[25] Percentages may not total 100 due to rounding.

people of that very religion or party.[26] This simple principle justifies a prediction: Whenever people think that the motivations of the choice architect are illicit, they will disapprove of the nudge. To be sure, that prediction might not seem terribly surprising, but it suggests an important point, which is that most people will not oppose (e.g.,) default rules and warnings as such; everything will turn on what they are nudging people *toward.*[27]

By contrast, we will see that mandates do run into some opposition simply because they are mandates, and that opposition cuts across partisan lines. When there are partisan differences in judgments about nudges, it is usually because of partisan disagreements not about nudges, but about whether the relevant motivations are legitimate. Resolution of such disagreements would of course depend on judgments having nothing to do with nudging as such.

Second, people oppose nudges *that are inconsistent with the interests or values of most choosers.* The most direct evidence is the finding that while most people support an automatic name change for women, they reject an automatic name change for men. The evident reason is that the former tracks people's interests and values (at least in general), while the latter countermands them.[28] Any default rule, of course, is likely to harm at least some people; some people will want, for good reason, to opt out, and some people who want to opt out will not do so, perhaps because of inertia and procrastination. This point is a potential objection to default rules in general. By itself, however, that fact is not enough to produce public opprobrium. Recall that there is majority approval for automatic voter registration and automatic enrollment in pension plans and green energy, apparently because respondents think that those nudges are in most

---

[26] We could, of course, imagine a nation in which favoritism on the basis of religion or party would attract widespread support and might be seen as analogous to a default rule in which a woman's last name changes to that of her husband (which was approved, it will be recalled, by a majority of respondents here). In such a nation, a default rule in favor of the most popular party, or the dominant religion, might be taken to track people's preferences and values and not to be a violation of the governing conception of neutrality at all.

[27] The striking findings of "partisan nudge bias" are fully consistent with this claim. *See* the discussion later of David Tannenbaum, Craig Fox, and Todd Rogers, *On the Misplaced Politics of Behavioral Policy Interventions* (2014), *available at* http://home.uchicago.edu/~/davetannenbaum/documents/partisan%20nudge%20obias.pdf.

[28] Here as well, we could easily imagine a population that would reverse these results. Suppose that one believes that automatically assuming that wives take their husbands' last names undermines sex equality, and that automatically assuming that husbands take their wives' last names promotes sex equality. For those who have these beliefs, and are committed to sex equality, reversing the majority's views might seem attractive.

people's interests.[29] Recall too that most respondents are favorably disposed toward public education campaigns designed to combat obesity and discrimination on the basis of sexual orientation. By contrast, most people oppose public education campaigns to encourage women to stay at home and to inform people that they can change their gender, apparently on the ground that those campaigns are inconsistent with what people regard as prevailing interests and values.[30]

When people are deciding whether to favor default rules, the size of the group of disadvantaged people undoubtedly matters. If a default rule harms a majority, it is unlikely to have much appeal. If the disadvantaged group is large (but not a majority), people might reject a default rule and favor active choosing instead. The precise nature of this principle remains to be tested, but most respondents appear to accept an important third principle: *Before certain losses can occur, people must affirmatively express their wishes.* The principle forbids the state from taking certain goods by default.[31] Actual consent is required. It is instructive here that most respondents favor a state requirement that when obtaining their driver's license, people indicate whether they want to be organ donors (and thus favor active choosing) – even though other surveys, discussed later, find that most Americans reject a default rule in favor of being an organ donor. For organ donations, affirmative consent is required, even if people will favor some kind of "prompt" to nudge people to express their wishes.

Note in this regard that strong majorities of people reject automatic charitable donations of diverse kinds. The apparent concern is that as a result of inertia, procrastination, or inattention, people might find

---

[29] Note, however, that savings defaults are importantly different from green defaults. The former are adopted because they are in the interest of choosers; money that would go to take-home pay goes into savings, and so choosers do not lose anything on net (while also saving for retirement). The latter are adopted because they help to solve a collective action problem. With respect to green defaults, the question did not specify whether people would have to pay for green energy. Not surprisingly, people are more likely to opt out if they would. *See* Simon Hedlin and Cass R. Sunstein, *Does Active Choosing Promote Green Energy Use? Experimental Evidence,* ECOLOGY L.Q. (forthcoming).

[30] To be sure, there is an ambiguity in these findings. Do respondents reject nudges that are (a) inconsistent with *their own* interests or values or (b) inconsistent with the interests or values of *most choosers*? On this question, the findings here do not provide a clear test. When respondents reject nudges, they probably believe that the nudges that are inconsistent with their own interests or values are also inconsistent with the interests or values of most choosers. It would be interesting, and possible, to pose questions that would enable us to choose between (a) and (b).

[31] Whether this principle is triggered will depend on a theory of entitlement, from which any account of "losses" will flow. In the questions here, that issue is not especially complicated. If a default rule will ensure that people give money to specified charities (subject to opt out), it will impose a loss. But we could imagine harder cases – as, for example, with adjustments in the social security program, where losses and gains might not be self-evident, and might be subject to framing.

themselves giving money to a charity even though they do not wish to do so. We might therefore complement the third principle with a fourth and narrower one, which can be seen as a specification: *Most people reject automatic enrollment in charitable giving programs, at least if they are operated by public institutions.* The case of carbon offsets can be understood in similar terms. While it does not involve a charitable donation, and instead might be seen as an effort to prevent a harmful act (pollution), Americans appear to want active consent. We do not yet know the exact boundaries of apparent public skepticism about default rules that would take away people's money without their active consent, but there is no doubt that such skepticism exists.

We have seen that people generally favor disclosures that, in their view, bear on health and safety (salt content, GMOs). At the same time, the results leave open the question whether and when people will favor mandatory disclosures that involve political issues associated with production of a product (rather than the health and environmental effects of product itself.) Americans seem closely divided on that question. With repeated violations of the nation's labor laws and nations that harbor terrorism, such disclosure achieved majority support – but not with products coming from Communist nations. People might well demand a certain threshold of egregiousness, in terms of the behavior of those who produce a good or service, before they will want to require disclosure of that behavior. On this question, partisan differences are to be expected, because people will disagree about whether the relevant threshold has been met and about what it exactly is.

It is tempting, and not inconsistent with the data, to suggest that people's reactions to nudges also show the influence of a fifth principle: People reject nudges *that they regard as unacceptably manipulative.* The subliminal advertising finding can be taken as support for this principle. But what counts as unacceptable manipulation? Most people are in favor of graphic warning labels on cigarettes; they like default rules (if consistent with people's values and interests); a majority favors mandatory cafeteria design meant to promote healthy eating; people approve of a graphic campaign to discourage distracted driving; with respect to obesity, a majority favors a somewhat tendentious public education campaign, one that could plausibly be characterized as manipulative. No one likes manipulation in the abstract, but there do not appear to be many cases in which most people are willing to reject nudges as unacceptably manipulative, at least if they have legitimate ends and are taken to be in the interest of most choosers.

Partisanship

What is the role of partisan differences? Democrats and Republicans will sometimes disagree, of course, about whether the goals of a particular nudge are illicit, and they will also disagree, on occasion, about whether a nudge is consistent with the interests or values of choosers. For example, those who disapprove of abortion will be especially likely to support nudges that are designed to discourage abortion; those who do not disapprove of abortion will be unlikely to support such nudges.

Imagine an anti-abortion nudge in the form of a law requiring pregnant women seeking abortions to be presented with a fetal heartbeat or a sonogram. (Some American states do impose such anti-abortion nudges.) We can predict, with a high degree of confidence, that Democrats would show lower approval ratings than Republicans. My own study, on Amazon's Mechanical Turk, finds exactly that: About 28 percent of Democrats approve, compared to 70 percent of Republicans.[32] With respect to a public education campaign informing people that they can change genders, the significant difference between Democrats and Republicans should not come as a big surprise.

But there is another and more general division as well. Even when majorities of Democrats, Republicans, and independents support a particular initiative, the *level* of support is sometimes higher within one group than within another. Even if the underlying end is broadly shared – as it is, for example, in the area of public health – some subset of Republicans sometimes seems skeptical of government nudges, taken as such, and *will therefore disapprove of them even if they do accept the legitimacy of the end and do not think that the nudge is inconsistent with choosers' interests or values.* Some Republicans, and undoubtedly some Democrats and independents, appear to support another principle: *There should be a rebuttable presumption against nudging, at least if the government can avoid it.* The survey does not provide conclusive evidence that some people embrace this principle, but it is highly suggestive. Many people reject graphic health warnings on cigarette packages (26 percent), an educational campaign for childhood obesity (18 percent), an educational campaign for distracted driving (15 percent), and a traffic light system for food (36 percent). It is reasonable

---

[32] The precise question asked people whether they approve or disapprove of a "state requirement that pregnant women must see a sonogram of their fetus, and hear its heartbeat, before proceeding to have an abortion." Interestingly, only about one-third of independents approved, essentially the same as Democrats.

to infer that those who oppose such nudges agree that they have legitimate ends and are in the interest of most choosers – but nonetheless do not favor government intervention. They can be seen as "reactors," in the sense that they rebel against such intervention, even when it maintains freedom of choice.

It is important to see that the strength of any anti-nudge presumption will vary with the particular issue, with partisan affiliations, and with competing views about the role of government. In some of the cases, Republicans are more skeptical of nudges than are Democrats. With calorie labels and childhood obesity campaigns, for example, there are significant differences in the levels of support within the two groups, even though majorities of both are supportive. But in some cases, Republicans are undoubtedly more enthusiastic about nudges than are Democrats, as shown by the example of the anti-abortion nudge. The fact that few such cases are found here is an artifact of the particular questions. If the issue involved automatic enrollment in programs by which high-income earners automatically receive capital gains tax benefits, for example, we can predict, with some confidence, that Republicans would be more supportive than Democrats. Evidence supports that prediction.[33]

Nationally representative surveys in Europe find strikingly similar results. In the United Kingdom, Germany, Denmark, Hungary, France, and Italy, citizens are broadly supportive of nudges that attract support in the United States and generally oppose nudges that Americans oppose (such as subliminal advertising and default payments to charities). Indeed, the levels of support are extremely close to those in the United States, suggesting the possibility that in a wide array of nations, people are in essential agreement.[34] To be sure, there are some differences. Puzzlingly, nudges attract somewhat lower levels of support in Denmark and Hungary than in other nations. But the basic story seems to be one of an international consensus, at least across those nations for which we have data.

Nudges vs. Mandates

I have suggested that many people are skeptical of mandates, even if they have legitimate ends. To test that proposition, I used Amazon's Mechanical Turk (with 309 participants) to explore people's reactions to three pairs of initiatives, with exactly the same goals but in the form of either nudges

---

[33] Tannenbaum, Fox, and Rogers, *On the Misplaced Politics of Behavioral Policy Interventions* (2014).
[34] *See* Reisch and Sunstein, *Do Europeans Like Nudges?* (unpublished manuscript 2016).

(with opt-out rights) or mandates (with no such rights). The initiatives involved savings (with a 3 percent contribution rate); safe sex education; and education about intelligent design (meant as an alternative to evolution). In all cases, the nudge was far more popular than the mandate (and received majority support) – and indeed, in all cases, the mandate ran into majority disapproval.

So long as people could opt out, the savings initiative received 69 percent approval; same-sex education, 77 percent; and intelligent design, 56 percent. But as mandates, the three fell to approval rates of 19 percent, 43 percent, and 24 percent respectively. Similar results have been found in Denmark, with significantly more support for nudges (including information provision) than for more aggressive instruments.[35]

It follows that many people do oppose mandates as such, even when they are enthusiastic about the underlying ends, and are supportive of nudges that are designed to promote those ends. We have seen that majorities of Americans have no general view about nudges as such; their assessments turn on the principles outlined here. With mandates, people do have a general view, in the form of a presumption, and it is not favorable, at least across a range of cases. Of course it is also true that people would support mandates of various kinds, especially when harm to others is involved (as in the case of the criminal law and many regulatory requirements).

An independent study by Janice Jung and Barbara Mellers reaches similar conclusions.[36] They ask about twenty-three nudges, including automatic enrollment in savings plans, graphic warnings for cigarettes, spending alerts for consumers whose credit card balance is approaching the limit, default displays in grocery stores that make healthy goods conspicuous and easier to reach, and default food orderings in school cafeterias, with salads and lower calorie foods to promote healthy choices. One of their central findings was that majorities of Americans supported most of these nudges. I will return to their study, because it has some important wrinkles.

Sweden and the United States

Surveying 952 people in Sweden and the United States, William Hagman, David Anderson, Daniel Vastfjall, and Gustav Tinghog find that strong

[35] *See* Sofie Kargh Pederson et al., *Who Wants Paternalism*, 66 BULLETIN OF ECONOMIC RESEARCH S147 (2014).
[36] *See* Janice Jung and Barbara A. Mellers, *American Attitudes toward Nudges*, 11 J. JUDGMENT AND DECISION MAKING 62 (2016).

majorities of both Swedes and Americans favor a variety of nudges.[37] The significance of the conclusion is fortified by the fact that along many dimensions, Swedes and Americans differ – and yet their ethical evaluations are remarkably similar. Consider five examples, each involving classic nudges from private or public institutions:

1. Avoiding tax evasion (appealing to conscience). *Many countries have a problem with its citizens not paying taxes, which costs society a considerable amount of money. Some countries have therefore started to send out information to the taxpayers with the encouraging message "To pay your taxes is the right thing to do." The idea with this intervention is to give tax evaders a bad conscience and therefore increase their motivation to pay their taxes.*

2. Smoking discouragement (graphic warnings). *Smoking often leads to addiction and has a negative effect on the health of the individual. To more clearly show the negative effects of smoking, many countries have started to add deterrent pictures on the cigarette packages. These images display damaged organs that can be a consequence of long-term smoking. The idea with this intervention is to discourage people to start smoking and motivate people that are smokers to quit.*

3. Cafeteria (accessibility). *Overconsumption of calorie-rich food can lead to deteriorating health. In an attempt to get their employees to eat healthier, a company rearranged its cafeteria. Healthy food was placed at eye level and easily available for the visitors of the cafeteria. Unhealthy food, such as candy or snacks, was placed behind the counter to make them less visible and accessible for the visitors in the cafeteria. The idea with this intervention is to encourage the consumption of healthier alternatives to improve the health of the employees.*

4. Energy conservation (social norms). *Most households today are over-consuming energy, which leads to a waste of resources both for the household and society. Therefore energy companies that succeed in decreasing the average energy consumption among households receive government subsidies. To motivate households to lower energy consumption, an energy company attached some complementary information to the energy bill. The information added contained a comparison of energy consumption between the customer's household and other households in the neighborhood.*

If the costumer's energy consumption was lower than the neighbors', a happy smiley face was shown on the bill. However, if the customer's energy consumption was higher than the neighbors', a sad face was shown. The idea

---

[37] William Hagman et al., *Public Views on Policies Involving Nudges*, 6 REV. OF PHIL. AND PSYCHOL. 439 (2015).

with this intervention is that the feedback that these faces give will have a positive effect on the energy consumption of the households.

5. Food labeling (disclosure). *It can be difficult to tell which food products are healthy and which are not; therefore a food chain started to label their products with stickers that look similar to a green and red stoplight or traffic signal. Healthy food, which is rich in minerals and vitamins and has a low amount of fat and sugar, is marked with a green tag. Unhealthy food, which is rich in fat and sugar and has a low amount of minerals and vitamins, receives a red tag. The idea with this intervention is to make it easier to make healthy choices.*

Hagman et al. find that over 80 percent of both Swedes and Americans think that the tax evasion policy is acceptable. Over 80 percent also favor disclosure to promote healthy choices (86.9 percent of Swedes and 83.8 of Americans). Hagman et al. find comparably high levels of support for both the smoking discouragement policy (81 percent of Swedes and 72.6 percent of Americans) and cafeteria redesign (82.6 percent of Swedes and 76.4 percent of Americans). About two-thirds of both Swedes (66.4 percent) and Americans (67.1 percent) support the energy conservation nudge.

Consistent with expectations, Swedes are generally a bit more enthusiastic than Americans about these nudges, but only two of the tested nudges fail to attract majority support in either country, with 42.9 percent and 45.7 percent of Americans (but over 60 percent of Swedes) favoring these:

4. Organ donation (default rule). *There is currently a lack of organ donors in many countries. In some places, to become an organ donor the individual has to make an active choice and register as an organ donor with the appropriate authority. If no choice is registered, the individual is assumed to be unwilling to donate in event of an accident (so called Opt-In). In previous surveys most people report that they are willing to be an organ donor but have not registered.*

One way to increase the number of organ donors could be to automatically enroll people as organ donors unless otherwise specified (so called Opt-Out). In other words, it is up to the individual to register at the appropriate authority if they are unwilling to donate their organs in the event of a fatal accident. The aim with this intervention (Opt-Out) is to increase the number of organ donors.

5. Climate compensation (default rule). *Carbon dioxide emissions in connection with flying have a negative effect on the environment. To compensate for this, there is usually a voluntary fee that travelers can add to the final price. The money from this fee goes to projects to reduce emissions of carbon dioxide to a corresponding level of the emission caused by the flight. To increase the number of travelers that choose to pay the climate compensation fee, it can*

automatically be added to the final price. Then, if a traveler does not want to pay the fee, the traveler instead has to make an active choice not to pay the fee (also known as Opt-Out). The idea with this intervention (Opt-Out) is to increase the number of travelers that compensate for climate change.

What accounts for the majority's rejection of these nudges in the United States (and significant opposition in Sweden as well)? It is reasonable to speculate that the answer lies in an ethical principle that we have already seen previously: *Before certain losses can occur, people must affirmatively express their wishes.* Here is a close cousin of that principle: *Choice architects should not use people's inertia or inattention against them.* For decisions that have a significant degree of moral sensitivity (organ donation) or sheer cost (climate change compensation), many people reject a default and favor active choosing. The apparent idea – for which more empirical testing would be desirable – is that if a default rule would lead people to end up with an outcome that is morally troubling (to them) or expensive (for them), that rule is objectionable and active choosing is much better.

Consistent with the findings in my own surveys, we could confidently predict widespread disapproval of a default rule announcing that voters will, by default, be assumed to support incumbent politicians (subject to opt-out), or that employees will, by default, give 10 percent of their earnings to their employer's children or to their employer's favorite charity. We have seen that in evaluating defaults, people are sensitive to the question whether the result is to track the desires and values of all or most of the population that is subject to them.

That lesson is a significant one, but the most important finding is the apparently widespread endorsement of nudges, whether the goal is to protect third parties (as in the case of tax evasion) or the self (as in the case of smoking discouragement).[38] In general, Hagman et al. find that larger percentages of people are more supportive of third-party nudges, but

---

[38] A qualitative study in the specific context of health behavior finds similar results. *See* Astrid F. Junghans et al., *Under Consumers' Scrutiny – An Investigation into Consumers' Attitudes and Concerns about Nudging in the Realm of Health Behavior*, 15 BMC PUB. HEALTH 336 (2015). The central conclusion is that "most consumers approve of the concept, especially in the realm of health behavior, given particular conditions: 1. Nudges should be designed for benefiting individuals and society; 2. consumers comprehend the decision-making context and the reasoning behind the promotion of the targeted behavior. Interviews revealed very limited concerns with manipulative aspects of nudges." *Id.* at 336. The authors add, "For governments currently employing or considering the implementation of nudges and paternalistic strategies into their range of policy instruments the findings speak in favor of such strategies despite criticisms from some scholars and media while simultaneously call for more information about nudges." *Id.* at 349.

the difference is not big, and many nudges that are designed to protect the self receive substantial support. Hagman et al. also tested whether those with an "individualistic worldview" are less likely to embrace nudges. To find out if people have such a worldview, they used a short version of the Cultural Cognition Worldview Group scale, which asks people whether they agree or disagree with such statements as this: *The government interferes far too much in our everyday lives.* Not surprisingly, those with a high score, agreeing with statements of this kind, are more likely to reject nudges.

More strikingly, Hagman et al. find that respondents *who are more prone to analytical thinking are less likely to see nudges as intruding on freedom of choice.* It may be that analytical thinkers are more able to see that the relevant nudges sufficiently preserve freedom, whereas less analytical thinkers have a more immediate and visceral reaction, leading to more skeptical (and erroneous?) conclusions.

The Swedish-U.S. differences remain noteworthy even in the midst of the general agreement between people in the two nations (and an assortment of others). It would of course be valuable to test diverse categories of nudges and to see what kinds of division might emerge. For some nudges, Americans will probably be more supportive than Swedes; on certain social issues (such as abortion), significant numbers of Americans might favor nudges than Swedes would reject. From the data, it is tempting to think that Swedes are generally more supportive of nudges than are Americans, but the temptation should be resisted. It is possible that Americans, or some subset, have a degree of skepticism about nudging, making for a distinction from Swedes, but the evidence does not support that conclusion. Hagman et al. tested particular nudges that Swedes are somewhat more likely to approve that Americans, and with a different set of nudges, the disparity might flip in the opposite direction.

It would also be valuable to explore in more detail whether people react differently to "harm-to-self" nudges than to "harm-to-others" nudges. For reasons we have explored, the former might well prove more controversial than the latter, at least as a general rule. Perhaps people have at least a degree of skepticism when government seeks to help people to protect themselves – and far less when government seeks to prevent harm to others. But we have seen that people are enthusiastic about many "harm-to-self" nudges. Some of those nudges, such as calorie labels and automatic enrollment in pension plans, might well attract more support than some "harm-to-others" nudges, such as default rules that promote use of environmentally-friendly (but expensive) energy providers.[39]

We could also test whether people reject nudges that involve especially sensitive spheres of life – for example, those that attempt to influence highly personal or intimate choices. It is fair to assume that both Swedes and Americans would be unhappy with a system of "default spouses." It is also fair to assume that Swedes and Americans would reject nudges that seem not to promote, or to reduce, the welfare of those they affect. Consider nudges that would actually promote dangerous activities or unhealthy eating or that would encourage behavior that people generally believe to be harmful to third parties or otherwise unethical.

Nudging System 1?

We have seen that in behavioral science, it has become standard to distinguish between two families of cognitive operations in the human mind: System 1, which is fast, automatic, and intuitive, and System 2, which is slow, calculative, and deliberative. With the distinction between deliberative and automatic processing in mind, we might want to distinguish between nudges that address System 1 and nudges that address System 2. Many of the most vigorous arguments against nudging appear to focus on "System 1 nudges" and to suggest that they are distinctly objectionable.[40] If government or the private sector is attempting to influence people by targeting or exploiting their automatic systems, or by enlisting their biases, it might seem to be engaged in manipulation and to be treating people without respect (see Chapter 5). It might also appear to be disparaging their agency. On this view, nudges that inform System 2 might seem far better, because they help people to reflect, or to improve their deliberative capacities.

But do people actually care about the difference? Exactly when and how? These questions can be tested. I have undertaken some initial tests, asking about 300 people on Amazon Mechanical Turk this:

(A) Which of these policies do you prefer, as part of an antismoking campaign?
(1) graphic warnings, with vivid pictures of people who are sick from cancer
(2) purely factual information, giving people statistical information about the risks from smoking

---

[39] *See generally* Simon Hedlin and Cass R. Sunstein, *Does Active Choosing Promote Green Energy Use?* 43 ECOLOGY L.Q. (forthcoming 2016).
[40] This is one way to read Till Grine-Yanoff and Ralph Hertwig, *Nudge Versus Boost: How Coherent Are Policy and Theory?*, 25 MIND & MACHINES 1 (2015).

(B) Which of these policies do you prefer, as part of a campaign to encourage people to save for retirement?

(1) automatic enrollment of employees in savings plans, subject to "opt out" if employees do not want to participate

(2) financial literacy programs at the workplace, so that employees are educated about retirement options

(C) Which of these policies do you prefer, as part of a program to reduce pollution?

(1) automatic enrollment of customers in slightly more expensive "green" (environmentally friendly) energy, subject to "opt out" if customers want another, slightly less expensive energy source

(2) educational campaigns so that consumers can learn the advantages of green (environmentally friendly) energy

(D) Which of these policies do you prefer, as part of a program to combat childhood obesity?

(1) redesigning school cafeterias so that healthy, low-calorie options are in the most visible locations

(2) educating parents about the problem of children obesity and how to combat it

In all of these questions, we can think of (1) as System 1 nudges, and (2) as System 2 nudges. System 2 nudges were more popular for the first three questions, attracting 59 percent, 62 percent, and 61 percent support respectively. Perhaps because it involved children, the fourth question produced 55 percent support for the System 1 nudge. But the basic finding is that strong majorities were inclined to prefer nudges that appeal to people's deliberative capacities and that can be counted as "boosts." Apparently majorities are concerned, at least in part, about individual agency and favor nudges that promote it (even if they would also approve of System 1 nudges).

I also attempted to see how people's answers might shift if they were explicitly told to assume that the System 1 nudge was "significantly more effective" in achieving the goal (e.g., fewer smokers, more participation in saving programs). This information produced shifts for three of the four questions: 53 percent favor graphic warnings, 50 percent favor automatic enrollment in savings, and 68 percent favor cafeteria design. (There was no shift for green energy.) Apparently people's preference for System 2 nudges can be reduced or eliminated if System 1 nudges work much better. The preference for active agency, or boosting, exists, but for most people it is only a presumption. In a sense, it has a price, and the price might be too high to pay. Undoubtedly people vary in their judgments along this dimension.

Gidon Felsen and his colleagues have undertaken a different kind of test, with broadly compatible results.[41] Notice, for example, the difference between two scenarios, involving nudges that are designed to increase savings.

(1)   *The new design works like this – with every annual salary increase you are provided information in the form of a series of icons representing tropical beaches that shows how much extra leisure you are likely to be able to afford during your retirement by investing different percentages of your increased salary; larger investments now translate into more retirement savings later. You can still choose to keep the entire salary increase instead of investing it, but the information provided results in a subconsciously driven bias toward investment; in other words, the decision to invest is made more likely as a result of subconscious deliberation. Studies have shown that implementing this policy leads to an increase in retirement savings.*

(2)   *The new design works like this – with every annual salary increase you are provided information in the form of a detailed table of your earnings that shows how much extra money you are likely to have during your retirement by investing different percentages of your increased salary; larger investments now translate into more retirement savings later. You can still choose to keep the entire salary increase instead of investing it, but the information provided results in a consciously driven bias toward long-term investment; in other words, the decision to invest is made more likely as a result of conscious deliberation. Studies have shown that implementing this policy leads to an increase in retirement savings.*

The difference is that (1) exploits a "subconsciously driven bias" whereas (2) does not. Or consider the difference between two approaches designed to promote healthy eating:

(1)   *The new design works like this – the cafeteria has been revamped so that unhealthy foods, such as candy bars, potato chips, and the like, are not as conveniently located. You can still choose whichever foods you would like, but moving the location of the unhealthy food in the cafeteria results in a subconsciously driven bias toward healthy eating choices; in other words, the decision to eat healthy foods is made more likely without the need for conscious deliberation. Studies have shown that implementing this policy leads to healthier eating habits.*

---

[41] *See* Gidon Felsen et al., *Decisional Enhancement and Autonomy: Public Attitudes toward Overt and Covert Nudges*, 8 JUDGMENT AND DECISION MAKING 203, 203 (2012). I explore these issues in detail in Cass A. Sunstein, People Prefer System 2 Nedges (Kind of) (unpublished manuscript 2016)

(2) *The new design works like this – the cafeteria has been revamped so that all foods have their nutritional content clearly displayed. You can still choose whichever foods you would like, but the nutritional information results in a consciously driven bias toward healthy eating choices; in other words, the decision to eat healthy foods is made more likely as a result of conscious deliberation. Studies have shown that implementing this policy leads to healthier eating habits.*

Here as well, the difference is between an approach that targets "a subconsciously driven bias" and one that focuses on "conscious deliberation." Such questions allow for a test of this hypothesis, connected with the earlier discussion of manipulation: *people are more likely to object to nudges that appeal to unconscious or subconscious processes.* Surveying 2,775 people in Canada and the United States, Felsen et al. find that people do indeed show a modest preference for nudges that lack that characteristic.[42] In a range of cases – involving not only healthy eating and savings but also wise investing and prudent online purchasing – people are moderately more likely to favor approaches that involve reflection and deliberation.

In the experimental design, subjects were not asked directly whether they preferred one nudge to another. Instead they were asked whether they would be more or less likely to accept a job offer from a company that offered one or another nudge or instead a company that did not (the neutral condition). For about half of the respondents, the comparison was between a System 1 nudge and the neutral condition. For the other half, the comparison was between a System 2 nudge and the neutral condition. The relevant scale ranged from 1 to 10, with 1 meaning "much less" likely to accept a job offer, and 10 meaning "much more." The authors compared the effect of the System 1 nudge and the System 2 nudge on people's likelihood of accepting a job offer. They found that in aggregate, people showed an increased willingness to accept job offers with a System 2 nudge (on average, around 8 on the 1–10 scale) as compared to those with a System 1 nudge (on average, around 6 on the 1–10 scale).[43]

It is important to see that while people were more favorably disposed to System 2 nudges, they found System 1 nudges to be a positive inducement as well, generally concluding that they would increase the likelihood that they would accept a job offer. Nonetheless, System 2 nudges were

[42] *Id.* at 205, 208.
[43] *Id.* at 205. I am simplifying some aspects of their analysis; *see id.* at 203–205 for details.

preferred. Why? A possible reason is that people think that when nudges appeal to unconscious or subconscious processes, they compromise individual agency. In strong support of this speculation, Felsen et al. find that when conscious processing is involved, people believe that the resulting decisions are more "authentic," evidently in the sense that those decisions reflect the chooser's own agency. They conclude that their evidence supports "the idea that preserving the individual's capacity for making authentic decisions is an important condition for the acceptability of decisional enhancement programs."[44]

Recall, however, that the difference in people's reactions is relatively modest; it is not as if people systematically approve of System 2 nudges and systematically disapprove of System 1 nudges. Moreover, there is reason to suspect that when people believe that some kind of behavioral bias – such as a self-control problem – is genuinely at work, they will become more receptive to nudges that target unconscious or subconscious processes. Felsen et al. find intriguing support for this suspicion, for in one scenario (involving eating), people were equally favorable to System 1 and System 2 nudges *when they wanted help*.[45] (The particular question, with answers on a nine-point scale, was "To what extent do you feel like you could use help making healthier eating choices in the face of the availability of unhealthy but tasty foods?") If people are aware that they are suffering from a problem of self-control, and if they want to overcome that problem, an approach that targets System 1 might be unobjectionable or even welcome. The conclusion might well be fortified if people believe that existing decisions are already a product of unconscious processing. In such cases, it might be acceptable to meet fire with fire.

As Felsen et al. suggest, "covertly influencing decision processes such that the resulting decision is *aligned with higher-order* desires may actually enhance autonomy, especially in situations in which the target population is known to want help with a given behavior."[46] They suggest that "respondents who wanted help with eating decisions may have been more likely to recognize that food choices are often subconsciously driven, and were therefore just as likely to favor the decisional enhancement program

---

[44] *Id.* at 206.

[45] *Id.* at 206–207. Note that when people wanted help, they were (not surprisingly) more likely to favor some kind of nudge over the neutral option. *Id.* at 206. But in most of the scenarios, they continued to show a relative preference for the System 2 nudge; the healthy eating scenario was the exception. *Id.* at 207 ("the less respondents wanted help, the more favorable they were to the conscious than the subconscious influence").

[46] *Id.* at 207.

with covert influences as the program with overt influences, whereas respondents who did not want help with food choices reverted to the expected preference for overt influences."[47]

It would be valuable to obtain much more evidence on this question, but we might speculate that people's evaluations of System 1 nudges would very much depend on whether they believe that it is necessary to counteract a self-control problem. Interestingly, a study in Denmark finds no link between support for nudges and strong or weak self-control – but it does find that as compared with people with weak self-control, those with strong self-control are more favorably disposed toward mandates and bans.[48] This is a somewhat surprising finding. One might expect that people with self-control problems would be more enthusiastic about mandates, at least if they could provide real help. But perhaps those who suffer from poor self-control do not want to be coerced by the state. Findings on this topic continue to emerge, with some evidence that smokers who seek to quit are more likely to support mandates than are smokers who have no such plans.[49]

Values, Systems, and Reactance

My own study involved more direct questions, asking them to compare System 1 nudges to System 1 nudges. Recall that Janice Jung and Barbara Mellers studied twenty-three nudges and found that Americans supported most of them.[50] At the same time, they gave System 1 and System 2 versions of essentially the same nudges. For example, consider this:

(a) *System 1. Suppose that when you pay your credit card bills online, the government requires the credit card companies to select the default payment option of full payment. You can pay other amounts, but you need to specify those by selecting different options. The default policy is designed to help you enjoy the benefits of no interest fees and good credit scores.*

(b) *System 2. Suppose that when you pay your credit card bills online, the government requires the credit card companies to provide information*

[47] *Id.* at 208.
[48] *See* Pederson et al., *Who Wants Paternalism*, 66 BULLETIN OF ECONOMIC RESEARCH S147 (2014).
[49] *See* Joni Hersch, *Smoking Restrictions as a Self-Control Mechanism*, 31 J. RISK AND UNCERTAINTY 5 (2005).
[50] *See* Jung and Barbara A. Mellers, *American Attitudes toward Nudges*, J. JUDGMENT DECISION MAKING 62 (2016).

that makes it easy to understand the benefits of paying the total amount due. The information encourages you to pay the entire bill by telling you that full payment helps you enjoy the benefits of no interest fees and good credit scores.

Or this:

(a) *System 1. Suppose that when you are at a hotel, the government requires the hotel to select a default policy of "environment-friendly rooms" in which towels left on the racks are not washed. If you want your towels washed, you must place them on the floor. The plan helps you save water and avoid water waste that leads to a less sustainable environment.*

(b) *System 2. Suppose that when you are at a hotel, the government requires the hotel to provide you with information about a "environment-friendly" policy in which towels left on the racks are not washed. To get towels washed, you must place them on the floor. The information makes it easier to understand how to participate in the water conservation program. You are encouraged to take part and told that the policy is designed to help you save water and avoid water waste, which results in a less sustainable environment.*

In my study, people were asked to choose between System 1 and System 2 nudges. By contrast, Jung and Mellers asked people to rate them both kinds on a numerical scale. In general, they found significantly higher levels of support for System 2 nudges than for System 1 nudges. To be sure, people often approved of System 1 nudges as well. Majorities gave positive support to System 1 nudges (in the form of default rules) to promote health insurance coverage, retirement savings, credit card payments, and water conservation – and also to promote healthy eating at cafeterias and grocery stores and to increase privacy on the Internet. But for the most part, the level of approval was higher for System 2 nudges. People are apparently a bit more comfortable with them. In the authors' words, Americans "distinguish between System 1 and System 2 nudges and prefer System 2 nudges with informational reminders and educational opportunities over System 1 nudges with defaults and sequential ordering."[51] This conclusion is important, but it must be qualified by a recognition of the sparse informational foundations of people's reactions in the surveys (what if a System 1 nudge is, in fact, more effective?) and by a reminder that many System 1 nudges also attract majority support.

---

[51] *Id.* at 71–72.

Jung and Mellers also found some intriguing differences among people with varying attitudes and political orientations. They asked participants to take certain tests for individualism (similar to that in Hagman et al.), for reactance, for empathy, and for "desire to control." They also tested for differences between liberals and conservatives. Not surprisingly, they found that individualists tended to oppose both System 1 and System 2 nudges, and that conservatives tended to oppose them as well. (Recall, however, that it would be possible to design a set of nudges that conservatives would be more likely to support than liberals; the finding here by Jung and Mellers is an artifact of the particular nudges that were tested, which are more likely to be favored by liberals than conservatives.) Those who showed empathy tended to support both System 1 and System 2 nudges. Participants who showed an inclination to reactance were fine with System 2 nudges – but they opposed System 1 nudges. The same was true for those who showed a strong desire for control. In general, people said that System 1 nudges were more threatening to autonomy than System 2 nudges. (Recall, however, that many System 1 nudges attracted majority support.)

Surveying students in Israel, the United States, and Germany, Ayala Arad and Ariel Rubinstein offer similar findings. In particular, they tested people's reactions to educative nudges (understood to target System 2) and to noneducative ones (understood to target System 1).[52] As I did, they also tested people's evaluations of hard mandates, which are of course not nudges at all.

Their central finding is that people are more likely to approve of System 2 nudges than System 1 nudges. Educative interventions received widespread endorsement in all three nations. Strong majorities favored an informational campaign about healthy foods and also a smartphone app created by the government that includes information about the nutritional value of items on every restaurant's menu. By contrast, participants were significantly less likely to favor a law requiring restaurants to order the items on a menu from healthiest to unhealthiest – or a law forcing employers to set 8 percent as a default saving rate for their employees (with participants needing to decide whether to opt out of the arrangement). There were also intriguing and relatively consistent differences across the three nations.

---

[52] Ayala Arad and Ariel Rubinstein, *The People's Perspective on Libertarian-Paternalistic Policies* 8 (2015), *available at* www.tau.ac.il/~aradayal/LP.pdf.

With respect to savings, substantial numbers of people said that they felt "negatively" about government mandating the default – 42 percent of Americans, 28 percent of Israelis, and 66 percent of Germans. With respect to healthy food choices, significant minorities of people were willing to prefer the educational intervention to the "menu order" requirement at restaurants *even if the former was less effective*. About 37 percent of Germans showed that preference, compared to 35 percent of Americans and 21 percent of Israelis. Importantly, however, majorities in the United States (66 percent) and Israel (55 percent), and 50 percent in Germany, said that they would favor the more effective intervention. And interestingly, small minorities favored the "menu order" requirement even if it was *less* effective (9 percent of Israelis and 13 percent of both Germans and Americans).

Arad and Rubinstein also find that people in all three countries are relatively averse to both mandates and taxes. About 83 percent of Germans prefer the app to a prohibition, even if the latter is more effective. The same is true for about 66 percent of Americans and about 73 percent of Israelis. About 51 percent of Germans prefer the app to a "fat tax" even if the latter is more effective; the same is true for 41 percent of Americans and 51 percent of Israelis. In both Israel and Germany, majorities prefer information to a tax even if the latter is more effective (65 percent and 59 percent respectively), as do nearly half of Americans (48 percent).

Do people's negative reactions to noneducative nudges translate into people's predicted behavior? Arad and Rubinstein find that it does. With respect to savings, a significant percentage of people in all three countries say that they would opt out of the default, apparently in reactance against government intervention. As we have seen, a default rule is not an order; people can reject it. Nonetheless, reactance might occur, at least on the part of those people who regard a default itself as a kind of top-down imposition. Arad and Rubinstein thus offer a surprising and even stunning result, which is that an opt-in design produces a higher participation rate than does opt-out. From this, they reach a bold conclusion, which is that *if people are informed that the government is nudging them, a significant number may respond negatively and opt out for that very reason.*[53]

Because the real-world evidence shows that default rules are very powerful, including in the context of savings, this conclusion should be taken as highly speculative; it might well be a product of the survey setting. But to the extent that it makes onto actual behavior, it is the mirror image of a

[53] *Id.* at 22.

common explanation for the effectiveness of defaults. Under that explanation, a default contains an informational signal about what it makes sense for people to do, and people do not opt out because they hear that signal; we might call that mechanism "receptance." Arad and Rubinstein suggest an intriguing contrary possibility, which is that some people will not much like that signal and will opt out accordingly.

An experimental study, conducted by Simon Hedlin and me, offers a similar finding,[54] also in the context of a survey, which is that *active choosing is more effective in producing green energy use than are green energy defaults*. This result, which we did not anticipate, appears to be a product of the interaction between guilt and reactance. With active choosing, participants said that they felt particularly guilty about not enrolling (as we found by asking a direct question about guilt). With a green energy default, some participants were resentful that the government automatically enrolled them in green energy – and hence they opted out. Their resentment cancelled out their guilt. At the same time, and interestingly, we found that respondents were less likely to *approve* of the active choosing policy than of the green energy default policy. The reason might be that the active choosing required them to make a decision – and also to feel guilty about not enrolling. The upshot is that compared to green energy defaults and standard energy defaults, active choosing was the most effective policy and the most guilt-inducing policy – and the least popular policy.

These findings are complex, but they suggest a simple lesson, which is that if people see default rules as some kind of imposition, they might rebel, and hence the nudge will be less effective than would otherwise be anticipated. But experimental findings of this kind, involving mere surveys, should be taken with a great deal of caution. There might well be a large difference between what people say they would do and what they would actually do. Asked in surveys whether they would opt out of a policy produced by government, they might say "yes," even if they would not do so in reality – either because of inertia and procrastination or because of social norms and guilt (receptance). It is easy to say "yes" on a survey; there are barriers to doing so in the real world, even if opting out is free. The real-world evidence is that green defaults are very sticky indeed (see Chapter 7), and contrary to what Arad and

---

[54] Simon Hedlin and Cass R. Sunstein, *Does Active Choosing Promote Green Energy Use? Experimental Evidence* 43 Ecology L. Q. (Forthcoming 2016).

Rubinstein find, opt-out savings policies are much more effective than opt-in policies.[55]

Partisan Nudge Bias

Do political judgments matter to people's assessment of nudges? Casual observation suggests that that they do. When the Obama administration used behaviorally informed tools, those who were inclined to oppose the Obama administration were not likely to love those tools. Consider this hypothesis: *At least across a wide range, people have no considered view about nudges as such. Their evaluations turn on whether they approve of the politics of the particular nudge, or the particular nudges that come to mind.*

In a series of studies, David Tannenbaum, Craig Fox, and Todd Rogers found what they call "partisan nudge bias."[56] Focusing on policies favoring automatic enrollment in pension plans, they randomly assigned people to conditions in which they learned that such policies had been implemented by the Bush administration, the Obama administration, or an unnamed administration. After informing participants about the policy nudge, Tannenbaum et al. specifically reminded them that defaults could be used "across a wide range of policies beyond the illustration above" and asked how they felt, setting the particular application aside, "about actively setting default options as a general approach to public policy."

The basic finding was that on that *general* question, people were much influenced by whether Bush or Obama was responsible for the particular nudge that they read about. When participants were told that the pension default had been implemented by Obama, liberals tended to display relative support for the use of defaults as a general policy tool, whereas conservatives tended to oppose them. But when told that the same policy had been implemented by Bush, that pattern was reversed; liberals displayed relative opposition to the use of defaults, whereas conservatives supported them.

Tannenbaum et al. also asked respondents about a series of nudges that would predictably trigger different reactions from liberals and conservatives. These included increasing participation by low-income individuals in existing food stamp and supplemental nutrition assistance programs (liberal

[55] RICHARD THALER AND CASS R. SUNSTEIN, NUDGE (2008) at 109; BENARTZI, SAVE MORE TOMORROW (2012), at 12.
[56] Tannenbaum, Fox, and Rogers, *On the Misplaced Politics of Behavioral Policy Interventions* (2014), at 1.

valence); making it easier for high-income individuals to claim existing capital gains tax breaks (conservative valence); increasing participation in educational programs for high-school children, involving safe sex and use of contraceptives (liberal valence); increasing participation in educational programs for high-school children, involving "intelligent design" (conservative valence); and a generic, context-free policy illustration (no valence). There were five different types of policy nudges: (1) automatic enrollment defaults, (2) implementation intentions, (3) public commitments, (4) highlighting losses, and (5) descriptive social norms. As in their first study, Tannenbaum et al. asked people about their *general* views about nudges, after seeing the relevant example. Participants were specifically reminded that the approach was general and could be used across a wide range of policies.

The result was unambiguous: *People are significantly more likely to approve of nudges in general when they favor the particular political objectives used to illustrate them.* When the nudges were applied to traditionally liberal policies (food stamps, safe sex), liberals were relatively supportive of nudges as policy tools, while conservatives were relatively opposed to their general use. This pattern reversed when those same nudges were applied to traditionally conservative policy goals (capital gains programs, intelligent design education programs).

Interestingly, and importantly, when nudges were attached to a *generic* policy objective, there was no association between political orientation and people's evaluation of nudges. Apparently conservatives and liberals do not disagree on that general question – a finding that supports the conclusion that the results in Jung and Mellers, suggesting that conservatives like nudges somewhat less, were a result of the particular nudges tested. An especially striking finding in Tannenbaum et al. was that while libertarians were less likely to approve of nudges than those without libertarian dispositions, attitudes about particular policies turned out to be a far more significant predictor than attitudes about libertarianism in general.

Tannenbaum et al. used the same basic strategy to test the responses of actual policymakers, consisting of U.S. city mayors and high-level public servants in state and local governments. They asked the participants to read about two kinds of automatic enrollment defaults. Half read a scenario in which low-income earners were automatically defaulted to receive supplemental food assistance benefits, and half read a scenario in which high-income earners were automatically defaulted to receive capital gains tax benefits. Policymakers were explicitly reminded that the task was the evaluation of nudges as general-purpose policy tools. The usual pattern held: The overall assessments of policymakers were greatly affected by the political valence of the examples.

In sum, "people find nudges more ethically problematic when they are applied to policy objectives they oppose, or when applied by policymakers they oppose, while they find the same nudges more acceptable when they are applied to political objectives they support or by policymakers they support."[57] It would not of course be surprising to find that people favor nudges that support their own goals and reject nudges that undermine those goals. What is more interesting is that many people seem not to have strong or firm judgments about nudges, taken simply as such. Particular examples drive their general views – perhaps because the examples create some kind of affective reaction to the broad category, perhaps because the examples are taken to convey information about how nudges would actually be used (which should of course bear on the overall evaluation). In this respect, people use the examples as heuristics, or mental shortcuts, in answering the broader and more difficult question. (This finding reflects a form of "attribute substitution," of the kind that has been found in many contexts.)

There is a clear implication here for the political economy of nudging: Citizens' judgments about the ethics of nudging, and even the general enterprise, are likely to be, in significant part, an artifact of their substantive judgments about the specific directions in which they think that people are likely to be nudged. It is noteworthy that in the United Kingdom, nudging has been prominently associated with the Conservative Party (and Prime Minister David Cameron), which has likely reduced concern from the right (and perhaps heightened concern from the left). To be sure, this point should not be taken too far. As we have seen, even those who strongly support an incumbent president would be likely to object strenuously if he imposed a nudge that entrenched himself (as, e.g., through a system of default voting). In egregious cases of self-dealing, or of violations of widely held social norms, citizens of a free society (or even an unfree one) might well be outraged whatever they think of the underlying substance. But within broad limits, political assessments are likely to reflect political judgments.

The Effects of Transparency

If people are explicitly informed that they are being nudged, does their behavior change? This question does not ask about people's ethical

---

[57] Id. at 1.

evaluations – at least not directly. Instead it tests a seemingly plausible hypothesis, consistent with the findings in Arad and Rubinstein, which is that if people are told that they are being nudged, they will react adversely and resist (and hence be nudged less or not at all). That hypothesis much bears on the ethical issues: If people resist nudges when they are told about them, then we have some reason to think that they might believe that nudges are ethically questionable, at least in some respects. And that possibility bears on the ethics of influence more broadly. Suppose that people are not only influenced, but told that they are being influenced, and why, and how. Would they be less likely to be influenced? Possibly. And when that is so, do we have reason to question the kinds of influences for which transparency turns out to be self-defeating?

On one view, challenging one of my central arguments here, the effectiveness of nudging *depends* on at least a degree of nontransparency. In an exceptionally illuminating essay, the philosopher Luc Bovens suggests broadly that the underlying psychological mechanisms "typically work better in the dark. If we tell students that the order of the food in the Cafeteria is rearranged for dietary purposes, then the intervention may be less successful. If we explain the endowment effect to employees, they may be less inclined to Save More Tomorrow."[58] And indeed, some people have contended that nudging is ethically questionable for that reason.[59]

But we have seen that even without empirical testing, we should be careful before accepting this claim. Most nudges are fully transparent, and all of them should be; they are hardly in the dark. Disclosure, reminders, warnings, uses of social norms – none of these is exactly hidden, and they need to be transparent in order to work. In general, public officials should inform people about what they are doing. But we have also seen that the very idea of transparency is not self-defining. Is a transparency requirement satisfied merely because the nudge itself is not secret? Is there an obligation to inform people about the specific psychological mechanisms that make

---

[58] Luc Bovens, *The Ethics of Nudge*, in Preference Change 207 (Till Grune-Yanoff and S. O. Hansson eds., 2008).

[59] *See generally* Riccardo Rebonato, Taking Liberties: A Critical Examination of Libertarian Paternalism (2012), for a series of objections, some of which involve this claim. In a related vein, Sarah Conly contends that when nudges are at work, "Rather than regarding people as generally capable of making good choices, we outmaneuver them by appealing to their irrationality, just in more fruitful ways. We concede that people can't generally make good decisions when left to their own devices, and this runs against the basic premise of liberalism, which is that we are basically rational, prudent creatures who may thus, and should thus, direct themselves autonomously." Sarah Conly, Against Autonomy 30 (2012).

nudges effective? (That appears to be Bovens's concern.) Is there any such obligation at the time that people are choosing?

We might ask, with Bovens, whether explicit warnings ("you are about to be nudged" or "we are exploiting loss aversion") would turn out to undermine the whole enterprise. It is reasonable to wonder about the effects of certain kinds of transparency. Consider this: "We know that people tend to do what other people do, and so we are telling you about the social norm in order to get you to do what other people do." Would that kind of transparency prove self-defeating? Or consider this: "We know that because of inertia, default rules stick. So we are using a default rule to affect your life – with the hope that it will stick." A statement of this kind might well make the nudge less effective, but perhaps not; perhaps the disclosure would increase the effect, or perhaps it would be immaterial.

There is not a great deal of evidence on these questions, and we need much more, but an important study by George Loewenstein, Cindy Bryce, and David Hagmann offers the following finding, at least in the context of end-of-life care: *When people are specifically informed that a default rule has been put in place, and that it might be otherwise, that information has little effect on what people end up doing.*[60]

As Loewenstein et al. designed the experiment, people were given one of these default options: (a) "I want my health care providers and agent to pursue treatments that help me to live as long as possible, even if that means I might have more pain and suffering." (b) "I want my health care providers and agent to pursue treatments that help relieve my pain and suffering, even if that means I might not live as long." In the experiment, one or the other of these was preselected as the default, but participants could change it by selecting a different alternative and confirming the change with their initials. Note that this is an exceedingly weak default, not only in the sense that it is exceptionally simple to change it, but also in the sense that the option to switch is made highly salient to participants, so that the problem of procrastination and inertia, which often makes defaults "sticky," is greatly reduced. More familiar defaults (e.g., automatic enrollment in pension or health care plans) are more likely to stick, in part because it is simple for people to ignore the question whether to depart from them, or to decide that they will consider that question at some future time.

---

[60] *See* George Loewenstein, Cindy Bryce, David Hagmann, and Sachin Rajpal, *Warning: You Are About to Be Nudged*, 1 BEHAVIORAL SCIENCE AND POL. 35 (2015).

Here is the disclosure provided by Loewenstein et al., letting people know that they have been defaulted: "The specific focus of this research is on 'defaults' – decisions that go into effect if people don't take actions to do something different. Participants in this research project have been divided into two experimental groups."[61] Having received this information, participants were also told "If you have been assigned to one group, the Advance Directive you complete will have answers to questions checked that will direct health care providers to help relieve pain and suffering even it means not living as long. If you want to choose different options, you will be asked to check off different option and place your initials beside the different option you select." Participants were informed as well that "if you have been assigned to the other group, the Advance Directive you complete will have answers to questions checked that will direct health care providers to prolong your life as much as possible, even if it means you may experience greater pain and suffering."

Notably, this information had little effect on participants' ultimate choices. With respect to particular medical instructions, the default itself had a significant effect; as predicted, more people chose "comfort" when it was the default. But even when people were specifically given the disclosure, signalling "the specific focus of this research" *before* they made their choices, there was no significant consequence for where they ended up.

A possible explanation is that participants thought something like "yeah, whatever" when they read the disclosure. For some of the same reasons that default rules stick – inertia and inattention – disclosures of this kind might have little influence on people's decisions. Here, then, is a general hypothesis: *Even if people are informed that they are being nudged, the effects of the nudge will usually not be reduced, either because people do not care, or because they will not expend the effort to focus on that information.*

But the finding in Loewenstein et al. must be taken with some caution. It involved an online questionnaire, with a low participation rate, and it asked people to consider whether they would make certain choices (which they did not, in fact, have to make in reality). In some contexts, the hypothesis probably will not hold. And it is important to ask how people would react if they were told not only that a default has been chosen and tend to be sticky, but also that it was chosen to promote specific ends, and that it tends to be sticky because many people procrastinate or suffer from inertia. There is a great deal to learn here, and it bears on the ethical questions.

[61] *Id.* at 38.

Informing people that the choice architect has set the default to achieve certain ends could have no effect, but it could actually amplify the effect of the default, or it could reduce that effect by triggering reactance. Suppose, for example, that people were told "Most people do not change the default rule. We want you to save money, and we are automatically enrolling you in a pension plan. We think that you will not opt out, because most people don't; one reason is that they procrastinate." Some disclosures of this kind might make a default stickier, even much stickier, because it increases the informational signal that it contains. A credible explanation, or perhaps any kind of explanation, can fortify the influence of a nudge. But some people might react negatively, thinking, "Oh, you're manipulating people. I don't like that. I'll opt out." How the disclosure is framed could undoubtedly increase the likelihood of one or another reaction. And different subgroups might well react differently.

Or consider transparency with respect to the use of social norms: "Over 70 percent of people engage in behavior X. We are telling you that because we want you to engage in behavior X, and because people like to do what most people do." In that case, the disclosure of the specific motivation for the nudge might increase its impact, but it might also reduce it. Recall that Bovens himself is concerned with transparency about the psychological mechanisms behind nudges. He thinks that if those mechanisms are not "in the dark," nudges will be less effective, and Arad and Rubinstein, discussed earlier, find some indirect support for this claim, especially in Germany.

On this count, Loewenstein et al. did not offer an empirical test. It would be interesting to know if their results would have been different if people had been told something like this: "Default rules often have significant effects on behavior, because of the force of inertia, and because people often think that such rules reflect what most people do." We cannot exclude the possibility that people would rebel if they were informed of the mechanisms that account for the effects of defaults. An understanding of those mechanisms might lead people to be on their guard.

If so, we would want to distinguish between three kinds of nudges: those for which disclosure of the psychological mechanisms would be perceived as innocuous, those for which such disclosure would increase effectiveness, and those for which such disclosure might arouse suspicion and thus decrease effectiveness. Provision of information, reminders, and warnings generally fall in the first or second category. For them, the psychological mechanisms are fairly obvious, and it is hard to see why anyone would be troubled by them. For default rules and uses of social norms, it is possible that disclosure of the mechanisms would produce at least a degree of concern. That question remains to be tested.

It would also be valuable to know if the setting of end-of-life care is distinctive in this respect, and if larger effects, from the disclosure in the Loewenstein et al. experiment, would be found in other contexts. For particular medical instructions, end-of-life care is complex and unpleasant to think about, and for that reason, a default might be especially likely to stick whatever the accompanying disclosures. Consider in this regard the fact that some disclosures have little impact precisely because it is effortful to process them.[62] In contexts that involve less effort, and clearer antecedent preferences, default rules are less likely to stick, and disclosures might make them less sticky still.

Almost certainly, a great deal depends on whether participants believe that choice architects are trustworthy, and also on whether they are generally rebellious "types." If people are told that a self-interested choice architect has chosen a default rule for them, and that default rules usually stick and were chosen for that reason, they might well be willing to reject the rule in question. Recall that some people are "reactors," and if they think that someone is trying to influence them, they might do whatever they can to take their own path.

Even for default rules, the possibility of reactance must be taken into account. But the findings by Loewenstein at al. make it reasonable to speculate that at least in many contexts, disclosure that a nudge is in place, and could be otherwise, would not much affect outcomes.

Five Conclusions

Let me offer five conclusions. First, there is widespread, cross-national support for nudges, at least of the kind that democratic societies have adopted or seriously considered in the recent past. Second, support diminishes when people distrust the motivations of the choice architects, or when they fear that because of inertia and inattention, citizens might end up with outcomes that are inconsistent with their values or their interests. Third, there appears to be greater support for System 2 nudges than for System 1 nudges, though there can be widespread approval of the latter as well, especially if they are meant to combat self-control problems; recall broad support for graphic warning labels for cigarettes.

---

[62] Ryan Bubb, *TMI? Why the Optimal Architecture of Disclosure Remains TBD*, 113 MICH. L. REV. 1021, 1022 (2015).

Fourth, people's assessment of nudges in general can be greatly affected by the political valence of the particular nudges that they have in mind (or that are brought to their minds). Fifth, transparency about nudging should not, in general, reduce the effectiveness of nudges, because most nudges are already transparent, and because people will not, in general, rebel against nudges. The principal qualification to the last point, supported by preliminary evidence, is that in some cases, reactance cannot be ruled out, especially if people do not like or trust the choice architect, and if they believe that they are being tricked or manipulated.

CHAPTER 7

Green by Default? Ethical Challenges for Environmental Protection

I have yet to focus, in detail, on any particular kind of nudge. We can make more progress, and avoid the trap of abstraction, if we explore the ethical issues in a particularly controversial area: environmental protection. In that area, choice architecture has prompted a great deal of recent discussion, with intense focus on ethical questions, not least because of the problem of climate change. One of the distinctive features of environmental problems is that they typically involve externalities, as when the decisions of producers or consumers inflict harms on third parties (in the form, say, of air pollution, water pollution, or waste).

We have seen that while many nudges are meant to reduce the risk that people's decisions will impair their own lives, many other nudges are designed to prevent people from harming others. Such externality-reducing nudges might be a complement to mandates or bans, or corrective taxes; they might be a substitute for them. In either case, the environmental context is an important and illuminating one for considering the ethical issues. Let us now undertake a kind of case study, focusing on possible uses and abuses of choice architecture in that context.

Suppose that in a relevant community, there are two sources of energy, crudely denominated "green" and "gray." Suppose that consistent with its name, "green" is much better than gray on environmental grounds. Those who use green energy emit lower levels of greenhouse gases and of conventional pollutants. Suppose that those who use gray energy save money. Which will consumers select, if they are specifically asked to make a choice?

The obvious response is that the answer will depend on the magnitude of the relevant differences. Suppose that green energy is far better than gray on environmental grounds and that gray energy costs only very slightly less. If so, consumers will be more likely to choose green energy than if it is only slightly better on environmental grounds and if it costs far more. Individual preferences certainly matter. Across a reasonable range of imaginable differences in magnitudes, we would expect to see a great deal of diversity across people, nations, and cultures. Some people do not much care about the environment, and the monetary figures will drive their choices. For other people, environmental protection is an important value; such people are willing to pay a great deal to make the environmentally preferred choice. On standard assumptions, people's decisions will depend on the relationship between economic incentives and underlying preferences.

The standard assumptions are not exactly wrong, but as we have seen, they disregard important variables that do not involve strictly economic incentives. One question involves prevailing social norms.[1] What choices are other people making, and why? If choosers know that most other choosers are selecting green energy, there will be an increase in the likelihood that they will themselves choose green energy. If, by contrast, environmentalists lament the fact that few people are choosing green energy, the result might well be to aggravate the very problem that environmentalists are seeking to solve, by drawing attention to, and thus reinforcing, a social norm that they hope to change.[2] And if there is a widespread belief that reasonable and good people select environmentally preferable products, that norm will exert pressure in favor of green energy.[3] Social norms may well lead behavior in a green or gray direction even in the face of significant economic incentives.[4]

---

[1] See Hunt Alcott, Social Norms and Energy Conservation, 95 J. PUB. ECON. 1082 (2011); Hunt Alcott and Todd Rogers, The Short-Run and Long-Run Effects of Behavioral Interventions (Nat'l Bureau of Econ. Research, Working Paper No. 18492, 2012), available at www.nber.org/papers/w18492.

[2] Robert B. Cialdini et al., Managing Social Norms for Persuasive Impact, 1 SOC. INFLUENCE 3, 10–12 (2006).

[3] See id. at 12. Note in particular the finding that drawing public attention to the existence or pervasiveness of undesirable behavior can actually increase such behavior:

> It is worthy of note that our most ineffective persuasive message simulated the sort of negatively worded, descriptive norm message that ... is regularly sent by public health and community service officials regarding a wide variety of social problems. Our results indicate that appeals of this type should be avoided by communicators in their persuasive undertakings. Unfortunately, this is not always the case. ... For instance, after we reported the outcomes of the present study [showing the ineffectiveness of park signs containing negatively worded, descriptive normative messages] to park administrators, they decided not to change the relevant aspects of their signage. ... We were disappointed – but, truth be told, not surprised – that park officials weighted visitors' subjective responses more than our empirical evidence in their signage decision.

Id.

[4] It is possible, of course, that an emphasis on social norms will trigger adverse reactions and potentially resistance, perhaps especially among younger people. See the discussion of "deviant subcommunities" in Robert A. Kagan and Jerome H. Skolnick, Banning Smoking: Compliance without Enforcement, in SMOKING POLICY: LAW, POLITICS, AND CULTURE 69, 72 (Robert L. Rabin and Stephen D. Sugarman eds., 1993).

My principal topic here is the role of default rules. In the example with which we began, people are asked to make an active choice between green and gray energy. But it is easy to imagine a different approach, one in which choice architects set a default rule in one direction or another, while allowing people to depart from it. In short, social outcomes might be automatically green. Apart from creating a default rule, choice architects may or may not seek to influence people's choices. In fact there is a continuum of possible approaches, whose poles are active choosing (with neutral presentation) and firm mandates (with no ability to opt out), and whose multiple intermediate points include the following:

- active choosing accompanied by self-conscious framing or related influences (meant to encourage either green or gray),
- a pro-green default with costly opt-out,
- a pro-green default with costless opt-out,
- a pro-gray default with costless opt-out,
- a pro-gray default with costly opt-out.

As we shall see, green defaults may well have major effects on environmental outcomes – in some contexts comparable to the effects of mandates and bans, and potentially far larger than the effects of information, education, moral exhortation, and even significant economic incentives.[5] If the goal is to protect the environment, and to save money in the process, default rules are an important tool in the regulatory repertoire, and they may be able to achieve a great deal more than other tools. Especially in a period in which the standard tools – mandates, bans, and economic incentives – sometimes face serious economic and political obstacles, default rules deserve careful attention.

When do they raise ethical problems? When do they intrude on autonomy or compromise dignity? When do they undermine consumer welfare? One of the primary advantages of green defaults is that they can have beneficial effects while maintaining freedom of choice and hence respect for heterogeneity. Suppose, for example, that a relevant population contains a number of people who are facing serious economic difficulty. If so, and if green energy is more expensive than the alternative, it may well be important to allow consumers to opt out (at least if energy subsidies are

---

[5] Raj Chetty et al., *Active vs. Passive Decisions and Crowd out in Retirement Savings Accounts: Evidence from Denmark* (Nat'l Bureau of Econ. Research Working Paper No. 18565, 2012), *available at* www.nber.org/papers/w18565. For electricity products in Germany, *see* Josef Kaenzig et al., *Whatever the Customer Wants, the Customer Gets? Exploring the Gap between Consumer Preferences and Default Electricity Products in Germany*, 53 ENERGY POL'Y 311 (2013).

unavailable). But from the standpoint of social welfare, complications arise by virtue of the fact that default rules are typically selected because they benefit choosers, not third parties; in the environmental context, externalities are frequently involved.

This point suggests that the choice of default rules should turn on an assessment not only of consumer welfare but also of a set of other costs and benefits. If, for example, a green default would have modest costs for consumers, but produce significant social benefits from emissions reductions, it would (by hypothesis) be justified on cost-benefit grounds.

The largest point is that default rules with environmental consequences are pervasive, and they might be green, gray, or somewhere between. When existing defaults are relatively gray, it is not because nature so decreed, but because of emphatically human choices, and these might be otherwise. If public and private institutions seek to make progress on environmental problems – whatever their magnitude – they might well be able to do so by becoming far more self-conscious about selection of the appropriate defaults. Default rules of multiple kinds are already in place, alongside other forms of choice architecture, and they have large effects on outcomes, both economic and environmental, even if they have not been subject to careful scrutiny. Especially in a period in which the world is concerned with the problem of climate change, green defaults deserve serious attention.

Green Defaults: An Illustrative Survey

Daily life is increasingly accompanied by the equivalent of green defaults, replacing grayer ones. Consider motion detectors that turn out the lights when people do not appear to be in the room. In this way, motion detectors create the equivalent of an "off" default. Or consider appliance and computer settings that turn the equipment off when it is not in use. If the default setting on office thermometers is turned down in winter, and up in summer, we should expect significant economic and environmental savings, at least if the default setting is not so uncomfortable that people will take steps to change it.[6] Both policy and technology are making green defaults of this kind readily available. For purposes of illustration, consider four domains in which choice architects may or may not select such defaults.

---

[6] Zachary Brown et al., *Testing the Effects of Defaults on the Thermostat Settings of OECD Employees*, 39 ENERGY ECONOMICS 128 (2013).

Paper

Human beings use a lot of paper, and paper requires use of a large number of trees. Suppose that a private or public institution wants both to save money and to protect the environment by reducing its use of paper. It could, among other things, educate people about the potential value of use reductions ("just the facts"); attempt moral suasion by appealing to economic and environmental values; impose some kind of charge or fee for the use of paper; or impose ceilings on the total amount of paper used by relevant individuals or groups (with an inventive approach being a kind of cap-and-trade system).

But consider a much simpler intervention: Alter the institution's default printer setting from "print on a single page" to "print on front and back." A number of years ago, Rutgers University adopted such a double-sided printing default. In the first three years of the new default, the result was to reduce paper consumption by well over fifty-five million sheets, which amounted to a 44 percent reduction, the equivalent of 4,650 trees.[7] An impressive experiment at a large Swedish university also found a substantial reduction, with a significant and immediate effect in the form of a 15 percent drop in paper consumption, with that effect staying stable over time.[8]

It is evident that if private and public institutions decided in favor of a simple change of the default, they would have a large impact on paper usage. Many people use far more paper than they need only because of the "single page" default; a change would produce significant savings at negligible costs in terms of convenience and changing reading habits. At least in the face of weak preferences, the default has a large effect, even when switching costs are negligible. Notably, that large effect can be found even though strong efforts to encourage people to use double-sided printing have essentially no impact.[9] Also notably, the effect of the double-sided default has been found to be far larger than that of a 10 percent tax on paper products, which would produce a mere 2 percent reduction.[10]

---

[7] *See Print Management Information*, RUTGERS.EDU, *available at* www.nbcs.rutgers.edu/ccf/main/print/transition.php.

[8] *See* Johan Egebark and Mathias Ekström, *Can Indifference Make the World Greener?* (2013), *available at* www2.ne.su.se/paper/wp13_12.pdf.

[9] *Id.*   [10] *Id.* at 20.

Green Energy

I began with a choice between utility suppliers. It is far too simple, of course, to suggest that the available possibilities fall in two dichotomous categories of "green" and "gray." There are multiple options, and the environmental and economic consequences of diverse sources of energy require careful investigation; disputes are easy to find. Recall that the very label "green" can affect consumers, even for candy bars, whether or not the underlying good or service is healthy or protective of the environment. For present purposes, it is sufficient to stipulate that from the environmental point of view, some sources are preferable to others, and consumers might want to consider environmental factors when choosing energy, especially if they can save (or do not lose) money at the same time.

Many jurisdictions do offer some kind of choice. In some nations (including the United States), people are generally defaulted into a particular source, with the option to opt out. Typically, the default is relatively gray (perhaps because some of the green options continue to be expensive). To use green energy, people have to seek out relevant information and choose it affirmatively.[11] The deterrent effects of that requirement are large, even in circumstances in which people would give serious consideration to green options if presented with the choice unaccompanied by a default.

A personal story: Not long ago, my own electricity provider sent me a note, inviting me to send in a form to change to green energy. The form was short and simple, and the idea of switching seemed to me attractive. I decided that I would focus on the issue and send in the form, within a day or two. But of course I lost the form.

What would be the effects of switching to a green default? The question has been examined through studying actual behavior and a series of laboratory experiments.[12]

Actual behavior. In Germany, many people say that they would use green energy if presented with a choice, but for a long period, few consumers actually opted for green; in almost all communities, the green usage rate was at one point under 1 percent (though it has significantly increased in recent

[11] For one example, *see* Mass Energy Consumers Alliance, *Frequently Asked Questions,* www.massenergy.org/renewable-energy/FAQ.
[12] Daniel Pichert and Konstantinos V. Katsikopoulos, *Green Defaults: Information Presentation and Pro-environmental Behaviour,* 28 J. ENVTL. PSYCHOL. 63 (2008).

years).[13] But even when the green usage rate was generally close to zero, two communities showed usage rates well above 90 percent. The reason is simple: They used green defaults.

The first such community is Schönau in the Black Forest, consisting of about 2,500 people and (notably) dominated by conservatives, with a weak Green Party (receiving only about 5 percent of ballots in the relevant time period).[14] In the aftermath of the Chernobyl disaster in the 1980s, a citizen referendum established an environmentally friendly energy supply, in which the Schönau Power Company became the incumbent utility and many of the Schönau citizens became owners of the cooperative. That company promotes solar energy and places a great deal of reliance on renewables. Customers are allowed to opt out and to use other energy sources, but they have to find relevant information in order to identify alternatives. Almost no one opts out: In many years, the opt-out rate was only slightly above 0 percent.

The second natural experiment involves Energiedienst GmbH, which supplies energy to an area in southern Germany. In 1999, the company established three separate tariffs. The default was green, and it turned out to be 8 percent cheaper than the previous tariff. The second option was less green but cheaper (by an additional 8 percent), and the third was greener but more expensive (by an additional 23 percent). If customers did not respond, they would remain with the default. About 94 percent of customers so remained, with 4.3 percent switching to the cheaper tariff, and the rest switching either to the greener alternative or to a different supplier.

These results testify to the extraordinary power of defaults. Recall that elsewhere in Germany, the use of green energy was at the time of the study less than 1 percent, even though many consumers said that they would be willing to pay a premium for it. But outside of the two areas just described, people were required affirmatively to select green energy, and overwhelmingly they did not. It is fair to speculate that at least within a large range, the default rule determines the kind of energy that people use.

A more recent and especially impressive study, based on a later time period, finds the same results.[15] In a large randomized trial, again in Germany, setting the default to green energy increased use of somewhat more expensive green energy nearly *tenfold*. In an opt-in design, political

---

[13] *Id.* at 64.   [14] *Id.* at 66.
[15] Felix Ebeling and Sebastian Lotz, *Domestic Uptake of Green Energy Promoted by Opt-Out Tariffs,* J Nature Climate Change 868 (2015), *available at* www.nature.com/nclimate/journal/vaop/ncurrent/full/nclimate2681.html.

preferences greatly mattered, which is hardly surprising: Being a member of the Green Party was a strong predictor of whether people would opt in. But with a green default, political preferences no longer mattered. Stunningly, the default completely eliminated the effect of environmental preferences.

With that finding, it would be possible to worry that the green default was affecting outcomes without people's conscious awareness, in a way that would raise troubling ethical questions. But follow-up experiments found that worry to be baseless. People were fully aware that they were relying on the green default, and they consciously decided not to opt out. One reason, as we will see, is that a green default triggers feelings of conscience.

Experiments and surveys. Experimental and survey results should be taken with many grains of salt, because they may not predict actual behavior, but they can be informative – and they also find a large effect from green defaults.[16] In one laboratory study, people were presented with a choice between two suppliers. The first, called EcoEnergy, was described in this way: "EcoEnergy sells clean energy, generated from renewable electricity sources. Contribute to climate protection and environmental protection!" The second, called Acon, was described in this way: "We offer low-priced electricity tariff – you cannot beat our prices. Save money with Acon!" The default turned out to matter a great deal. When EcoEnergy was the default, 68 percent of participants stuck with it, but when it was the alternative, only 41 percent of people chose it. Interestingly, about the same percentage of people chose EcoEnergy under conditions of active choice as it was the default.

A related experiment found a significant disparity in economic valuations.[17] Asked how much they would be willing to pay to switch to green energy, people gave a mean value of 6.59 euros. Asked how much they would be willing to *accept* to switch away from green energy, they gave a median value of 13 euros. Interestingly, this difference precisely tracks the standard difference between willingness to pay and willingness to accept; the latter is usually double the former.

In a survey, mentioned in Chapter 6, Simon Hedlin and I found that significantly more people said that they enroll in green energy when it is the default than when they have to opt in.[18] We also found that with a

---

[16] Daniel Pichert and Konstantinos V. Katsikopoulos, *Green Defaults: Information Presentation and Pro-environmental Behaviour*, J. ENVTL. PSYCH., 28, 63–73 (2008).

[17] *Id.*, at 70.

[18] Simon Hedlin and Cass R. Sunstein, *Does Active Choosing Promote Green Energy Use? Experimental Evidence*, ECOLOGY L.Q. (forthcoming), *available at* http://papers.ssrn.com/sol3/papers.cfm?abstract_id=2624359.

green energy default, people feel more guilty about not using green energy than they do with a gray default – and guilt is a good predictor of what people will do. As also noted in Chapter 6, active choosing produced even higher green energy usage rates than green defaults, apparently because of reactance. Recall, however, that survey evidence might well find higher levels of opt-out than would be observed in reality. We cannot know for sure, but my own prediction is that in most real-world settings, automatic enrollment would be far more effective than active choosing. If green is the goal, green defaults are probably best.

Energy Efficiency

Many consumers use products that are significantly less energy efficient than available alternatives. For public policy, a central question is whether and when they will to switch to products that are more efficient and less expensive (at least in the long run). And in some cases, people do have energy-efficient products, and it is possible that they will switch less energy-efficient products that are less expensive (at least in the short run). Independent of the expense of the switch itself, does the default matter?

A series of experiments attempted to answer this question.[19] People were asked to choose between two kinds of light bulbs. One is the efficient but costly compact fluorescent light bulb (CFLB); the other is the inefficient but inexpensive incandescent light bulb (ILB). The choice between the two greatly matters. If every home in the United States changed merely one ILB to a CFLB, the result would be to save over $600 million in annual energy costs, to eliminate greenhouse gas emissions equal to those of more than 800,000 cars, and to save energy that would light over three million homes annually.[20]

In the relevant studies, subjects were told that they were undergoing a significant amount of remodeling of their home and that the contractor had outfitted the light fixtures with either the ILB or the CFLB. Subjects were asked whether they wanted to switch, at no cost, to the alternative. They were also given a great deal of information about the costs and benefits of the two options. For example, the CFB would cost $11 in electricity per 10,000

---

[19] Isaac Dinner et al., *Partitioning Default Effects: Why People Choose Not to Choose*, 17 J. EXPERIMENTAL PSYCHOL.: APPLIED 332 (2011).
[20] *See id.* at 332, citing EnergyStar, *Light Bulbs, available at* www.energystar.gov/products/certified-products/detail/light-bulbs.

hours, whereas the ILB would cost $49 per 10,000 hours. The CFB would cost $3 per bulb whereas the ICB would cost $0.50 per bulb.[21]

The central finding is that the default greatly mattered. When energy-inefficient ICBs were the default, they were chosen nearly 44 percent of the time. When the CFLBs was the default, the ICBs were chosen only 20.2 percent of the time.[22] The disparity is especially noteworthy in view of the fact that in these experiments, people were not in the standard real-world situation of having to overcome inertia and to make a change. They were asked, more simply, whether they would do so, and in that sense they were forced to choose. If they had the option of postponing the decision and simply sticking with the status quo, the disparity would almost certainly be larger.

Smart Grids

Smart grid technology is of considerable interest in many nations,[23] and in Germany in particular, it is a prerequisite for the radical expansion of the share of renewable energy that is needed to realize the German *Energiewende* (a transition in the uses of energy). Such technology has the potential to provide a better balance of the supply and demand of electricity and to make the grid more flexible, efficient, and reliable. In particular, smart meters have increasingly been seen, by the public and private sectors alike, to be useful tools to develop smart energy use patterns through the provision of immediate feedback.[24] The explicit binding goal of the European Union's "Third European Energy Liberalization Package" is that by 2020, smart meter systems will be installed in 80 percent of households.[25] But there are serious obstacles to achievement of this goal, including data privacy concerns and perceived risks of reduced home comfort (part of the electricity consumption is remotely controlled by the energy provider). As a result, many consumers are reluctant to accept this new technology in their homes, and the 80 per-cent target currently seems to be a distant prospect.[26]

---

[21] *Id.* at 341.   [22] *Id.* at 335.

[23] *See, e.g.,* Peter Fox-Penner, Smart Power: Climate Change, the Smart Grid, and the Future of Electric Utilities (2012).

[24] *See id.*

[25] Directive 2009/72/EC, of the European Parliament and of the Council of 13 July 2009 concerning common rules for the internal market in electricity and repealing Directive 2003/54/EC (Text with EEA relevance), 2009 O.J. (L 211) 91; *see also* Institute for Energy & Transport Joint Research Centre, *available at* http://ses.jrc.ec.europa.eu/.

[26] Austrian Energy Agency, *European Smart Metering Landscape Report* (2011), *available at* www.piio.pl/dok/European_Smart_Metering_Landscape_Report.pdf.

If the goal is to get close to the target, what might be done? An experimental study, based on a nationwide panel in Denmark, shows that the implied default greatly affects consumer behavior. More specifically, the acceptance rate to install a smart meter is significantly higher if offered in an "opt-out" frame ("No, I would not like to have a smart meter with remote control installed in my home") than in an opt-in frame.[27] The study confirms that the framing of the question, and the implied default, are likely to have a substantial impact on the share of a population that accepts smart grid installation.

Why Default Rules Matter

Why do default rules have such a large effect on outcomes[28]? There appear to be four contributing factors. While we have briefly encountered each of them, they have distinctive characteristics in the context of green defaults and therefore deserve brief elaboration here.

Suggestion and endorsement. The first factor involves an *implicit suggestion or endorsement* on the part of those who have devised the default rule.[29] Suppose that choice architects, whether private or public, have explicitly chosen a green default. If so, choosers may believe that they have been given an implicit recommendation from people who know what they are doing, and that they should not reject it unless they have reliable private information that would justify a change. If the default choice is double-sided printing or green energy, it is tempting to think that experts, or sensible people, believe that this is the right course of action. Those who are deciding whether to opt out might trust the choice architects well enough to follow their lead.

Many people appear to think that the default was chosen by someone sensible and for a good reason. Especially if they lack experience or expertise and/or if the product is highly complex and rarely purchased,

---

[27] Folke Ölander and John Thøgersen, *Informing or Nudging, Which Way to a More Effective Environmental Policy?*, in Marketing, Food and the Consumer 141 (Joachim Scholderer and Karen Brunsø eds., 2013).

[28] *See, e.g.*, William G. Gale, J. Mark Iwry and Spencer Walters, *Retirement Savings for Middle- and Lower-Income Households: The Pension Protection Act of 2006 and the Unfinished Agenda*, in Automatic 11, 13–14 (William G. Gale et al. eds., 2009); Dinner et al., *Partitioning Default Effects* (2011); Gabriel D. Carroll et al., *Optimal Defaults and Active Choices*, 124 Q. J. Econ. 1639, 1641–1643 (2009).

[29] *See* Craig R. M. McKenzie, Michael J. Liersch, and Stacey R. Finkelstein, *Recommendations Implicit in Policy Defaults*, 17 Psychol. Sci. 414, 418–419 (2006); Brigitte C. Madrian and Dennis F. Shea, *The Power of Suggestion: Inertia in 401(k) Participation and Savings Behavior*, 116 Q. J. Econ. 1149, 1182. Of course it is not true that all defaults are chosen because they produce the best outcomes for people.

they might simply defer to what has been selected for them. The point suggests that default rules are less likely to have an effect when people consider themselves to be experienced or expert, and indeed there are findings to this effect among environmental economists, who reject selected defaults.[30]

Outside of the environmental context, there is strong evidence that a lack of information on the part of choosers, including a lack of information about alternatives, helps to account for the power of defaults.[31] In one study (involving savings behavior), over half of those who stuck with the default specifically mentioned an absence of private information as one of their reasons for doing so.[32] An implication of this explanation is that if choosers do not trust the choice architect, in general or in the particular instance, they will be far more likely to opt out. And indeed, there is evidence for this proposition as well.[33] If choice architects select a green default for reasons that are perceived as self-serving, elitist, preachy, or foolish, we would expect to see an increase in the rate of opt-out. Green defaults are more likely to stick if choosers trust those who have selected them, or at least perceive no reason to distrust them. As we have also seen, people who are prone to reactance, or who generally distrust choice architects, might not be so interested in the recommendation that they have offered.

Inertia. The second explanation involves inertia and procrastination (sometimes described as "effort" or an "effort tax"[34]). To change the default rule to either green or gray, people must make an active choice to reject that rule. They have to focus on the relevant question, which is whether and how they should trade off environmental, economic, and perhaps other goods. Especially but not only if the question is difficult or technical, and if the trade-off is complex or morally charged, it may be tempting to defer the decision or not to make it at all. In view of the power of inertia and the tendency to procrastinate, people may simply continue with the status quo.

---

[30] Asa Lofgren et al., *Are Experienced People Affected by a Pre-set Default Option – Results from a Field Experiment*, 63 J. ENVTL. ECON. AND MGMT. 66 (2012).

[31] *See* Jeffrey Brown et al., *The Downside of Defaults* (unpublished manuscript) (2011), *available at* www.nber.org/programs/ag/rrc/NB11-01%20Brown,%20Farrell,%20Weisbenner%20FINAL.pdf.

[32] *See id.*

[33] *See* David Tannenbaum and Peter Ditto, *Information Asymmetries in Default Options* 11–17 (unpublished manuscript) (2012), *available at* https://webfiles.uci.edu/dtannenb/www/documents/default%20information%20asymmetries.pdf.

[34] *See* Eric Johnson and Daniel Goldstein, *Decisions by Default*, in THE BEHAVIORAL FOUNDATIONS OF POLICY 417 (Eldar Shafir ed., 2013).

A striking example can be found in Germany. In periods in which increasing energy prices were headline news in German media, and caused considerable concern to consumers, most households remained in the basic tariff of the energy provider. This is so even though the basic tariff is usually more expensive than one fitting the household's actual use patterns and may also be more expensive than green energy.[35] In a two-year period only 22 percent of German households switched their tariff or provider – strong evidence of the power of inertia.[36]

In many cases involving environmental values, the decision whether to select green energy involves some thinking, some risk, and a potentially complex (and morally charged) assessment of economic and environmental considerations. The choice of an electricity provider is not exactly intuitive; it may well be cognitively demanding. The default rule might stick simply because people do not want to engage in that thinking, take that risk, or make that trade-off. Studies of brain activity find that when decisions are complex and difficult, people are more likely to stick with the default.[37] Even if people in some sense want to investigate the issue and possibly to make a change, they might decide that they will do so tomorrow – and tomorrow never comes.

Reference point and loss aversion. A third and especially interesting explanation stresses the fact that the default rule establishes the *reference point* for people's decisions. Recall the behavioral finding of loss aversion. People dislike losses far more than they like corresponding gains,[38] and whether a loss or a gain is involved does not come from nature or from the sky. The default rule determines what counts as a loss and what counts as a gain.

---

[35] *See* regular product tests and price comparisons of energy providers offers conducted by the Stiftung Warentest, *available at* www.test.de; *see, e.g., Stiftung Warentest empfiehlt Versorgerwechsel,* Stiftung Warentest (November 20, 2012), *available at* www.test.de/presse/pressemitteilungen/Hoehere-Strompreise-Stiftung-Warentest-empfiehlt-Versorgerwechsel-4472100-0/.

[36] Infas Energiemontor 2012, *available at* www.infas.de/fileadmin/images/aktuell/infas_Abb_Energiemarktmonitor.pdf.

[37] S. Fleming, C. L. Thomas, and R. J. Dolan, *Overcoming Status Quo Bias in the Human Brain,* 107 PROC. NAT'L ACAD. OF SCI. 6005–6009 (2010).

[38] *See* Richard H. Thaler, Daniel Kahneman, and Jack L. Knetsch, *Experimental Tests of the Endowment Effect and the Coase Theorem,* in RICHARD H. THALER, QUASI RATIONAL ECONOMICS 167, 169 (1994); A. Peter McGraw et al., *Comparing Gains and Losses,* 21 PSYCHOL. SCI. 1438, 1444 (2010). Vivid evidence of loss aversion can be found in David Card and Gordon B. Dahl, *Family Violence and Football: The Effect of Unexpected Emotional Cues on Violent Behavior,* 126 Q. J. ECON. 103, 105–106, 130–135 (2011) (finding an increase in domestic violence after a favored team suffers from an upset loss in football).

To appreciate the power of loss aversion and its relationship to default rules, consider an illuminating study of teacher incentives.[39] Many people have been interested in encouraging teachers to do better to improve their students' achievements. The results of providing economic incentives are decidedly mixed; many of these efforts have failed.[40] But the relevant study enlists loss aversion by resetting the default. The authors gave teachers money in advance and told them that if students did not show real improvements, *the teachers would have to give the money back.* The result was a significant improvement in math scores – indeed, an improvement equivalent to what would result from a substantial improvement in teacher quality. The underlying idea here is that losses from the status quo are especially unwelcome, and people will work hard to avoid those losses.[41]

Return in this light to default rules and the question of energy efficiency. Suppose that as compared to the gray (energy-inefficient) choice, the green option costs $200 more upfront but saves $210 over five years. If the gray option is the default, people are likely to focus on the immediate loss of $200, and they will be highly reluctant to incur that loss. Perhaps the $210 savings will overcome their reluctance – but the immediate $200 loss will likely loom large. If, by contrast, the green option is the default, people are more likely to focus on the eventual loss of $210, and they will be highly reluctant to incur that loss. In the environmental context, loss aversion may have an especially significant effect, certainly in the case of green defaults.

In this respect, the default may well interact with, and help to establish or reinforce, prevailing social norms. Recall that some people make environmentally friendly choices because they want to "make a statement." If opting out produces environmental as well as economic harm, it may entail a statement that consumers do not want to make – and this is so even if they would not have opted in.

---

[39] *See* Roland Fryer et al., *Enhancing the Efficacy of Teacher Incentives through Loss Aversion* (Nat'l Bureau of Econ. Research, Working Paper No. 18237, 2012), *available at* www.nber.org/papers/w18237.pdf.

[40] *See id.*

[41] For a valuable discussion of loss aversion and its importance, *see* Tatiana A. Homonoff, *Can Small Incentives Have Large Effects? The Impact of Taxes versus Bonuses on Disposable Bag Use?* (unpublished manuscript) (March 27, 2013), *available at* www.human.cornell.edu/pam/people/upload/Homonoff-Can-Small-Incentives-Have-Large-Effects.pdf. Homonoff shows that small, five-cent tax on the grocery bags, in the District of Columbia, has had a significant effect in reducing grocery bag use – but that a small, five-cent bonus for using reusable bags had essentially no effect.

Guilt. A final factor, of particular importance in the environmental setting, is guilt. Some decisions have an evident moral component, and a default rules can press moral buttons. Consider the case of cheating. Most people will not take action to cheat the government or their fellow citizens. But if the government or a fellow citizens makes a mistake in your favour, and if profiting from that mistake is the default, you might be willing to stick with it.

Empirical evidence suggests that when the default is green, people can feel quite guilty about opting out – at least if they think that there are good moral reasons to stay with the default, as in the cases of reusing towels at hotels or receiving electronic, rather than paper, statements.[42] In the environmental context, green defaults might trigger intense feelings of guilt and be especially effective for that reason. People might also feel moral compunctions about not switching from gray energy to green energy – but if the default is gray, the level of guilt, from sticking with the status quo, might not be high.

When Default Rules Do Not Stick

In some cases, people are willing to switch the default and possibly to reject the greener outcome. To see why, consider an illuminating study of the effects of a default thermostat setting on employees of the Organisation for Economic Co-operation and Development (OECD).[43]

During the winter, the experimenters decreased the default setting by one degree Celsius. The result was a significant reduction in the average chosen setting, apparently because most employees were not much bothered by the new default and hence did not take the time to change it. Small as it was, the cost of that effort did not justify the bother, because people were not uncomfortable enough to act. But when the default setting was reduced by two degrees Celsius, the reduction in the average chosen setting was actually smaller – apparently because sufficient numbers of employees thought that it was too cold and so returned the setting to the one that they preferred.

The basic lesson here is simple and profound: *People will generally go along with the default, except when it makes them too cold.* We should

---

[42] Aristeidis Theotokis and Emmanouela Manganari, *The Impact of Choice Architecture on Sustainable Consumer Behavior: The Role of Guilt*, 131 J. Bus. Ethics 423–437 (2014).

[43] Zachary Brown et al., *Testing the Effects of Defaults on the Thermostat Settings of OECD Employees*, 39 Energy Econ. 128 (2013).

understand the idea of "too cold" as a metaphor for a range of negative reactions, including a loss of money or a threat to personal values. If a default rule really makes people uncomfortable, they will reject it. Note as well that when experienced people – environmental economists attending a conference – were presented with a default number for carbon dioxide offsets for flying, they were unaffected by that number.[44] The reason is that the environmental economists knew what they wanted, and they chose it, whatever the default. And in the study of energy-efficient light bulbs, the default rule was only mildly sticky. Even when it was the default, the energy-inefficient light bulb was rejected by about 56 percent of choosers.[45] We could easily imagine populations that would reject the energy-efficient choice in equal or higher numbers, especially if the less efficient option cost a great deal less and if, in that population, environmental considerations did not loom large.

When default rules do not stick, the reason is usually straightforward: People have clear preferences that run counter to them. If preferences are clear, people are less likely to be influenced by the endorsement in the default rule. Inertia may well be overcome. Loss aversion will be far less relevant, in part because the clear preference helps define the reference point from which losses are measured. And if people know what they want, they will not feel guilty in trying to get it.

Suppose that consumers are defaulted into an energy source that costs 50 percent more than the alternative. Unless social norms or inertia are particularly strong, consumers will reject that default. For supportive evidence, consider both the evidence presented earlier and a study in the United Kingdom, which found that most people opted out of a savings plan with an unusually high (and therefore unattractive) default contribution rate (12 percent of before-tax income).[46] Only about 25 percent of employees remained at that rate after a year, whereas about 60 percent of employees shifted to a lower default contribution rate. Notably, people with lower incomes were more likely to stay at the unusually high contribution rate.[47] Similar findings have been made elsewhere, with growing

---

[44] Lofgren et al., *Are Experienced People Affected by a Pre-Set Default Option – Results from a Field Experiment* (2012).

[45] Recall, however, that the study was a laboratory experiment, not a randomized trial. If people actually had to take steps to change the default – rather than merely answering questions about whether they would do so – the switch rate would likely have been smaller.

[46] *See* John Beshears et al., *The Limitations of Defaults* 8 (unpublished manuscript) (Sept. 15, 2010), *available at* www.nber.org/programs/ag/rrc/NB10-02,%20Beshears,%20Choi,%20Laibson,%20 Madrian.pdf.

[47] *Id.*

evidence that those who are less educated, and less sophisticated, are more likely to stick with the default.[48] Note as well the finding that while school children could well be nudged (through the functional equivalent of default rules) into healthier choices, researchers were not able to counteract the children's strong preference for (unhealthy) French fries.[49]

The clear implication is that highly unwelcome defaults are less likely to stick. It follows that green defaults that are perceived as foolish, wrong, harmful, expensive, or the imposition of some high-minded environmentalist elite may well be rejected by many consumers. A more puzzling and somewhat troubling implication, based on the lower incomes of those who stayed with the default in the savings study described earlier, is that default rules may be more sticky for low-income workers than for their higher-earning counterparts. One reason may be that low-income workers have a great deal to worry about[50] and so are less likely to take the trouble to think through and to alter the default rule.

Of course it is true that wealthy people may have many decisions to make, but they can also take a lot for granted. An "effort tax" may seem especially high for, and have an especially large adverse effect on, people who are already facing a large number of difficult or life-stabilizing decisions and costs. Supportive evidence can be found in Germany, where low socioeconomic status (SES) households tend to stay with their energy provider while higher SES households tend to switch.[51]

This point suggests that a costly green default may have a regressive impact, both because poor people have less money and because they may well be especially likely to stick with it. And indeed, there is general evidence that when people are highly informed and experienced, and hence know what they want, they are far less likely to be affected by the default rule.[52] One reason is that the effort tax is worth incurring. Another reason is that some people actually enjoy searching extensively and making their choice independently of defaults.

---

[48] Jeffrey Brown et al., *The Downside of Defaults* (unpublished manuscript) (2011), *available at* www.nber.org/programs/ag/rrc/NB11-01%20Brown,%20Farrell,%20Weisbenner%20FINAL.pdf.

[49] *See* David J. Just and Brian Wansink, *Smarter Lunchrooms: Using Behavioural Economics to Improve Meal Selection*, 24 CHOICES (2009), *available at* www.choicesmagazine.org/magazine/pdf/article_87.pdf.

[50] *See* ABHIJIT BANERJEE AND ESTHER DUFLO, POOR ECONOMICS (2010); Shah et al., *Some Consequences of Having Too Little*, 338 SCIENCE 682–685.

[51] Infas Energiemontor (2012), http://perma.law.harvard.edu/0AWnxhdhJrk.

[52] *See* Åsa Lofgren et al., *Are Experienced People Affected by a Pre-Set Default Option – Results from a Field Experiment*, 63 J. ENVTL. ECON. & MGMT. 66 (2012).

Green or Gray?

Now turn to this question, with evident ethical dimensions: Which default rule should choice architects select? A full analysis of policy instruments must consider the effects of those instruments on social welfare, and that analysis is not provided by a demonstration that, say, a green default rule significantly increases use of green energy. Among other things, it is necessary to understand the social benefits of any such increase. Are the effects on environmental quality (including human health) large or small? Is there a significant reduction of greenhouse gas emissions? What is the social cost of carbon? It is also necessary to understand the costs. Are consumers paying more? If so, how much more? In view of the answers to these questions, a switch to green energy may or may not have significant net benefits.

In addition, a corrective tax, or some system of cap and trade, is usually the preferred instrument for producing an optimal level of pollution.[53] By definition, such an approach should be efficient. A default rule in favor of green energy, in the abstract, is likely to be inferior to a corrective tax (including a carbon tax). Nonetheless, efforts to increase use of green energy are an important part of the mix of policy instruments, and they might avoid some of the political constraints that apply to both corrective taxes and cap-and-trade.

Consumers (Without Externalities)

For purposes of simplification, begin with the case in which the only concern is the welfare of the chooser and there are no (or only modest) externalities. For reasons explored in Chapter 3, the preferred approach is to select the default rule that reflects what most people would choose if they were adequately informed. If we know that a particular default rule would place people in the situation that informed people would select, we have good reason to select that default rule (with the understanding that those who differ from the majority may opt out). This test respects people's autonomy; it does not offend their dignity; and it is likely to promote their welfare.

In the easiest cases, the answer is entirely clear once we specify the likely effects of the options in question. If green energy would both cost less and reduce environmental harm, it is safe to say that most informed people

---

[53] For clear and superb discussion, *see* WILLIAM NORDHAUS, CLIMATE CASINO (2014).

would choose it. It should certainly be default. Under the specified circumstances, those who want consumers to make different choices will not find it easy to explain their views. Indeed, some options should be ruled out of bounds because they are obviously in no one's interest.

Now suppose that the trade-off is not so self-evident, but that we have reason to believe that 80 percent of people, given a great deal of information, would choose green energy. This might be the case if either (1) green energy is far better on environmental grounds but only very slightly more expensive or (2) the relevant population is known to have strong environmental commitments. In either case, there is a strong reason to favor automatic enrollment in green energy. But if gray energy would cost significantly less than green, and if it would be only slightly worse on environmental grounds, a gray energy default would seem best.

To be sure, it might well be necessary to do a great deal of empirical work in order to identify the approach that informed people would choose. (As we shall see, this is a point in favor of active choosing.) On this count, actual evidence – about what informed choosers do – is extremely important. It would be useful to assemble information about the level of opt-out under various alternatives. Perhaps experiments or pilot programs would provide such information. If only 2 percent of people opt out if green energy is the default, and 50 percent opt out if gray energy is the default, we have reason to believe that green energy is better.

Of course it is possible that majority rule is too crude. Suppose that there are two default rules, green and gray. Suppose that 55 percent of informed people would be relatively indifferent between green and gray but would slightly prefer green. Suppose too that because of their unusual situation (perhaps they are poor), 45 percent of people would strongly prefer gray. It might be best to select gray, because almost half of the population would much like it, and the (narrow) majority only cares a little bit. The example shows that it is important to ask not only about which approach would be preferred by informed people, but also about the intensity of their preferences. Of course it is also true that people with intense preferences are more likely to opt out, which makes for a reasonable argument, in the case just given, on behalf of green.

Consumers and Third Parties

In the environmental context, externalities are pervasive; they may well be the principal motivation for a green default rule. Choosers may also face a collective action problem. Asked individually, they might rationally select gray energy, but they might prefer green energy if everyone else were doing so as well (a possibility that argues for a firm mandate rather than a mere default rule). If choice architects are deciding among defaults in the presence of externalities and collective action problems, they must investigate the full set of costs and benefits, not only the welfare of choosers. If a default rule turned out to stick, what would be the costs and what would be the benefits?

Consider the question whether the default rule should favor one-sided paper or two. We would need to know something about the relevant population to know which of these would be best from the individual standpoint. In the abstract, the answer is not obvious. Perhaps choosers are generally indifferent as choosing between one-sided and two-sided copies; perhaps they strongly favor one or the other. If choice architects have no idea, they might ask people to choose. But it is easy to imagine situations in which individuals are relatively indifferent and the externalities are decisive. The best approach would be to quantify those effects. If the effects are significant, they will argue strongly for a double-sided default even if the majority of choosers would prefer single-sided. It is of course relevant that those who dislike the default can opt out. And it is true that if the externalities are especially large, a mandate starts to look more attractive on economic and ethical grounds.

Or return to the case of green energy. Even if most choosers would select gray because it is less expensive, green might be the better default if it would avoid significant costs. Perhaps certain energy sources produce far less in the way of air pollution. If so, there would be strong reason to select a default rule that reduces such pollution. Suppose that we focus narrowly on greenhouse gas emissions. In recent years, a great deal of work has been done to attempt to specify the social cost of carbon (SCC).[54] In 2010, a technical working group in the United States settled on an SCC of about $23 (2013 dollars)[55]; in 2013, the number was updated to about $37.[56] We

---

[54] *See* Interagency Working Group on Social Cost of Carbon, *Technical Support Document: Social Cost of Carbon for Regulatory Impact Analysis under Executive Order 12866* (2010), *available at* www.epa.gov/oms/climate/regulations/scc-tsd.pdf. For an illuminating critique, *see* William Nordhaus, *Estimates of the Social Cost of Carbon* (unpublished manuscript), *available at* www.econ.yale.edu/~nordhaus/homepage/documents/CFDP1826.pdf.

[55] *See* Interagency Working Group on Social Cost of Carbon, *Technical Support Document: Social Cost of Carbon for Regulatory Impact Analysis under Executive Order 12866* (2010).

[56] Interagency Working Group on Social Cost of Carbon, *Technical Support Document: Updated Social Cost of Carbon for Regulatory Impact Analysis under Executive Order 12866* (2013), *available at* www.whitehouse.gov/sites/default/files/omb/inforeg/social_cost_of_carbon_for_ria_2013_update.pdf.

could easily imagine cases in which the avoidance of greenhouse gases would produce significant gains, so that a green default would be simple to justify even if it turned out to be more expensive for users. Ideally, choice architects would monetize all of the relevant costs associated with relevant energy users and set a default rule accordingly. Of course it is true that the assessment could create serious empirical challenges both in monetizing the relevant benefits and in projecting the level of opt-out.

Distributional issues may be important as well. Suppose, for example, that the cost-benefit analysis argues in favor of a green default, but that the selection of that default imposes net costs on consumers, including poor people. Suppose too that poor people are unlikely to opt out, perhaps because they are busy and occupied with other matters, perhaps because they are not confident that opting out makes best sense. If poor people would in fact be net losers but would not opt out, the argument for a green default is weakened. If it is chosen, it may be important to explore the possible of financial subsidies for those who pay for it or to make the possibility of opt-out both salient and clear, at least if the latter can be achieved without endangering the goals that led to the default rule in the first instance.

Active Choosing, Influenced Choice, and Personalization

We have seen that choice architects might dispense with a default rule entirely. For example, they might require people to make an active choice between green and gray options. Markets provide an array of active choices, and while the relevant architecture affects what consumers ultimately select, no default rule need be involved.

Consider a "menu approach" to the question of energy efficiency and fuel economy, in which people have a wide range of options, and they may select what best fits their preferences and situations (perhaps with legal restrictions on the most energy-inefficient possibilities). The menu approach captures a great deal of the current situation. For example, there is active competition in the markets for motor vehicles and appliances, and energy efficiency is one dimension along with producers compete. No default rule is generally in place for private households.

Neutrality and Active Choice

With active choices, people are required to make an actual decision among the various options; they are not defaulted into any particular alternative.

In the environmental domain, active choosing has a number of significant advantages, certainly over opt-in (requiring consumers to reject the default to arrive at the environmentally preferred result), and sometimes over opt-out as well.

Green by choice? The first point is that because an actual decision is required, active choosing promotes agency and personal responsibility, and it also overcomes inertia. In these respects, it might be better than either opt-in or opt-out. Suppose that people are using gray energy not because they have affirmatively decided to do so, but because gray is the default, and they have not focused on the options. If inertia and procrastination are playing a significant role, active choosing may be far preferable to opt-in. We have also encountered several arguments on behalf of "boosts." In the environmental context, active choosing might be accompanied by educative nudges, which could stand people in good stead for all of their lives.

Active choosing is also a safeguard against uninformed or self-interested choice architects. When choice architects lack relevant information, so that the chosen rule might be harmful to some or many, there are significant advantages to active choosing. If public officials are biased or inadequately informed, and if the default rule is no better than a guess, that rule might lead people in the wrong direction. We have seen that the choice between green and gray defaults may well create serious empirical challenges. In the face of those challenges, the best route might be to ask consumers what they would like (again, in the absence of significant externalities).

There is also a strong argument against a default rule, and in favor of active choosing, when self-interested private groups are calling for government to select it even though it would not benefit those on whom it is imposed. In the environmental context, it is easy to imagine a high degree of interest-group jockeying, in which self-interested producers argue vigorously on behalf of a default rule that would benefit them; the choice of energy sources may well invite that kind of jockeying. Active choosing would reduce the risks on this count, because it would not allow public officials to default consumers into any particular source.

Finally, and in some cases most important, active choosing appropriately handles diversity. As compared with either opt-in or opt-out, active choosing can have major advantages when the relevant group is heterogeneous, so that a single approach is unlikely to fit diverse circumstances. (The issue of personalization is taken up later.)

No panacea. Notwithstanding its important advantages and the frequent appeal of the menu approach, active choosing will sometimes run into legitimate objections, especially in the environmental context. The initial objection is not obscure: In the face of significant externalities, it may seem odd to ask consumers to choose for themselves. Of course some consumers may attend to those externalities and make their selections accordingly. Social norms, moral convictions, self-perception, and signaling may well incline them in that direction. But if a central goal is to reduce air pollution and emissions of greenhouse gases, active choosing may well be inadequate.

An independent problem is that active choosing can impose large burdens on choosers. That burden may be costly or unwelcome. Suppose that an environmental question is unfamiliar and complicated. Suppose that consumers lack information or experience. In the context of energy choices, many consumers may welcome a default, which will relieve them of the duty of having to focus on an issue that they would like to ignore. At the same time, active choosing can impose large burdens on providers. Defaults can be desirable and even important for those who provide goods or services. Without default rules, significant resources might have to be devoted to patient, tedious explanations and to going through the various options with consumers or users, who might not welcome the exercise.

A final point is that active choosing can increase errors. The goal of active choosing is to make people better off. But if the area is unfamiliar, highly technical, and confusing, active choosing might have the opposite effect. If consumers are required to answer a set of technical questions about energy options, and if the choice architects know what they are doing, then people will probably enjoy better outcomes with defaults. Perhaps it would be best to rely on experiments or pilot studies that elicit choices from informed people, and then to use those choices to build defaults. But if choice architects have technical expertise and are trustworthy, there is a question whether this exercise would be worthwhile.

A very simple conclusion. Notwithstanding imaginable debates, a sensible conclusion is that if choice architects have reason to be confident that a particular default would be fit with the interests and the values of choosers, they should select it. But if the assessment is difficult, and if their judgment is highly tentative, they should rely on active choosing, at least if the externalities are not large.

An intermediate approach, perhaps the best of both worlds, might be called *simplified active choosing*. With this approach, people are asked whether they want to make their own choice or instead rely on a default rule. The beauty of simplified active choosing is that if people want to go with the default, they can easily do so – but they are not put in a position in which inertia or procrastination might place them in a situation that they do not like. With simplified active choosing, people can, in effect, actively choose the default. The most serious problem with that approach is that sometimes people would not like to do even that; they would much prefer a default rule. And of course simplified active choosing may not be enough in cases of significant externalities.

Influenced Active Choosing

It is possible to imagine a variety of variations on active choosing. For example, active choosing might be "enhanced," or influenced, in the sense that one of the choices might be highlighted or favored, perhaps through the use of behaviorally informed strategies.[57] If choice architects intend to avoid a default rule but nonetheless want to promote selection of a green option, they might list it first, or use bold or a large font, or adopt verbal descriptions that make it especially salient or appealing.

Consider a relevant study in which choice was enhanced, in the sense of being influenced, by enlisting loss aversion to discourage selection of the option disfavored by the experimenters.[58] The experimenters introduced several different messages in the following way:

> We would like you to imagine that you are interested in protecting your health. The Center for Disease Control indicates that a flu shot significantly reduces the risk of getting or passing on the flu virus. Your employer tells you about a hypothetical program that recommends you get a flu shot this Fall and possibly save $50 off your bi-weekly or monthly health insurance contribution cost.

In the *opt-in condition*, people were asked to "Place a check in the box if you will get a flu shot this Fall." In a *neutral active choice condition*, people were asked to "Place a check in one box: I will get a flu shot this Fall or, I will not get a flu shot this Fall." With *enhanced or influenced choice*, people were asked to choose between two alternatives: "I will get a flu shot this Fall to reduce my risk of getting the flu and I want to save $50 or, I will not get a flu shot this Fall even if it means I may increase my risk of getting the flu and I don't want to save $50." Compared to opt-in, the active choice condition led to a significant increase in the percentage of people who would get a flu shot – and the percentage was highest when active choice was influenced.

[57] *See* Punam Anand Keller et al., *Enhanced Active Choice: A New Method to Motivate Behavior Change*, 21 J. CONSUMER PSYCHOL. 376 (2011).
[58] *Id.*

We could easily imagine analogues in the environmental context. If a green default is rejected, but if there is nonetheless good reason to promote the green option, loss aversion and framing might be enlisted to encourage people to select it. The result would almost certainly be to increase the number of people who choose that option. The general point is that active choosing can be more or less neutral with respect to green and gray options. As the choice architect becomes decreasingly neutral, active choosing starts to look closer to a default rule. But so long as choosing is active, those who favor agency and personal responsibility should be comfortable with it.

Green Personalization? Gray Personalization?

Thus far the assumption has been that default rules apply to all of a relevant population ("mass defaults"), but some default rules are highly personalized. Personalized defaults draw on available information about which approach is sought by, or best suits, different groups of people, and potentially each individual person, in the relevant population. In the context of travel preferences, personalized defaults are increasingly familiar. A website might know where you like to sit, which airline you prefer, and how you like to pay. A bit like a close friend, a sibling, a partner, or a spouse, it defaults you into your preferred choices while allowing you to opt out.

In the fullness of time, the same will be possible for a wide range of consumer products. Personalization might also be possible for choices that affect the environment. Choice architects might know, for example, that certain people like single-sided or double-sided printing, or are highly likely to be drawn to green or gray energy. The best evidence would be their past choices. If consumers have made green choices in the past, we might expect that they will do so in the future and set defaults accordingly (while of course allowing opt out). Lacking that evidence, choice architects might know relevant demographic or other factors, suggesting that certain people or certain communities would or would not prefer green energy.

If the goal is to reflect the likely choices of consumers, personalized default rules have significant advantages. But a potential problem remains: If there are significant externalities, the interests of choosers are not the only consideration, and the default rule should be chosen only after consideration of the full set of social effects. And of course any effort to promote personalization must contain sufficient safeguards for personal privacy.

A Framework

We have now seen a large number of options that choice architects might consider, and it will be useful to offer a brief sketch of a general framework, based on the discussion thus far, that might be used to select among the various options. The framework is designed for situations in which environmental factors are particularly relevant, but it might well be adapted more generally.

Choice architects might be in a position to choose among a continuum of nine stylized possibilities, marked from most green to most gray:

(1) green mandate or ban;
(2) green default with costly opt-out;
(3) green default with costless opt-out;
(4) active choosing with pro-green presentation of some kind;
(5) active choosing with neutral presentation;
(6) active choosing with pro-gray presentation of some kind;
(7) gray default with costless opt-out;
(8) gray default with costly opt-out;
(9) gray mandate or ban.

As we have seen, an appealing general framework is rooted in some kind of cost-benefit analysis, bracketing some of the debates over that contested idea. And of course the ideas of "green" and "gray" are not unitary and include possibilities that can themselves be arrayed along a continuum; the same is true of "costless" and "costly" opt-out.

An implication of the discussion thus far is that without a market failure of some sort, the argument for any kind of mandate or ban is usually weak. If the interests of choosers are all that is at stake, their own freedom should generally be preserved, so long as their choices are properly informed (see Chapter 8 for more details). On the continuum, this conclusion rules out the more aggressively regulatory poles (1) and (9). The choice among the remaining options depends on an analysis of which approach is in the interest of choosers and the confidence that choice architects have about their conclusion on that count. If they have reason for real confidence that a green or gray default is best (from the standpoint of all or most informed choosers), they should choose that default (perhaps with personalization, if feasible). In such cases, the decision costs and error costs associated with active choosing may well be too high to justify that approach.

If choice architects lack such confidence, the set of reasonable options narrows to points (2) through (6) (the middle of the continuum). Active choosing with neutral presentation is appealing if choice architects do not know which approach is best, perhaps because they lack information, perhaps because the relevant population is heterogeneous. If choice architects know enough to favor one or another approach, but not enough to set a default, they might use active choosing with some kind of non-neutral presentation, meant to incline choosers in a particular direction.

Of course the analysis must be different in the face of externalities. If the decisions of choosers would impose significant costs on others, the argument for a mandate or a ban is significantly strengthened and may be convincing (with an acknowledgment that mandates and bans come in different forms, and some approaches are less costly and more choice-preserving than others). Sometimes, however, mandates or bans are not feasible for political reasons, and sometimes there is a reasonable dispute about whether they are justified. In such cases, there is a serious argument for a green default, even if it is not necessarily in the interest of choosers themselves. The strength of that argument depends on whether the externalities are large and whether choosers would be significantly helped, or instead hurt, by a green default. A form of cost-benefit analysis is indispensable here. In the face of externalities, the "less green" points on the continuum lack much appeal, and the only potential argument in their favor is that the externalities are modest and that choosers would be far better off with a grayer approach.

Distributional questions must also be considered. If a mandate would have serious adverse effects on those at the bottom of the economic ladder, those effects should be taken into account. We have seen that a personalized approach, exempting those who cannot easily bear the relevant costs, might well make sense. And in the face of a well-justified mandate or ban, perhaps steps could be taken to give economic help to those who need it.

Environmental Ethics

Economic incentives are of course exceedingly important, but with respect to the environment, consumer choices are greatly affected by a wide range of influences, including social norms and the applicable default rule. When the automatic choice is not green, it might well take a great deal of work for people to identify and to select environmentally preferable approaches. Even when that work seems relatively easy, people may not do it (in part because of inertia and procrastination), and the results may include both economic and environmental harm.

Green defaults are easiest to justify when they will simultaneously save money and protect the environment; consider motion detectors, automatic "off" defaults, and double-sided printing defaults. No one should favor a situation in which choice architects select defaults that cost consumers a great deal (perhaps in terms of money, perhaps in terms of privacy) and deliver only modest environmental benefits. Some of the hard cases arise when the green default would cost consumers a nontrivial amount but would also produce significant environmental benefits.

In such cases, choice architects have two reasonable options. The first is to call for active choosing (and to inform consumers in the process). The second is to assess costs and benefits and to select the default rule on the basis of the assessment. The choice between the reasonable options depends on whether choice architects have justified confidence in the assessment of costs and benefits. If they do, and if the assessment demonstrates that the green default is unambiguously superior, they should choose it.

However the hardest cases are resolved, the basic point is clear. In important contexts, outcomes are harmful to the environment and to the economy, not because consumers have actively chosen to impose those harms, but because of the relevant choice architecture. In some cases, the architecture cannot be changed by individual consumers, and some kind of collective action, whether private or public, is necessary to supply a corrective. In other cases, the architecture is effectively a default rule, as in the cases of double-sided printing and gray energy sources. In such cases, active choosing may well have significant advantages.

At least some of the time, however, the best approach is automatically green. Well-chosen default rules, attentive to the full set of costs and benefits, are likely to emerge as a significant contributor to efforts to protect human health and the environment – potentially more effective, in many cases, than either information and education or substantial economic incentives. In an era in which public officials all over the world are focussing on the problem of climate change, green defaults deserve serious and sustained attention.

CHAPTER 8

Mandates

Nudges preserve freedom of choice. But in light of behavioral findings, demonstrating the occasional human propensity to blunder, some people have been asking whether mandates and bans have a fresh justification, with a newly firm ethical foundation.[1] The motivation for that question is clear: If we know that people's choices lead them in the wrong direction, why should we insist on freedom of choice? Is such freedom always in people's own interests? In the face of human errors, isn't it odd, or even perverse, to insist on that form of freedom? Isn't especially odd to do so if we know that in many contexts, people choose not to choose?

It should be agreed that if a mandate would clearly increase social welfare, there is a strong argument on its behalf. Of course we would have to specify what social welfare means,[2] but if we can agree on a rough definition, we will find many cases where mandates make sense. Following Mill, we can see that the argument on their behalf is most secure when third parties are at risk. As we have seen, no one believes that nudges are a sufficient approach to the problem of violent crime. No one thinks that people get to choose whether to steal or to assault. We have also seen that in the face of a standard market failure, coercion has a familiar justification; consider the problem of air pollution. It is true that even in such contexts, nudges may have an important role; recall the possibility of default rules in favor of clean energy. But the effects of nudges, taken by themselves, might well prove too modest for the problem at hand, and they hardly exhaust

---

[1] *See* SARAH CONLY, AGAINST AUTONOMY (2012); Ryan Bubb and Richard Pildes, *How Behavioral Economics Trims Its Sails and Why*, 127 HARV. L. REV. 1593 (2014).

[2] I am bracketing the question of definition but note that freedom of choice is, on any reasonable account, an important ingredient in social welfare. *See* Björn Bartling et al., *The Intrinsic Value of Decision Rights* (U. of Zurich, Dep't of Econ. Working Paper No. 120, 2013), *available at* http://papers.ssrn.com/sol3/papers.cfm?abstract_id=2255992. For valuable discussion of foundational issues, *see* MATTHEW ADLER, WELL-BEING AND FAIR DISTRIBUTION: BEYOND COST-BENEFIT ANALYSIS (2011).

the repertoire of appropriate responses. Mandates, incentives, and subsidies might turn out to be better.

We have seen that there are behavioral market failures as well. If people are suffering from unrealistic optimism, limited attention, or a problem of self-control, and if the result is a serious welfare loss for those people, there is an ethical argument for some kind of public response. When people are running high risks of mortality or otherwise ruining their lives, it might make sense to coerce them. After all, people have to get prescriptions for certain kinds of medicines, and even in freedom-loving societies, people are forbidden from buying certain foods, or running certain risks in the workplace, because the dangers are too high. We could certainly identify cases in which the best approach is a mandate or a ban, because that response is preferable, from the standpoint of social welfare, to any alternative, including nudges.

Of course it is true that those who emphasize autonomy or dignity might have a quite different view. They might believe that even if people's welfare would be promoted by a mandate, they have a right to choose for themselves and to make their own mistakes. Those who believe in welfare might accept this view if they think that mistakes produce learning, and hence benefits over a lifetime. But if autonomy and dignity are central, mandates might be unacceptable whether or not people learn. If (some) nudges can compromise dignity, the same would appear to be even more clearly true of mandates, which might fail to treat people as agents deserving of respect.

One question, suggested earlier, is whether people would delegate a degree of discretion to government under certain conditions. Would they grant informed officials – say, at some food safety agency – the authority to forbid foods whose consumption causes serious health problems? Some preliminary research suggests that a majority of people (Americans) would indeed.[3] Would they grant informed officials – at some financial regulatory agency – the authority to require employees to participate in pension plans and thus forbid them to opt out? Some preliminary research suggests that a majority of people (Americans) would not.[4] If we think that such research is relevant, we might have a way to test objections from the standpoint of autonomy and dignity: Perhaps there is a serious offense to either value only if many or most people do not want the government to be undertaking the relevant action.

---

[3] *See* Oren Bar-Gill and Cass R. Sunstein, *Regulation as Delegation*, 7 J. LEGAL ANALYSIS 1 (2015).
[4] *Id.*

Of course these points take us into challenging philosophical waters. Some forms of autonomy or dignity are not alienable. For example, people are not allowed to sell themselves into slavery. True, we are not speaking here of anything nearly so extreme, but perhaps the public is willing to approve of prohibitions in circumstances in which they ought to be making their own choices. There are also questions about whether and when majorities should be authorized to bind minorities. Suppose that most people support certain bans, on food safety grounds, but that many people abhor those bans and would like to be free to make their own choices. Is it so clear that the majority should be allowed to rule? The only point is that insofar as mandates and bans reflect the desires of large segments of the public, the objection from autonomy and dignity is becomes more questionable.

Against Mandates

Nonetheless, there are excellent reasons to think that whatever our foundational values, nudges have significant advantages and are often the best approach, at least when the interest of choosers is all that is involved. In a slogan: Influence yes, coercion no, at least as a presumption.

The first point is that freedom-preserving approaches tend to be best in the face of diversity. By allowing people to go their own way, nudges reduce the problems associated with one-size-fits-all solutions, which mandates usually impose. With respect to diet and exercise, for example, people have their own tastes and values, which they should usually be allowed trade off as they see fit. A nudge might inform them, or put some salutary pressure on behavioral biases, but if some subgroup wants to go its own way, it remains entitled to do so. A mandate does not have that virtue; it might impose a stifling uniformity. I have referred to Mill's celebration of "experiments of living," a celebration spurred in part (I think) by his own unconventional relationship with Harriett Taylor.[5] But whether we are speaking of intimate choices or less intimate ones, it is important, in a free society, to allow such experiments. A central reason involves welfare: If people really want to take their own path, they might well know what will make their lives go best. It is true that people show behavioral biases, but there is a distinction between genuine mistakes on the one hand and personal tastes and values on the other. If people choose high-calorie

[5] Cass R. Sunstein, *John and Harriet: Still Mysterious*, NY REV. OF BOOKS (April 2, 2015), *available at* www.nybooks.com/articles/2015/04/02/john-stuart-mill-harriet-taylor-hayek/.

foods, or current consumption over savings, it may be because that is why they like.

Second, those who favor nudges are alert to the important fact that public officials have limited information and may themselves err (recall the knowledge problem). To be sure, nudges may themselves be based on mistakes. A default rule might not fit people's situations; an information campaign might be based on mistakes about facts . Influencers often go wrong. But even when this is so, the damage is likely to be significantly less severe than in the case of mandates, because people are free to ignore nudges. An information campaign can be disregarded. If a default rule poorly fits people's situations – say, because they need money now, rather than for retirement – they are permitted to opt out. If social norms do not point people in good situations, they can decide to flout social norms. So long as their own lives are all that is involved, that right is an important safeguard against official error. Hayek's own emphasis on the knowledge problem was rooted in a concern for welfare. Mandates, imposed on complex systems, can produce all sorts of unintended adverse consequences, and it should be unnecessary to belabor the point that any mandate might have effects that public officials cannot foresee.

Third, nudges respond to the fact that public officials may be affected by well-organized private groups (recall the public choice problem). Even if such officials have a great deal of knowledge, they might not have the right incentives, even in the most well-functioning democracies. For their own selfish reasons, powerful private groups might want officials to impose particular nudges, and sometimes they can convince officials to act as they wish. If so, the fact that people can go their own way provides real protection, certainly when compared with mandates. The most egregious examples of interest-group authority over government processes involve prohibitions. A presumption in favor of choice-preserving approaches is a significant way of reducing interest-group power, well suited to situations in which conventional market failures are not involved.

Fourth, nudges have the advantage of avoiding the distinctive kind of welfare loss that people experience when they are deprived of the ability to choose. That loss takes the form of a felt diminution of both autonomy and respect, and in some cases, it is severe. If your government tells you that you may not engage in some activity, or purchase some product, you might feel that you are being treated as a child. As we have seen, people often want to choose, and when they are forbidden to do so, they might be frustrated, angered, or worse. A nudge avoids that kind of loss.

There is a closely related point: When people dislike bans, they may respond with reactance. If so, achieving compliance with bans may prove challenging; people might disobey. Because they do not force anyone to do anything, nudges are far less likely to create reactance (though as we have seen, reactance cannot be ruled out). Existing research, summarized here, finds that significant parts of the population are indeed prone to reactance and that majorities often oppose bans even when they support nudges in the same direction. On welfare grounds, nudges have a significant advantage insofar as they do not trigger the distinctive kind of loss that comes when government tells people what they cannot do.

Fifth, nudges recognize that freedom of choice can be seen, and often is seen, as an intrinsic good. Many people insist that autonomy and dignity have independent value and are not merely part of a large category of goods that people enjoy. If government is to respect people's autonomy, or to treat them with dignity, it should not deprive them of freedom. It should treat them as adults, rather than children or infants.

Illustrations

The five arguments on behalf of choice-preserving approaches will have different degrees of force in different contexts. They suggest reasons to favor nudges over mandates, but those reasons may not be decisive. They should not be wielded as all-purpose challenges to mandates. In some settings, the interest in freedom of choice has overwhelming importance. In others, people do not much care about it, and its intrinsic value is only modest. Consider some illustrative problems, from the relatively small and mundane to the much larger.

1. Suppose that a public university has long had a single-sided default for its printers, and it is deciding whether to change to double-sided. On the basis of careful investigation, suppose that it has learned that at least 80 percent of its students, faculty, and other employees would prefer a double-sided default, on the ground that they would like to save paper. Armed with this information, and aware of the economic and environmental savings that a double-sided default could bring, the university switches to that default.

Now suppose that some university administrators, enthusiastic about the savings, ask whether double-sided printing should be mandatory. The answer to that question is plain. About one-fifth of users prefer a single-sided default, and there is little doubt that single-sided printing is often best – for example, for PowerPoint presentations and for lecture notes.

The assessment might be different if the use of single-sided printing imposes significant costs on nonusers (e.g., very high paper costs on the university or environmental costs). If so, there is some weighing to be done. But if the welfare of those who use printers is the only or primary variable, a default is clearly preferable to a mandate. From the standpoint of users, a mandate would impose unnecessary costs and burdens in the face of heterogeneity across persons and projects. Here, then, is a clear case in which a default is much better than a mandate, and we can take it as illustrative of a wide range of problems with similar features.

2. A great deal of work explores the effects of automatic enrollment in retirement plans. We have also seen that automatic enrollment greatly increases participation rates, and thus people's savings, while also preserving freedom of choice. So far, so good. The problem is that if the default contribution rate is lower than what employees would choose (say, 3 percent, as it has been under many automatic enrollment plans in the United States), then the result of automatic enrollment might be to *decrease* average savings, because the default rate turns out to be sticky.[6] This seems to be a bad – and ironic – result for those who want to use defaults to increase people's welfare during retirement. Of course a full evaluation would require an assessment of what people's savings should be. But let us simply stipulate, as many people believe, that current levels are generally too low, and hence that a program that decreases average savings has a serious problem.

If so, the natural response is not to abandon default rules in favor of mandates, but to choose a better default. One possibility is "automatic escalation," which increases savings rates each year until the employee hits a predetermined maximum.[7] And in fact, there has been a significant increase in the use of this approach; automatic escalation is increasingly popular.[8] Another possibility is to select a higher default contribution. No one denies that defaults can go wrong.[9] If they do, the challenge is to get them right.

---

[6] *See* Bubb and Pildes, *How Behavioral Economics Trims Its Sails and Why* (2014).

[7] Shlomo Benartzi and Richard H. Thaler, *Behavioral Economics and the Retirement Savings Crisis*, 339 SCIENCE 1152 (2013). Bubb and Pildes note that the typical maximum contribution rate even after automatic escalation may still be too low (Bubb and Pildes, *How Behavioral Economics Trims Its Sails and Why*, 2014), but this problem too can be solved by simply raising the maximum contribution rate.

[8] In 2009, 50 percent of plans with automatic enrollment include escalation; by 2012, 71 percent did. *See Employers Expressing Doubt in Retirement Readiness of 401(k) Plan Participants, Towers Watson Survey Finds* (October 4, 2012), *available at* www.towerswatson.com/en/Press/2012/10/employers-expressing-doubt-in-retirement-readiness-of-401k-plan-participants.

[9] Note the important finding that default-induced improved choices, at the level of individuals, can undermine social welfare by substantially exacerbating adverse selection. *See* Benjamin Handel,

But there is a more fundamental objection to automatic enrollment in retirement plans, which questions freedom of choice altogether. Suppose that people opt out of pension plans for bad reasons, in the sense that the decision to opt out makes their lives go far worse. Perhaps the relevant people have a general (and unjustified) distrust of the financial system, or of their employer, and so they elect to save little or not to save at all. Perhaps they suffer from an acute form of present bias. Perhaps those who opt out are most likely to suffer as a result of doing so.

These are empirical questions, but if so, the argument for a mandate gains force on welfare grounds. If public officials know, from practice, that a behavioral market failure, or some kind of error, is really leading people to make self-destructive blunders, maybe government should mandate savings and eliminate the right to opt out. After all, most democratic nations have mandatory pension plans of one kind or another. Perhaps they should expand those plans, rather than working to allow or encourage voluntary supplementation. Several nations have been doing exactly that. Indeed, some observers might argue for some kind of comprehensive welfare assessment by public officials about optimal savings rates, and ask those officials to build mandates on the basis of that assessment.

This approach cannot be ruled out in principle; behavioral economics provides good reasons for fresh thinking about the nature and size of savings mandates. But in establishing new or bigger mandates, we have good reasons for caution. When assessing the rationality of those who opt out, public officials might be wrong. They might also be biased. As compared to a default, a mandate will get people into the system who would benefit from inclusion, because they will need the money later, but it will also get people into the system who would be harmed, because they need the money now. It is important, and it may be difficult, to know the size of the two groups. Those who opt out might do so not for bad reasons, or because they are ignoring their future selves, but because they are making a sensible trade-off between their current and future welfare.

To say the least, a comprehensive welfare assessment of optimal savings rates is exceedingly difficult, especially in view of diversity of the population and changes over time. What is the right savings rate for those who are twenty-five, or thirty, or forty, or sixty? Guidelines are helpful, and nudges too, but no single answer can be right, even within age groups. And how does the right savings rate change when people have to pay

Adverse Selection and Inertia in Health Insurance Market: When Nudging Hurts, 102 Am. Econ. Rev. 2643 (2013).

school loans or mortgages, or to pay for their children, young or old, healthy or not? And how does it change for people who earn $30,000 per year, or $60,000, or $100,000? And what is the impact of changing macroeconomic conditions?

Any such assessment would have to acknowledge that different approaches make sense for different people and over time. In a recession, for example, a lower contribution rate might be best, at least for relatively low-income people, than in a time of rapid growth. So too, those who have to pay off their college loans might not want to save while they are struggling to make those payments, and people who are reasonably spending a great deal on current consumption (perhaps they have young children, or children in college) might not want to save so much in that period. These points suggest the need for personalized rather than one-size-fits-all mandates, which would not be easy to design, and which would amount to a risky form of social engineering.

Moreover, any form of coercion will harm many choosers, who want to exercise their autonomy, and who would undoubtedly be frustrated to find that they cannot. And if freedom of choice has intrinsic value or can promote learning, then there are further reasons to avoid mandates. As we have seen, boosts can be the best nudges, and they might accompany defaults.

While these various points raise cautionary notes, they are not decisive. As I have noted, many nations compel savings through some kind of social security program, and for perfectly legitimate reasons. Perhaps existing programs should be expanded to increase the level of mandatory savings; such expansions could easily accompany automatic enrolment plans. If it could be demonstrated that those who opt out, under automatic enrollment, are making genuinely bad decisions, there would be a strong argument for mandates, or at least for constraining opt-outs in various ways. But even if so, private retirement plans have an important place for savers, and the question is whether the current voluntary system should become more coercive. The fact of heterogeneity and the risk of government error argue strongly for the conclusion that automatic enrollment plans, with freedom to opt out, have an important role.

3. Most motor vehicles emit pollution, and the use of gasoline increases national dependence on foreign oil. On standard economic grounds, there is a market failure, and some kind of corrective tax seems the best response, designed to ensure that drivers internalize the social costs of their activity (including the costs of greenhouse gases). Behaviorally informed regulators would be inclined to add that at the time of purchase, some consumers

may not give enough attention to the costs of driving a car. Even if they try, they might not have a sufficient understanding of those costs, because it is not simple to translate differences in miles per gallon or other measures into economic and environmental consequences. An obvious approach, preserving freedom of choice, would be a modest influence in the form of clear, simple disclosure of those consequences, with a fuel economy label that would correct that kind of behavioral market failure. And in fact, the Obama administration produced a label of exactly that kind, with a nudge specifying those economic and environmental consequences.[10]

But it would be reasonable to wonder whether such a label will be sufficiently effective; this is an empirical question. Maybe some or many consumers will pay little attention to it and hence will not purchase cars that would save them a significant amount of money. True, a corrective tax might help solve that problem. But if consumers really do neglect fuel costs at the time of purchase, it might be best to combine the tax with some kind of subsidy for fuel-efficient cars, to overcome consumer myopia. And if some or many consumers are insufficiently attentive to the costs of operating a vehicle (at the time of purchase), then it is even possible that fuel economy standards, which are strongly disfavored on standard economic grounds (as inefficient), might turn out to be justified. The reason is that such standards might end up giving consumers what they would want, if they were fully informed and did not suffer from behavioral biases.

That is a speculative argument, to be sure. To see if it is right, it would be useful to focus directly on two kinds of consumer savings from fuel economy standards, not involving externalities at all: money and time. In fact, the vast majority of the quantified benefits from recent fuel economy standards in the United States come not from environmental improvements, but from money that consumers save at the pump. Turned into monetary equivalents, the time savings are also significant. For one of the most ambitious of those standards, for example, the Department of Transportation projected consumer economic savings of about $529 billion; time savings of $15 billion; energy security benefits of $25 billion; carbon dioxide emissions reductions benefits of $49 billion; other air pollution benefits of about $14 billion; and less than $1 billion from reduced fatalities.[11] The total anticipated benefits are $633 billion over fifteen years, of which a remarkable 84 percent come

---

[10] *See* Cass R. Sunstein, Simpler: The Future of Government 81–86 (2013).

[11] Nat'l Highw. Traf. Safety Admin., *Final Regulatory Impact Analysis: Corporate Average Fuel Economy for MY 2017–MY 2025*, August 2012, table 13.

from savings at the pump, and no less than 86 percent from those savings along with time savings.

The problem is that on standard economic grounds, it is not at all clear that these consumer benefits are entitled to count in the analysis, because they are purely private savings and do not involve externalities in any way. The objection is that in deciding which cars to buy, consumers can certainly take account of the private savings from fuel-efficient cars; if they choose not to buy such cars, it might be because they do not value fuel efficiency as compared to other vehicle attributes (such as safety, aesthetics, and performance). Where is the market failure? If the problem lies in a lack of information, the standard economic prescription, which might be supported on ethical grounds, overlaps with the behaviorally informed one: *Provide that information so that consumers can easily understand it.* Again: Influence yes, coercion no. And this particular influence has a particular virtue, which is that it is educative.

In this context, however, there is a risk that any kind of choice-preserving approach will be inadequate. Even with the best fuel economy label in the world, some or many consumers might well be insufficiently attentive to those benefits at the time of purchase, not because they have made a rational judgment that the benefits are outweighed by other factors, but simply because they focus on other variables.[12] And how many consumers think about time savings when they are deciding whether to buy a fuel-efficient vehicle?

This question raises a host of empirical questions, to which we lack full answers.[13] But if consumers are not paying enough attention to savings in terms of money and time, a suitably designed fuel economy mandate – hard paternalism, and no mere default – might well be justified, because it would produce an outcome akin to what would be produced by consumers who are at once informed and attentive. If the benefits of the mandate greatly exceed the costs, and if there is no significant consumer welfare loss (in the form, e.g., of reductions in safety, performance, or aesthetics), then the mandate does serve to correct a behavioral market failure. And indeed, the U.S. government has so argued:[14]

---

[12] *See* Xavier Gabaix and David Laibson, *Shrouded Attributes, Consumer Myopia, and Information Suppression in Competitive Markets*, 121 Q.J. Econ. 505, 511 (2006).

[13] For a detailed discussion, see Hunt Allcott and Cass R. Sunstein, *Regulating Internalities*, 34 J. Pol'y Analysis & Mgmt 698 (2015).

[14] *See* Light-Duty Vehicle Greenhouse Gas Emission Standards and Corporate Average Fuel Economy Standards; Final Rule, Part II, 75 Fed. Reg. 25,324, 25,510–11 (May 7, 2010), *available at* www.gpo .gov/fdsys/pkg/FR-2010-05-07/pdf/2010-8159.pdf.

The central conundrum has been referred to as the Energy Paradox in this setting (and in several others). In short, the problem is that consumers appear not to purchase products that are in their economic self-interest. There are strong theoretical reasons why this might be so:

- Consumers might be myopic and hence undervalue the long-term.
- Consumers might lack information or a full appreciation of information even when it is presented.
- Consumers might be especially averse to the short-term losses associated with the higher prices of energy-efficient products relative to the uncertain future fuel savings, even if the expected present value of those fuel savings exceeds the cost (the behavioral phenomenon of "loss aversion").
- Even if consumers have relevant knowledge, the benefits of energy-efficient vehicles might not be sufficiently salient to them at the time of purchase, and the lack of salience might lead consumers to neglect an attribute that it would be in their economic interest to consider.
- In the case of vehicle fuel efficiency, and perhaps as a result of one or more of the foregoing factors, consumers may have relatively few choices to purchase vehicles with greater fuel economy once other characteristics, such as vehicle class, are chosen.

Of course we should be cautious before accepting a behavioral argument on behalf of mandates or bans. Behavioral biases have to be demonstrated, not simply asserted; perhaps most consumers do pay a lot of attention to the benefits of fuel-efficient vehicles.[15] The government's numbers, projecting costs and benefits, might be wrong; recall the knowledge problem. Consumers have highly diverse preferences with respect to vehicles. Even though they are not mere defaults, fuel economy standards should be designed to preserve a wide space for freedom of choice. The use of fleet-wide averages helps to ensure that such space is maintained.

With these qualifications, the argument for fuel economy standards, made by reference to behavioral market failures, is at least plausible. In this context, nudges (in the form of an improved fuel economy label) and mandates (in the form of standards) might march hand-in-hand. With an understanding of behavioral findings, a command-and-control approach, promoting consumer welfare, might turn out to be far better than the standard economic remedy of corrective taxes.

---

[15] Allcott and Sunstein, *Regulating Internalities*, 34 J. POL'Y ANALYSIS & MGMT 698 (2015). Hunt Allcott and Michael Greenstone, *Is There an Energy Efficiency Gap?*, 26 J. ECON. PERSP. 3 (2012).

Humility and Respect

The fuel economy example is important, but it should not be read for more than it is worth. It certainly does not establish that in the face of human error, mandates are *generally* preferable to choice-preserving alternatives. As we have seen, such alternatives reduce the costs of imposing solutions on heterogeneous populations, reduce the risks associated with government mistakes, and avoid the many problems associated with eliminating freedom of choice. In light of the frequently unanticipated and sometimes harmful effects of mandates, nudges are generally more humble and less risky. They are also more likely to treat people with respect and to recognize the dignity of free agents.

No one should deny that in the end, mandates might turn out to be justified. But in a free society, it makes sense to give careful consideration to less intrusive, choice-preserving alternatives, and at least where standard market failures are not involved, to adopt a rebuttable presumption in their favor – with the rebuttal available only if it can be shown that a mandate will clearly improve people's lives.

A Very Brief Recapitulation

I have covered a great deal of territory, and it will be useful to conclude by recapitulating the principal themes.

It is pointless to raise ethical objections to nudges and choice architecture as such. Human beings cannot live in a world without them. Social norms nudge, and a society cannot exist without social norms. Many such norms make life agreeable and even possible. They increase the likelihood that people will not abuse or mistreat one another, and they help solve collective action problems that would otherwise make human lives shorter, sadder, and worse. Such norms influence us every day, even when we do not notice them. They can emerge without any involvement from political actors, but the law has an expressive function, and what it expresses influences the content of norms. If a state takes violence seriously, and attempts to stop it, it can fortify norms against violence. And if a state takes steps to reduce discrimination on the basis of race, religion, sex, and sexual orientation, it will influence norms. Healthy behavior, including good diet and the avoidance of cigarettes and alcohol, is very much a product of choice architecture, emphatically including social norms.

Spontaneous orders have many virtues, but they nudge. Whether or not they are associated with liberty, properly conceived, they create multiple forms of choice architecture. Some people celebrate small groups, informality, and longstanding traditions that seem to have nothing to do with government. Other people deplore such groups and traditions. But whether they deserve celebration or something else, they produce choice architecture. The most minimal state creates such an architecture, and it will influence people's decisions even if it seeks not to do so. Recall the effects of default rules, of the sort that are pervasive in the law of property, contract, and tort. But while nudging itself is inevitable, many nudges are anything but that, and they can be avoided. Some forms of influence are not the appropriate business of public officials.

The modern regulatory state imposes numerous mandates and bans. Some of them are easily justified, as ways to solve collective action problems, to reduce externalities, or to response to people's lack of information. But some forms of coercion must be characterized as paternalistic. Consider the requirement that people obtain prescriptions before using certain medicines, or fuel economy and energy efficiency rules, or occupational safety and health laws; all these, and many others, have paternalistic features. Paternalistic mandates and bans are subject to obvious ethical concerns, many of them identical to those explored here. A central question involves the effects of mandates and bans on people's welfare. Another question is whether they insult people's autonomy – a problem that is likely to be diminished if government is requiring people to do what they would do if they were properly informed (and not subject to behavioral biases). Because nudges preserve freedom of choice, those concerns are weakened, though not eliminated.

We have seen that people's judgments about nudges generally make a great deal of sense and line up fairly well with the conclusions that follow from extended analysis. People do not oppose nudges as such. So long as they believe that the end is legitimate and important, and likely to be favored by choosers themselves, most people will support nudges in its direction. By contrast, people dislike those nudges that (a) promote what they see as illicit goals or (b) are perceived as inconsistent with either the interests or values of most choosers. Avoiding the trap of abstraction, people agree that the nature of the particular nudge in question is highly relevant to the ethics of nudging.

In addition, they tend to prefer nudges that target and improve deliberative processes to those that target unconscious or subconscious processes, and they may react against the latter – though they do not by any means rule the latter out of bounds and will often approve of them as well. When the political valence of nudging is clear, their evaluation of nudges very much turns on that valence: People on the political right tend to approve of nudges that move people in the directions that they favor, and people on the political left show the same tendency. This finding reinforces the view that in many cases, it is people's assessment of the ends of particular nudges, rather than of nudging as such, that settles their judgments. The most interesting qualification is that for a minority of people, predisposed to show reactance or to emphasize the importance of personal control, there is some evidence of a general inclination to reject nudges.

It is clear that any changes in choice architecture, including those that preserve freedom, can run into serious and even convincing ethical objections – most obviously, where the underlying goals are illicit. But where the goals are legitimate, nudges are less likely to run afoul of ethical constraints, not least because and when they promote informed choices and thus improve people's capacity to exercise their own agency (as in the case of disclosure of information, warnings, and reminders). Transparency and public scrutiny are important safeguards, especially when public officials are responsible for nudges and choice architecture. Nothing should be hidden or covert.

It remains true and important that some imaginable nudges are objectionable, even when legitimate goals are involved, even when freedom of choice is preserved, and even in the face of full transparency. Most important, some nudges can be counted as forms of manipulation, raising objections from the standpoint of both autonomy and dignity. We have seen that influences are manipulative when they do not sufficiently engage or appeal to people's capacity for reflective and deliberative choice. Such influences do not treat people with respect, and there is reason to suspect that they will not promote people's welfare. Most nudges do not fall in this category – but a few do. There is also a risk that if nudges do not build up people's own capacities, they will not have long-term effects.

These are cautionary notes against certain nudges. But even when nudges target System 1, it would strain the concept of manipulation to categorize them as such (consider a graphic warning). The concept of manipulation has a core and a periphery. Very few nudges fit within the core, somewhat more fit within the periphery, and most lie comfortably outside of both.

Many nudges, and many changes in choice architecture, are not merely permissible on ethical grounds. They are actually required. Far from being ethically questionable, they are ethically mandatory. On grounds of welfare, the point should be straightforward; much nudging promises to increase social welfare. A government that nudges people in directions that reduce their welfare is acting unethically. The same is true of a government that declines to create welfare-improving nudges.

The point holds for autonomy, dignity, and self-government as well. Many nudges promote people's ability to choose for themselves; they increase autonomy. Many nudges combat discrimination on the basis of race, religion, and sex, and help people who face severe economic deprivation; they promote dignity. A system of self-government can be compromised by bad nudges, such as those that discourage people from voting. It needs a good system of choice architecture, promoting the right to vote and making meaningful the greatest office of all, which is that of the citizen.

The history of freedom-respecting nations is full of changes in choice architecture that have permitted them to move further in the direction of their highest ideals. It should go without saying that those ideals have yet to be fully realized. In moving closer to them, new nudges, and new forms of choice architecture, will prove indispensable.

American Evaluations of Thirty-Four Nudges[*]

[*] This survey was administered in 2015 by Survey Sampling International. It included 563 Americans, invited via email, and paid a total of $2,073.

Nudge	All		Democrat		Republican		Independent		Significance between-party, all conditions (%)	Pairwise significance between parties
	Approve (%)	Disapprove (%)	Approve (%)	Disapprove (%)	Approve (%)	Disapprove (%)	Approve (%)	Disapprove (%)		
1. Mandatory labeling: GMOs	86	14	89	11	80	20	87	13	5	D/R ($p = .04$)
2. Mandatory calorie labels	85	15	92	8	77	23	88	12	1	D/R ($p < .001$); R/I ($p = .01$)
3. Public education campaign: distracted driving	85	15	88	12	80	20	84	16		
4. Public education campaign: childhood obesity	82	18	89	11	70	30	81	19	1	D/R ($p < .001$); R/I ($p = .04$)
5. Government-encouraged automatic enrollment: pension plan	80	20	88	12	73	27	75	25	1	D/R ($p = .002$); D/I ($p = .002$)
6. Public education campaign: sexual orientation discrimination	75	25	85	15	57	43	75	25	1	D/R ($p < .001$); D/I ($p = .03$); R/I ($p < .001$)
7. Mandatory graphic warnings on cigarettes	74	26	77	23	68	32	74	26		
8. Mandatory labels for high salt content	73	27	79	21	61	39	72	28	1	D/R ($p = .002$)

9. Government-encouraged automatic enrollment: "green energy"	72	28	82	18	61	39	66	34	1	D/R (p < .001); D/I (p = .001)
10. Mandatory automatic enrollment: pension plan	71	29	78	22	62	38	67	33	1	D/R (p = .01)
11. Mandatory choice: organ donors during driver's license registration	70	30	75	25	62	38	69	31	5	D/R (p = .04)
12. Mandatory automatic enrollment: green energy	67	33	79	21	51	49	63	37	1	D/R (p < .001); D/I (p = .001)
13. Mandatory "traffic lights"	64	36	71	29	57	43	61	39	5	D/R (p = .03)
14. Mandatory manufacturing labels for countries that violate labor laws	60	40	67	33	50	50	57	43	1	D/R (p = .006)
15. Default last name change upon marriage to that of husband	58	42	61	39	57	43	56	44		

Nudge	All		Democrat		Republican		Independent		Significance between-party, all conditions (%)	Pairwise significance between parties
	Approve (%)	Disapprove (%)	Approve (%)	Disapprove (%)	Approve (%)	Disapprove (%)	Approve (%)	Disapprove (%)		
16. Public education campaign: obesity as "terrible curse"	57	43	61	39	47	53	60	40	5	D/R (p = .04)
17. Mandatory healthy food placement	56	44	63	37	43	57	57	43	1	D/R (p = .001); R/I (p = .03)
18. Mandatory manufacturing labels for countries that have recently harbored terrorists	54	46	56	44	58	42	49	51		
19. Mandatory public education in movie theaters for healthy eating	53	47	61	39	41	59	51	49	1	D/R (p = .001)
20. Automatic enrollment: voting	53	47	63	37	39	61	50	50	1	D/R (p < .001); D/I (p = .03)
21. Automatically listing the incumbent politician first on ballots	53	47	58	42	47	53	51	49		

22. Public education campaign: Animal Welfare Society	52	48	59	41	34	66	11	89	1	D/R ($p < .001$); R/I ($p = .001$)
23. Mandatory manufacturing Communist country labels	44	56	47	53	43	57	42	58		
24. Mandatory subliminal ads in movie theaters	41	59	47	53	42	58	35	65	5	D/I ($p = .04$)
25. Public education campaign: transgender	41	59	49	51	29	71	38	62	1	D/R ($p = .001$)
26. Default charge for carbon emissions on airplane tickets	36	64	43	57	25	75	34	66	1	D/R ($p = .003$)
27. Public education campaign: stay-at-home mothers	33	67	33	67	31	69	33	67		
28. Default donation to Red Cross	27	73	30	70	20	80	28	72		
29. Default Democratic party registration	26	74	32	68	16	84	26	74	1	D/R ($p = .002$)

Nudge	All		Democrat		Republican		Independent		Significance between-party, all conditions (%)	Pairwise significance between parties
	Approve (%)	Disapprove (%)	Approve (%)	Disapprove (%)	Approve (%)	Disapprove (%)	Approve (%)	Disapprove (%)		
30. Default donation to Animal Welfare Society	26	74	30	70	20	80	25	75		
31. Default last name change upon marriage to that of wife	24	76	28	72	18	82	23	77		
32. Default employee donations to the United Way (majority of employees have agreed)	24	76	26	74	17	83	25	75		
33. Public education campaign: unpatriotic criticism	23	77	24	76	21	79	22	78		
34. Default assumption of Christianity for census data	21	79	22	78	27	73	17	83		

Note: Pairwise significance was obtained for those nudges with significant differences by party, using a Bonferroni correction.

Survey Questions[*]

1. Do you approve or disapprove of the following hypothetical policy?
The federal government requires calorie labels at chain restaurants (such as McDonald's and Burger King).

2. Do you approve or disapprove of the following hypothetical policy?
The federal government requires graphic warnings on cigarette packages (where the graphic warnings include pictures of people suffering from smoking-related diseases, such as cancer).

3. Do you approve or disapprove of the following hypothetical policy? The federal government requires a "traffic lights" system for food, by which healthy foods would be sold with a small green label, unhealthy foods with a small red label, and foods that are neither especially healthy nor especially unhealthy with a small yellow label.

4. Do you approve or disapprove of the following hypothetical policy? The federal government encourages (without requiring) employers to adopt a system in which employees would be automatically enrolled in a pension plan, but could opt out if they wish.

5. Do you approve or disapprove of the following hypothetical policy?
The federal government encourages (without requiring) electricity providers to adopt a system in which consumers would be automatically enrolled in a "green" (environmentally friendly) energy supplier, but could opt out if they wished.

6. Do you approve or disapprove of the following hypothetical policy?

[*] This survey was administered in 2015 by Survey Sampling International. It included 563 Americans, invited via email, and paid a total of $2,073.

A state law saying that on the ballot, the current senator, governor, president, or mayor must always be listed first.

7.   Do you approve or disapprove of the following hypothetical policy? A state law saying that citizens of a state are automatically enrolled as voters, and do not have to register as voters.

8.   Do you approve or disapprove of the following hypothetical policy? A state law requiring people to say, when they obtain their drivers' license, whether they want to be organ donors.

9.   Do you approve or disapprove of the following hypothetical policy? A federal law requiring companies to disclose whether the food they sell contains genetically modified organisms (GMOs).

10.   Do you approve or disapprove of the following hypothetical policy? A federal law assuming that people are Christian, for purposes of the census, unless they specifically state otherwise.

11.   Do you approve or disapprove of the following hypothetical policy? The federal government assumes, on tax returns, that people want to donate $50 to the Animal Welfare Society of America, subject to opt out if people explicitly say that they do want to make that donation.

12.   Do you approve or disapprove of the following hypothetical policy? A state law requires all large grocery stores to place their most healthy foods in a prominent, visible location.

13.   Do you approve or disapprove of the following hypothetical policy? A state law assumes that women want to take their husbands' last name upon marriage, while assuming that men want to retain their own last names; it also allows both women and men to retain or change their names if they explicitly say what they want.

14.   Do you approve or disapprove of the following hypothetical policy? A state law assumes that people want to register as Democrats, subject to opt out if people explicitly say that they want to register as Republicans or Independents.

15.   Do you approve or disapprove of the following hypothetical policy? To reduce deaths and injuries associated with distracted driving, the national government adopts a public education campaign, consisting of vivid and sometimes graphic stories and images, designed to discourage people from texting, emailing, or talking on their cellphones while driving.

16.   Do you approve or disapprove of the following hypothetical policy?

To reduce childhood obesity, the national government adopts a public education campaign, consisting of information that parents can use to make healthier choices for their children.

17. Do you approve or disapprove of the following hypothetical policy?

The federal government requires movie theaters to provide subliminal advertisements (i.e., advertisements that go by so quickly that people are not consciously aware of them) designed to discourage people from smoking and overeating.

18. Do you approve or disapprove of the following hypothetical policy?

A newly elected President is concerned that the public, and the press, will be unduly critical of what he does. He adopts a public education campaign designed to convince people that criticism of his decisions is "unpatriotic" and potentially "damaging to national security."

19. Do you approve or disapprove of the following hypothetical policy?

The federal government requires airlines to charge people, with their airline tickets, a specific amount to offset their carbon emissions (about $10 per ticket); under the program, people can opt out of the payment if they explicitly say that they do not want to pay it.

20. Do you approve or disapprove of the following hypothetical policy?

The federal government engages in a public education campaign to encourage people to donate to the Animal Welfare Society of America.

21. Do you approve or disapprove of the following hypothetical policy?

The federal government requires labels on products that have unusually high levels of salt, as in, "This product has been found to contain unusually high levels of salt, which may be harmful to your health."

22. Do you approve or disapprove of the following hypothetical policy?
The federal government engages in a public education campaign designed to encourage people not to discriminate on the basis of sexual orientation.

23. Do you approve or disapprove of the following hypothetical policy?

The federal government engages in a public education campaign designed to encourage mothers of young children to stay home to take care of their kids.

24. Do you approve or disapprove of the following hypothetical policy?

Your state enacts a law by which husbands automatically change their last names to that of their wives upon marriage, but they can retain their names if they explicitly say that they want to do so.

25. Do you approve or disapprove of the following hypothetical policy?

The federal government assumes, on tax returns, that people want to donate $50 to the Red Cross, subject to opt out if people explicitly say that they do not want to make that donation.

26. Do you approve or disapprove of the following hypothetical policy?

Your state government assumes that its employees want to donate money to the United Way, and it deducts $20 per month from their paychecks for that purpose; but it allows employees to opt out of the program if they explicitly say that they do not want to participate. (Assume that at least 60 percent of state employees have said that they do, in fact, want to give this amount to the United Way.)

27. Do you approve or disapprove of the following hypothetical policy?

The federal government requires all products that come from a Communist country (such as China or Cuba) to be sold with the label, "Made in whole or in part under Communism" in the specified country. (Assume that this label would not substitute for or displace any existing labels identifying where products are made.)

28. Do you approve or disapprove of the following hypothetical policy?

The federal government requires labels on products that come from companies that have repeatedly violated the nation's labor laws (such as laws requiring occupational safety or forbidding discrimination), as in, "This product is made by a company that has repeatedly violated the nation's labor laws."

29. Do you approve or disapprove of the following hypothetical policy?

The federal government requires labels on products that come from countries that have recently harbored terrorists, as in, "This product comes from a nation that was recently found to harbor terrorists."

30. Do you approve or disapprove the following hypothetical policy?

The federal government requires movie theaters to run public education messages designed to discourage people from smoking and overeating.

31. Do you approve or disapprove of the following hypothetical policy?

The federal government engages in a public education campaign designed to combat obesity, showing obese children struggling to exercise, and also showing interviews with obese adults, who are saying such things as, "My biggest regret in life is that I have not managed to control my weight," and "To me, obesity is like a terrible curse."

32. Do you approve or disapprove of the following hypothetical policy?

The federal government requires large employers (more than 200 employees) to adopt a system in which employees would be automatically enrolled in a pension plan, but could opt out if they wish.

33. Do you approve or disapprove of the following hypothetical policy?

The federal government requires large electricity providers (serving at least 500,000 people) to adopt a system in which consumers would be automatically enrolled in a "green" (environmentally friendly) energy supplier, but could opt out if they wished.

34. Do you approve or disapprove of the following hypothetical policy?

The federal government adopts a public education campaign informing people that it is possible for people to change their gender from male to female or from female to male, and encouraging people to consider that possibility "if that is really what they want to do."

35. With which political party do you most closely identify?

36. What is your race?

37. What is your gender?

38. What is your age?

39. What is the highest level of education you have completed?

40. In which state do you currently reside?

41. What is your combined annual household income?

Executive Order 13707: Using Behavioral Science Insights to Better Serve the American People

Executive Order – Using Behavioral Science Insights to Better Serve the American People

A growing body of evidence demonstrates that behavioral science insights – research findings from fields such as behavioral economics and psychology about how people make decisions and act on them – can be used to design government policies to better serve the American people.

Where Federal policies have been designed to reflect behavioral science insights, they have substantially improved outcomes for the individuals, families, communities, and businesses those policies serve. For example, automatic enrollment and automatic escalation in retirement savings plans have made it easier to save for the future, and have helped Americans accumulate billions of dollars in additional retirement savings. Similarly, streamlining the application process for Federal financial aid has made college more financially accessible for millions of students.

To more fully realize the benefits of behavioral insights and deliver better results at a lower cost for the American people, the Federal Government should design its policies and programs to reflect our best understanding of how people engage with, participate in, use, and respond to those policies and programs. By improving the effectiveness and efficiency of Government, behavioral science insights can support a range of national priorities, including helping workers to find better jobs; enabling Americans to lead longer, healthier lives; improving access to educational opportunities and support for success in school; and accelerating the transition to a low-carbon economy.

NOW, THEREFORE, by the authority vested in me as President by the Constitution and the laws of the United States, I hereby direct the following:

Section 1. Behavioral Science Insights Policy Directive.

(a)   Executive departments and agencies (agencies) are encouraged to:
   (i)   identify policies, programs, and operations where applying behavioral science insights may yield substantial improvements in public welfare, program outcomes, and program cost effectiveness;
   (ii)   develop strategies for applying behavioral science insights to programs and, where possible, rigorously test and evaluate the impact of these insights;
   (iii)   recruit behavioral science experts to join the Federal Government as necessary to achieve the goals of this directive; and
   (iv)   strengthen agency relationships with the research community to better use empirical findings from the behavioral sciences.
(b)   In implementing the policy directives in section (a), agencies shall:
   (i)   identify opportunities to help qualifying individuals, families, communities, and businesses access public programs and benefits by, as appropriate, streamlining processes that may otherwise limit or delay participation – for example, removing administrative hurdles, shortening wait times, and simplifying forms;
   (ii)   improve how information is presented to consumers, borrowers, program beneficiaries, and other individuals, whether as directly conveyed by the agency, or in setting standards for the presentation of information, by considering how the content, format, timing, and medium by which information is conveyed affects comprehension and action by individuals, as appropriate;
   (iii)   identify programs that offer choices and carefully consider how the presentation and structure of those choices, including the order, number, and arrangement of options, can most effectively promote public welfare, as appropriate, giving particular consideration to the selection and setting of default options; and
   (iv)   review elements of their policies and programs that are designed to encourage or make it easier for Americans to take specific actions, such as saving for retirement or completing education programs. In doing so, agencies shall consider how the timing, frequency, presentation, and labeling of benefits, taxes, subsidies, and other incentives can more effectively and efficiently promote those actions, as appropriate. Particular attention should be paid to opportunities to use nonfinancial incentives.

(c)   For policies with a regulatory component, agencies are encouraged to combine this behavioral science insights policy directive with their ongoing review of existing significant regulations to identify and reduce regulatory burdens, as appropriate and consistent with Executive Order 13563 of January 18, 2011 (Improving Regulation and Regulatory Review), and Executive Order 13610 of May 10, 2012 (Identifying and Reducing Regulatory Burdens).

Section. 2. Implementation of the Behavioral Science Insights Policy Directive.

(a)   The Social and Behavioral Sciences Team (SBST), under the National Science and Technology Council (NSTC) and chaired by the Assistant to the President for Science and Technology, shall provide agencies with advice and policy guidance to help them execute the policy objectives outlined in section 1 of this order, as appropriate.

(b)   The NSTC shall release a yearly report summarizing agency implementation of section 1 of this order each year until 2019. Member agencies of the SBST are expected to contribute to this report.

(c)   To help execute the policy directive set forth in section 1 of this order, the Chair of the SBST shall, within 45 days of the date of this order and thereafter as necessary, issue guidance to assist agencies in implementing this order.

Index

abortion, 133
abstraction, 26
  ethical, 15–16
accessibility, 136
accountability, 13
active choosing, 12, 26–7, 49–50, 60–2, 65–7, 161, 166–7
  environmental protection and, 179
  simplified and, 181–2
actual malice standard, 112
advertising, 21–2, 70, 78, 80–1
  affect heuristic and, 94
  associative political, 83–4
  manipulation and, 97–8
  subliminal, 82–4, 90, 102–7, 121, 132
affect heuristic, 94–5, 110–11
Affordable Care Act, 27–8
agency, 11–13, 32
aggregation, 37–8
air pollution regulations, 53–4, 178, 187–8
airports, 22
Akerlof, George, 97–8
alcoholism, 46–7
Anderson, David, 135–6
appealing to conscience, 136
Arad, Ayala, 147–9, 156–7
"as judged by themselves" standard, 43–5
  ex ante judgments and, 48–50
  ex post judgments and, 48–50
  informed judgments and, 45–6
  objectively good lives and, 50–2
  preferences about preferences and, 47–8
  self-control and, 46–7
associations, 84, 87
  in political advertising, 83–4
attention, 24
  inattention, 131–2, 138, 155
  selective, 82
attribute substitution, 152
Australia, 9–10
authoritarian nations, 15

automatic enrollment plans, 27–8, 31, 192–3
automatic escalation, 192
automatic voter registration, 14–15, 73, 125
autonomy, 3–4, 13–14, 20, 43, 45–6, 62–7, 188–9
  manipulation and, 84–110
  nudges and, 16–17, 63–5
  paternalism and, 62–3
  self-government and, 72–3
  time management and, 65
availability heuristic, 70, 75–6

bans, 5, 11–12, 63, 188–91
Barnhill, Anne, 88–90
Beauchamp, Tom, 87
behavioral biases, 34–5, 55–8, 61–2, 108–9, 144, 197
behavioral market failures, 19–20, 53, 187–8, 193, 196–7
behavioral public choice, 75–6
behavioral science, 1–4, 28–9, 214–16
  burden of justification and, 13–15
  ethics and, 11–13
  as growing movement, 5–11
  personal agency and, 11–13
Behavioural Insights Team (BIT), 8–10, 26
biases
  behavioral, 34–5, 55–8, 61–2, 108–9, 144, 197
  debiasing strategies, 29–30, 110–11
  of officials, 74–7
  partisan nudge, 150–2
  status quo policy, 48–9
  subconsciously-driven, 142–3
bigotry, 17
BIT. *See* Behavioural Insights Team
Blake, William, 15–16
boosts, 12, 29–30, 32–4, 167–80, 194–5, 200–1
  informed judgments and, 45–6
Bovens, Luc, 152–6
Brandeis, Louis, 72–3
Brave New World (Huxley), 60–1
Bryce, Cindy, 154–5

217